T0367874

Have You Ever Loved Someone Who Didn't Love You Back?

A great collection of sermons on God's great love

BEVERLY D. THOMAS

iUniverse LLC
Bloomington

Have You Ever Loved Someone Who Didn't Love You Back?
A great collection of sermons on God's great love

Scriptural references, unless otherwise noted, are from the King James Bible, printed in 1611.

iUniverse books may be ordered through booksellers or by contacting:

iUniverse LLC
1663 Liberty Drive
Bloomington, IN 47403
www.iuniverse.com
1-800-Authors (1-800-288-4677)

Because of the dynamic nature of the Internet, any web addresses or links contained in this book may have changed since publication and may no longer be valid. The views expressed in this work are solely those of the author and do not necessarily reflect the views of the publisher, and the publisher hereby disclaims any responsibility for them.

Any people depicted in stock imagery provided by Thinkstock are models, and such images are being used for illustrative purposes only.
Certain stock imagery © Thinkstock.

ISBN: 978-1-4917-2942-7 (sc)
ISBN: 978-1-4917-2945-8 (e)

Printed in the United States of America.

iUniverse rev. date: 04/22/2014

I Remember Momma

W. Louise Johnson
1941-2011

"Momma Left us a Wealthy Inheritance—
She Left us Love"

Love is rich, for by it our God gave His whole heart, His most precious
and brightest jewel. He gave us Jesus Christ. Christ gave us all—
He gave us His life's blood—that precious blood which purchased
our freedom and made a way for our mother to go to heaven.

See you in the morning, Momma.

FOR

Momma, Daniel, Juanita, Jimmy

Kenneth, May and Kiela

Table of Contents

Part 4—When A Sinner Dies

Part 5—This Is My Blood

ACKNOWLEDGMENTS

This book is dedicated to my Lord and Saviour Jesus Christ
who has redeemed me with His precious blood. I love you Jesus.

A Passion For Christ Ministries—your faithfulness is matchless. I love
you all. A special note of thanks to everyone who typed, proofed,
edited or contributed in any way toward the
completion of this great work.

To my pastor, teacher and evangelist, Reverend Ernest Angley of Ernest
Angley's Grace Cathedral, thank you for sharing your work with
me and allowing me to use that work in my books.

INTRODUCTION

"Have You Ever Loved Someone Who Didn't Love You Back?
A collection of sermons about God's great love" teaches about the
love of God, both the greatness of it as well as the fierceness of it.

God can *love* as much as He can **hate**.

There is a *special prayer* at the end of each part.

God bless you

Yours in His wonderful name,

Reverend Beverly D. Thomas

Pastor, Teacher and Evangelist
A Passion for Christ Ministries

Part 1

Why Can't We Stay In Love?

CHAPTER 1
LOVING SOMEONE VERSUS BEING IN LOVE

Loving someone versus being in love. Now, if you say "ain't that the same?" you're already in trouble. "Love" is such a dynamic word; it's such a powerful word. But the mismanagement of it has escalated.

What if the Lord said the following words to you, "*Thus saith Lord you either love me or you don't love me. I am your first love or I'm not your first love.*" The Lord is very "plain" with us. Yes or no? Yea or nay? "*You're either totally obedient to me or you're not obedient to me. You're really following in my steps or you're not following in my steps. You're really in my word or you're not in my word. You're really living according to my promises or you're not living according to my promises. I am caring for you as if you were a little one. I'm making plain paths for your feet. But I will just make them so long, because if you fail to walk my paths, I will not give you the plain paths. And the paths will be covered with fog and you won't be able to find my paths. You will seek them and you won't find them. Now is the time for you to walk in the light because I am beaming my light down upon your life and upon your paths that you are to walk.*" And what is that light? It's the truth that's in God's word.

"*I'm beaming down my light down upon your life and upon your paths that you are to walk. I'm showing you what you are supposed to do. I am directing your steps in this last and final hour. You either want me to direct your steps or you don't want me to direct your steps. And you must not be selfish in this hour. You must walk in my love as I walked when I was on planet Earth. You must have the same love that I showed on Calvary for you. And that's the love that I brought. And you must use my blood power and you must walk hand-and-hand with me."* Isn't that what you do when you are in love? *"And you must bury the old self. That's the old self that rebels. That's the old self that refuses to do my will. It's the old self that will not put me first. It's the old self that refuses to do my will. But the new self-created in the righteousness and the holiness of God puts self down completely. The old self, the new self-rises up to do all the will all the will all the will of your Lord.*

I am with you if you will be with me just like I promised my people years ago that I will be with them if they will be with me. But they failed to walk with me and they failed in the wilderness. Multitudes and multitudes and I had to wait to get the disobedient out of the way before I could take the younger ones on into the land of Canaan. And I will take my people, my obedient people into spiritual Canaan in this final hour. If you fail now you have failed." If you fail now, you have failed. Can you imagine the Lord speaking these words directly to you?

NO MAN CAN COME

John 6:44 makes it plain when it says, **No man can come to me, except the Father which hath sent me draw him**. John 15:16 says, **Ye have not chosen me, but I have chosen you, and ordained you, that ye should go and bring forth fruit, and that your fruit should remain.** Matthew 22:14 says, **For many are called, but few are chosen.** This is a deciding hour; so many are making final decisions, whether they know it or not. Many are making their final choice, God or the devil? Have you made yours? Loving someone versus being in love. *"I will take my people, my obedient people into spiritual Canaan in this final hour. If you fail now you have failed. If you fail now you will never do the work that I have called you to do saith the Lord."*[2]

---

[1] Prophecy #3, dated March 21, 1999 Ernest Angley's Grace Cathedral Akron, Ohio
[2] ibid

Do you love God or are you in love with Him? You are the only one who can answer that. Again, do you love God or are you in love with Him? While researching this very topic, I wanted to know and understand the difference so I could properly explain it. This author said, ". . . is it possible for you to love and adore someone yet not be in love with them?" Huh? I will summarize in my own words[3]. Is it possible for you to love and adore someone yet not be in love with Christ, the Son of God? Is it possible for you to love the Son of God and adore Him, but yet not be in love with Him; not love His ways; His plan for your life? This is indeed a confusing question for most people. Many people, for the most part, have been taught that loving someone is the same as being in love with him or her. However, that's wrong. There is a basic difference between loving and being in love. The author goes on to say that some people say when they are in love with each other but get tired of each other they can take a break.

YOUR RELATIONSHIP

Our lesson today is about your relationship with your Maker; the one who came and died for you. Some people take a break from paying their tithes; some people take a break from forgiving; some people take a break from long suffering and being kind, meek, gentle and tender, and yet those same people claim they are in love with God. They might love God, but they're not in love with God. One reader from the many articles I read, summed it up nicely, "Taking a break," he commented, "means not cutting ties to each other but just postponing the relationship temporarily to see where things are at." Now, remember we are talking about your relationship with God and the difference between loving someone and being in love. Found yourself already? Keep reading. Some say "taking a break" means taking a step back from a relationship that isn't meeting one or both partner's

---

[3]   Internet Search—different articles when searching for "Loving someone verses being in love" About.com Dating; Difference Between.net; Difference Between. com Bkirbykeith.wordpress.com

needs and reviewing how the relationship fits into their life's picture over the long-term. A person might think to him/herself, "I need to step back and see where we are going. I need to step back and see if this is really the woman/man for me," after you've slept together, unmarried, shacking up for two years. It's about re-evaluating or redefining a relationship without the stress of the relationship itself. *I'm going to cut things off and get by myself and think about this whole God thing. A godly thing, and Him loving me unconditionally, and I have to separate, and I have to love everybody. I have to love the souls of the white man and the black man, and be consistent, diligent and fervent, and to pray and fast and live in the word. I need a break! I need a break to examine things! I love God though just not in love with Him . . . today.*

You can't hide *real love*. That's what I'm telling you. And so when the other brother who was not her husband came around she would yid, "Ah, I see you don't love me today." One day, tired of the back and forth, she hung herself. What's the difference between loving someone and being in love?

Some authors conclude that the problem with "taking a break" is that few people actually define what it means for their relationship. Does it mean that one or both of you can see other people, other gods, other things, other times, go other places do other things when you should be in church? Is that it? I don't know. Or do you want to muddy the waters with more? What is it all about? Some say being in love is a feeling that is beyond description as one feels smitten, infatuated, enamoured, and ready to fall head over heels for someone. This is not the same as loving someone or something. Kind of reminds me of when I got saved. Somebody came along that loved me unconditionally. He didn't care about my past. He didn't care that I once had an addiction. He didn't care about what happened to me when I was little. He didn't care that I was skinny and had big lips. These things didn't matter. He loved me unconditionally. How could I not respond? I was infatuated at once and fell in love. What's the difference between loving someone and being in love? This author goes on to say that some spouses say they still love each other, but they are no longer in love with each other.

I have a problem with that. You may say, "That's your problem Reverend because I know where I stand." But hear me out. Again, the article [taken from the internet] states that many times we hear spouses say that they still love each other but they are no longer in love with each other.

YOUR GIRLFRIEND

What I have discovered in pastoring and counselling people for over 16 years is you have to, number one, make sure you get the "right" person. Secondly, marriage is the beginning not the end of dating. You should still be dating throughout your entire marriage. Your wife should still be your girlfriend and your husband should still be your boyfriend. You have to keep on working on your relationship. Your companion should be your best friend. You have to keep on working on your relationship. You have to be quick to forgive, quick to listen, and slow to give your opinion about what you think. If you say mean words or use profanity and do horrible stuff to one another, words are so powerful you will talk the love right out of your marriage. But we're talking about your relationship with the Lord.

What is the difference between loving someone and being in love? It is clear that being in love is kind of a spark or flame included in the feeling of love. It is when that flame dims that the people say that they are no longer in love with their spouse or girlfriend. Let's see how can I put that in a spiritual sense? In the high priestly prayer in John the 17th chapter, Jesus stated that He was talking to His father and said, "Lord I have not lost any. All of the ones that you have given me I still have. Why? Because they love me." But He never said that you couldn't leave. The ones that are still in the hands of Jesus, they are in love with Him. But those who have left the Lord; they may have loved Him at some point in their lives but were no longer in love with Him. Revelation backs this up when it says, **Nevertheless I have somewhat against thee, because thou hast left thy first love. Remember therefore from whence thou art fallen, and repent, and do the first works; or**

else I will come unto thee quickly, and will remove thy candlestick out of his place, except thou repent (Revelation 2:5). The Lord wishes us to be cold or hot, not indecisive. **I know thy works, that thou art neither cold nor hot: I would thou wert cold or hot. So then because thou art lukewarm, and neither cold nor hot, I will spue thee out of my mouth. Because thou sayest, I am rich, and increased with goods, and have need of nothing; and knowest not that thou art wretched, and miserable, and poor, and blind, and naked. As many as I love, I rebuke and chasten: be zealous therefore, and repent** (Revelation 15-17,19).

A STRONG FEELING

Love is a strong feeling of affection or attraction to somebody accompanied by a sense of liking, desire, and longing. With such an abstract experience such as love, people are wondering if there is a difference between being in love and loving someone. The answer is, in fact, that there are many differences between the two. Being in love is like being in a slightly altered state of mind. In such a condition, your focus shifts from yourself. Can I get an Amen? "Your focus shifts from yourself." It can feel as if you cannot live a day without that person. You eagerly want or need them to become part of your life. Save my soul, I'm so sorry that I sinned against you, Lord. We were shaped in iniquity, and in sin did our mother's conceive us. We were born needing to fall in love. Right? Moreover, being in love means that you are already looking at what you can do together with your partner, because you have become love struck. Who can I use as a witness? My boy, Jeremiah. He said Lord, ever since you called me they've been beating up on me. Ever since you called me to prophesy they've been putting me in one hole after another. And people have been blacking my eyes. Jeremiah's love he had for the Lord in his heart is undeniable. He tried it. He decided within himself that he was not taking any more black eyes! Matter of fact, he was not going to preach in the Lord's name. Jeremiah must have thought, "I am not going to prophecy in your name, I'm going to sit back and be quiet. But that love that I accepted from you is like fire! And if I don't preach your word, I am unhappy. So I'll take the consequences, because I'm in love with you. I'm going to keep on speaking." *Thus saith the Lord*! Yes! Who else was love struck? Stephen, ooh he was dying! But he said, "Oh my God, I see Jesus! They can only kill me one time but the next time I look up I'll be at the throne of the almighty God. You only can kill me once".

INFATUATION

Some will say that the initial stage of being in love is mostly infatuation. Some will still argue that it's a state wherein you're smitten, taken with, and besought. To say that being in love is not infatuation requires that you base your love for someone on the grounds of compassion, compromise . . . uh oh. Should I name them? OK, I'm going to do it. You convinced me. Compassion, compromise, respect, and dependability. Uh-oh. What's the difference between loving someone and being in love? Huh? John 15:13 says, **Greater love hath no man than this, than a man lay down his life for his friends.** You know, some people can meet somebody on a one-night stand and tell them that they love them for the few minutes they are together. Some people say, "I love you I love you I love you," but what they really mean is "I lust you. I lust you. I lust you. Ooh I gotta have them. I just gotta have them cause Reverend that's the one; that's the one Reverend." You done started tarrying off of it. That's the one that's the one that's the one that's the one that's the one that's the one that's the one whew! That's the one that's the one! Whew!

GOD SO LOVED

John 3:16-17 says, **For God so loved the world, that he gave his only begotten Son, that whosoever believeth in him shall not perish, but have everlasting life.** For God so loved the whole word. He fell in love with us, and He still is in love with us. He's in love with this world. The

Lord *loves* you but doesn't *like* the sinful things that you do. He thinks I'm married to a backslider. He loves the sinner; He just hates the sin that they do. The Lord has made us apart of Himself. I don't want somebody to just love me. I want them to be in love with me, because they'll be patient with me and kind towards me, and tolerable with me, and easy to forgive, and have my best interest at heart. When somebody loves you they might just only love you based on condition. But when you are in love, you don't fight over small things, and you don't complain over every little issue. You say lovely things and kind things and sweet things when you are in love. **God sent not his Son into the world to condemn the world; but that the world through him might be saved** (John 3:17).

FATHER AND SON

King Solomon started out in love with God. At the end of his life, he didn't even love Him. 1st Kings third chapter tells the story of David. So it says here David and Bathsheba came together. The Lord punished David for taking another man's wife. He took the baby from Bathsheba, because the baby was created in sin. The Lord said the child born in sin and had to die. But the Lord did not leave David. He loved David. And after David truly found forgiveness, the Lord forgave him and gave another son with Bathsheba, which was Solomon. David had it in his heart to build a temple for the Lord, but he was unable to because he had shed much blood. But the Lord said that he would use his son.

And so now Solomon is in charge. **And Solomon loved the Lord, walking in the statutes of David his father: only he sacrificed and burnt incense in high places. In Gibeon the Lord appeared to Solomon in a dream by night; and God said, Ask what I shall give thee. And Solomon said, Thou has shewed unto thy servant David my father great mercy, according as he walked before thee in truth, and in righteousness, and in uprightness of heart with thee; and thou hast kept for his this great**

kindness, that thou hast given him a son to sit on his throne, as it is this day (I Kings 3:3-4,5-6). Imagine how close two people would have to be in order for one person to want to meet all their needs. Think about how close the bride is to the Lord that we know He will do anything for us. In turn, because not only do we love Him and are in love with Him, we know we will do anything He asks us to do for His name's sake. The word declared in the book of John, ". . . if you love me [like you say] you will keep my commandments." That's what the book says, right?

IN A DREAM

Solomon finds himself in a situation where the God of the universe has come to him in a dream saying he can have anything at all he wants, God will give it to him. Now, there are two types of people around. You have those that look out for themselves and those that look out for others. And the Lord said here because He knew Solomon was going to ask according to His divine will. He asked, "What shall I give thee?" In the beginning, Solomon's heart was very tender toward God. This just tells you about his heart and dedication to the Lord. You can listen to some men talk about their wives and tell if they love them or are in love with them. They talk about their wives as being a queen, how well she takes care of him and the meals she makes. Or if they have a disagreement, they don't talk about it because it is not anyone else's business. In turn, listen to how some women talk about their husbands. How he watches over her, protects her, takes care of her, and meets her needs. But think about this. You could find out a lot of characteristics about people if you just have a brief conversation with them. They will tell you a lot about themselves. If they're unhappy, they're always looking. You have something going on in your relationship, you will never get it fixed looking over in the neighbor's yard. They only put the good stuff out. But they might be hoarders on the inside. Solomon finds himself in a position where the great God of the universe has asked him what He can do for him. He starts out so humbly by reminding the Lord

---

of His grace and His mercy towards his father. He says in verse six, "Thou hast, shewed unto thy servant David my father great mercy, according as he walked before thee in truth, and in righteousness, and in uprightness of heart with thee; and thou hast kept for him this great kindness, that thou hath given him a son to sit on his throne, as it is this day." What was Solomon doing Reverend Thomas? He was reminding the Lord that what He told his daddy He would do, He did it. And not only did He do it, but his daddy made sure he knew who did it. It was the Lord! And he thanked Him for it. Because if He had not moved for his daddy then, see, he wouldn't have been in a certain position later. Isn't that the word? The Lord gives us the strength to get the wealth we have. Isn't that the Lord that takes care of us, and wakes us up in the morning, and watches out for us, and gives us favor in the market, and makes even our enemies be at peace with us? It's God! It's God! But what did Solomon ask the Lord for? Now you can measure this up with your prayers? Do you love God or are you in love with Him? Solomon says give me your gifts. Give me wisdom and knowledge, which equals prophecy so that I can judge your people correctly. Give me a tool; give me a skill; give me the capability that will bless my people because if my people are fruitful, if my people are blessed, if my people are nurtured, that will bless me as a leader.

A MAN AFTER MY OWN HEART

The Lord says, ahh . . . a man after my own heart. He says here in verses 10 and 11, **And the speech pleased the Lord, that Solomon had asked this thing. And God said unto him, because thou hast asked this thing, and hast not asked for thyself long life**. The Lord was saying, *you didn't ask me for stuff for yourself. But you asked me for things that will magnify Me in your life*. Did you know that? Giving him wisdom and knowledge allowed the Lord to shine. It allowed the Lord to be lifted up. And isn't that the word, that if you lift me up I'll draw people unto me? Amen. Solomon asked for the Lord to continue to be glorified in his life. And the Lord said bam! I like that! Let me give you all this other stuff that I knew was in your heart, but you put me first. Here it is. Here it is. And he told him in verse 13, **And I have also give thee that which thou hast not asked, both riches, and honour: so that there shall not be any among the kings like unto thee all thy days.** Verse 14 says, there it is. **And if thou wilt walk in my ways, to keep my statutes and my commandments, as thy father David did walk, then I will lengthen thy days.** He's saying that if you will walk in My ways and in My statures; if you *continue* to love Me with your whole heart, soul, and mind then I will do this and that. You can't say you are in love with the Lord without serving Him with your whole heart, soul, and mind.

I LOVE YOU—I LUST YOU

Love is used so loosely in our society. Guys meet a girl on the first date, telling her "I love you." What they really mean is "I lust you. Let's go around the corner and get in the back of the car." Don't let these people lie to you. Girl, it's going on . . . all those visions of sugar cones. No! Nope! Nothing from nothing leaves nothing. (Singing) you gotta have something if you want to be with me. (Singing) What's the difference between loving someone and being in love?

Solomon seeks the Lord and the Lord promises to give him wisdom and knowledge. David ordained that Solomon, his son, become the next king. He then gave Solomon the plans for the temple. **And thou, Solomon my son, know thou the God of thy father, and serve him with a perfect heart and with a willing mind: for the Lord searcheth all hearts, and understandeth all the imaginations of the thoughts: if thou seek him, he will be found of thee; but if thou forsake him, he will cast thee off for ever. Take heed now; for the Lord hath chosen thee to build an house for the sanctuary: be strong, and do it. And the pattern of all that he had by the spirit** (I Chronicles 28:9-10,12). And people claim they can't understand the word. People claim they can't understand God.

You are not going to never understand somebody you don't spend any time with. Come on Reverend Thomas preach it girl. Preach it! That's what's wrong with a lot of marriages you gotta learn them outside the bedroom; you gotta learn them. ***Know the God of your father serve him with a loyal heart.*** The more you know the Lord, the more you'll love Him. People don't stay in there with the Lord because they don't know him. These people think some of this stuff going on is God's will He has nothing to do with it. But it's because you can't discern the difference, because you don't know enough about Him. That's because you love Him, but you have yet to fall in love with Him. For the Lord searches all hearts and understands all the intents of the thoughts. If you seek Him, there it is. He will be found by you. But if you forsake Him, He will cast you off forever. Consider now for the Lord hath chosen you to build a house for the sanctuary. Be strong and do it. Now, there are a lot of things going on in that verse about being in love with God. Notice, David made it so plain to Solomon that even though the Lord chose him, that doesn't mean anything. You gotta earn the fact that he chose you. You got to show up with the fact that he chose you. Just because he chose you don't mean anything. You gotta respond that He chose you. You gotta plead with Him and thank Him that He chose you. You gotta walk softly that He chose you! You gotta live as close to the Lord as you can because He chose you! Yes! That's being in love with the Lord. Everybody loves God at some time or another.

MY SON WOULD NOT LISTEN

And when my son was murdered, people were telling me from here to Zion that God had another plan for his life. I said, "Don't lie on God. Stop lying on God." The only way God is involved in this is that if God wasn't on the scene, Daniel probably could have died in January instead of July. God had another plan for him. God has nothing to do with death, except the death of one of His saints; to bring to home so that they won't keep suffering. We told Daniel to stay from around "those parts." But he was so smart. Gotta face the truth about everything in your life. You gotta face the truth about everything in your life. Some of you married couples need to get down to business. The problem lies within yourself and not with your companion. The problem is with yourself, not your companion. It takes a lot to be a man. Even though the Lord chose Solomon, David had to encourage his son to seek God for himself. He encouraged him to know God. David encouraged Solomon to stay with God. He encouraged him that the people weren't going to understand him. Stay with God! He encouraged him you gotta be strong and when you serve the true and the living God you gotta be tough! You gotta be strong! You gotta be bold because practically everybody else is not serving Him. And they'll try to bring you down. You can't be no punk when you in love. You can't be no punk I'm telling you! Cause people are going to try to talk you out of being saved. People are going to say you go to church too much. But when you were out in the world how much was you clubbing? When you were out in the world you were gambling on your phone. And now you're going to tell me I'm going to starve if I fast? No! That's the only reason why I'm lasting, because I'm fasting! Yes! Where were you when I was driving from hotel to hotel? Where were you when I was going from lounge to lounge? You weren't lifting up a flag then! Shut up and be quiet! Shut up and be quiet! People might say, "You are giving that church all your money." Well, you were giving it to a man, weren't you? "*Come on baby come on baby come on baby come on baby baby baby baby baby baby come on baby come on baby baby baby baby baby. (Lol) Don't act like that daddy give you a few more dollars. Come on baby baby baby baby baby. Come on daddy give you a few more dollars.*" That's what you want? Married and you buying sex from your companion; that's not right! What's the difference between loving someone and being in love?

TWO MOTHERS

After the Lord blessed Solomon, he became Israel's most magnificent King. The Queen of Sheba came to see him. Remember how his wisdom was tested with the two ladies who brought the babies? His fame spread all abroad. The Lord wants to bless some of you to be a financial blessing to the ministry. During Solomon's reign, the Lord made Israel a royal power, and a great wealth flowed into the kingdom. Solomon displayed such great wisdom from God that people came from distant lands to hear him. He taught many proverbs and wrote Ecclesiastics and some Psalms. Yet Solomon did more than any other king to breakdown the kingdom and destroy its true foundations. He was given so much, but he did so much damage. Solomon stopped being in love with the Lord. That close bond that close fellowship and close connection. He didn't need that anymore. He didn't need to talk to God. He didn't need to sacrifice. He didn't need to spend time away with God, or so he thought. But other things on the outside started getting Solomon's attention. He started idol gods for his foreign wives.

That the Lord appeared to Solomon the second time, as he had appeared unto him into Gibeon. And the Lord said unto him, I have heard thy prayer and thy supplication, that thou has made before me: I have hallowed this house, which thou has built, to put my name there for ever; and mine eyes and mine heart shall be there perpetually (I Kings 9:2-3). The Lord is warning Solomon again to be careful where to walk. Be careful where to tread. Be careful with who you associate with. Be careful where you go. Be careful who you let in your house and what you watch on TV. Be careful. The Lord wants His presence to stay with you. The Lord was letting Solomon and us know that this is what you have to do. If you want Him to be with you, if you want His favour to continue with you, this is what you have to do. You want His presence? The presence is the power. The presence brings the anointing's. The presence brings the healing. The presence brings deliverance. And so we have to make this house of God suitable for Him to dwell at any time. We want the glory of the Lord to fill our church. So, we have to do the work at home. We have to make sure we are kind and sweet and show love. We can't enter God's temple with hypocrisy in our hearts and minds. We women have to love our husbands. And men, you have to love your wives. We have to raise our children according to God's word. We have to do what's right. We have to have a family altar in our homes, leading our children to it, not just sending them. Lead them to the altar! Yes! Yes!

BUT IF YOU TURN

The Lord warned Solomon. He told him, Solomon, Solomon. I will establish your throne. Just follow me. Solomon I will establish your throne. And here it is in verse 6 **But if ye shall at all turn from following me.** There it is. There it is. **But if ye shall at all turn from following me; you or your children and will not keep my commandments and my statures which I have set before you. But go and serve other gods and worship them then will I cut off Israel out of the land which I have given them. And this house which I have hallowed for my name will I cast out of my sight. And Israel shall be a proverb and a byword among all the people. And at this house, which is high, everyone that passes by it shall be astonished, and shall hiss; and they shall say, Why has the Lord done this unto this land, and unto this house? And they shall answer because they forsook the Lord their God and who brought forth their fathers out of the land of Egypt and have taken hold upon other gods. And have worshiped them and served them therefore hath the Lord brought upon them all this evil** (I Kings 9:6-9).

I saw somebody in a store parking lot that used to come to church. The woman said to me she had been thinking about us; we had been on her mind recently. She asked us where the church is. We told her we're on the same block we've been for nearly 16 years. And the lady said, "Well you know what. That's something. Somebody told me you had moved." I said, "Nope. I'm still right there for nearly 15 years." I told her, "Not only are we here, but we're working on our fourth book. Not only are we here, but we're on two TV stations now. Not only are we here, but people are being healed, delivered and set free!" She said, "I'll be right on by." Isn't that something to think about? When you're doing right, don't worry about the chatter. God will look out for you. People, I believe, tried to tell this lady that we were no longer in existence but when you're doing right, don't worry about what people are saying. When you're doing right, God will stand by you. You don't have to prove yourself to anybody but God. When you're doing right, people are going to talk. You can't stop people's mouths. They're going to gossip and say this and that. I'm still here. Churches are going into bankruptcy, but we still on TV by the grace of God.

STRANGE WIVES

Solomon loved his many *strange* wives. **But King Solomon loved many strange women . . . Of the nations concerning which the Lord said unto the children of Israel, Ye shall not go in to them, neither shall they come in unto you: for surely they will turn away your heart after their gods: Solomon clave unto these in love. And he had seven hundred wives, princesses, and three hundred concubines: and his wives turned away his heart** (I Kings 11:1-3). Now, at the sunset of his life, Solomon lost everything. He started out so strong. He started out like many of you. He started out on fire for God. Solomon was really in love with the Lord. What's the key of staying in love? You gotta work at it. You gotta work at it every day. You must be dedicated and consecrated, devoted.

SELF-EXAMINATION

What's the key to a good marriage? Self-examination. Stop pointing your finger at the other person and look at what you're doing. The key to a successful marriage is that you are supposed to be a team; you have the same mission in mind. There shouldn't be any controlling women. "You going to do what I say. What kind of mess?" And a man should want his wife looking pretty. "I am not spending any money on them shoes." And you got to treat women with great love and passion. And the wife must treat the husband with respect and great love. Men and women are different when it comes down to love making. Women like gotta drop flowers and *hi hi hi honey. Hello I thought about you. What time you get off sweetie? [guy make say] Oh I don't know [lady may say]. Oh I'll pick ok [guy may say]. You want some black walnut [lady may say]? Um hmmm. Aww what do we have planned for today? Oh you know I have to help the kids with [lady may say]. I'll do it. I'll help them with their homework so you can rest [guy may say]. Ummm yeah. Oh yeah, I know. I know.* See, women, we take a little bit more prep time, but we're worth it. We're worth it. We're worth it. Man comes in from work all sweaty, grumpy, hot talking about "come on!" Now I'm not going on. You want honey, you gotta be sweet. You say good things to your wife that's you're companion. You show love. Supposed to be love making, not a fight. Some of you almost have it down to caveman mentality. *Come on here! I said come on here! Trying to block people out the room what kind of mess?* Women, you can't play the game, and then when you get married the poor guy doesn't know where "that other woman" went. You know what I mean. You played that game, but don't realize that whatever you did to get it, you have to do the same to keep. Hahaha. And then some of you will, as an act of vengeance, withhold yourself like that's some kind of weapon. You're a real dumb-dumb. You'll figure it out, but I pray it's not too late. You're a real dumb-dumb.

Solomon loved his wives. He had seven hundred wives and those wives led him astray. He started worshiping false gods instead of the one true God. Solomon's heart was no longer totally devoted to God. When you are in love with somebody you are totally devoted to that person. You are not easy to be talking about getting a divorce and moving out; always talking about moving out when you can't get your way. It's time to grow up. Remember, you always wanted to be grown, so be grown! You both stick it out—you stay together. Kids need both mother and father **BUT** I wouldn't recommend anyone stay with an abusive person.

TWO KIDS

Treat your children all as equals. If you have two kids, you can't take one kid's word over the other kid. You've got Johnny and Gina [hypothetically speaking], and Johnny is full of the devil. You need to godly discipline. Stop falsely accusing Gina! I got so many whippings as a child. I was the middle child in between two older siblings and two younger siblings. They always seemed to point their finger at me. I took many whippings for them, as well as for myself. Investigate. Find out who's doing what. If your kids tell you that the other one is doing something, take a moment to see if that child is telling the truth or not. You know if you have a rat or a skunk. You know it! The Bible says to bend the sap while it's young. It might be hard, but if you visit it enough, it will bend. I'm a witness. On my job, when it's a little bitty small space that only one person can crawl into, they call that "a confined space." Get that lovely child of yours in a confined space and remind him whose boss. He can't do anything else; he is in a confined space. You take the *work permit* right in there with you. Some of these kids are full of the devil. You don't want to be accused of showing favouritism. Watch it! Listen to what these kids say, because some of them can lie right to your face and not even blink. That child will grow up to hate you. I'm telling you. Some of you all are guilty and have to face yourself. Don't be deceived about who are. Self-deceit is the worst deceit there is. You listen.

Don't show partiality to one child. Listen to both until you get it all figured out. Momma would get me, no matter what time she got home. I could be sound asleep. Boy, she would bring me to life. Hahaha. I'm still standing here today. She didn't kill me. I needed every one of them whippings. I needed every one of them. And my daddy use to whip us *just in case*. "You take this for what you are going to do." You be like, "Daddy I did nothing wrong daddy." He said, "Yep, I'm going to get you for what you're going to do." And don't let my mama be whipping somebody else. Her memory will start going through the *Rolodex* about what you did. So, I want you to work on that. Some of you know your child is no angel. Some of these kids really are influenced by the stuff that's happening in these schools. When your kids get out for the summer, you gotta have a plan for them. When they get home, go through their room. What are they doing? You need to be more involved in what's going on. These kids will get taken out of your life right in front of your eyes.

Solomon started worshiping the false gods he built for his many wives. How sad. How tragic. Solomon's heart no longer was totally devoted to God. He even built special buildings for his wives false gods. God was very sad and angry with Solomon. He was hurt that Solomon no longer loved him, but was in love with him. He was hurt that Solomon no longer came to Him for help. They use to reason together, but sin destroyed that fellowship. God wanted to keep his relationship strong, but Solomon turned away from Him. Instead of listening to God, Solomon did things his own way. God told Solomon that because of his sin and his attitude, He would divide the kingdom into two parts. Just as God said when Solomon died, the kingdom was divided into two countries. The southern part was called Judah, and the northern part was called Israel. Each country had its own king. Unfortunately, most of the kings did not stay in love with God. Let's get those hands up and say the sinner's prayer. **Everybody saying, "Oh God! Oh God! Please forgive me for sinning against you. But I have come home. Never to leave you again. Lord I love you, but I need to be in love with you. Lord I love you, but I need to be in love with you. By faith in your blood Lord, save my soul! Save my soul! Save my soul! Help me Lord! I need your help!** And if you mean it today, you have the God of the universe on your side. God bless you. And if you need prayer today, the Levites will direct you, and I will be right around to pray for you.

CHAPTER 2
HAVE YOU EVER LOVED SOMEONE WHO DIDN'T LOVE YOU BACK?
CHANCE AFTER CHANCE

Have you ever loved someone who didn't love you back chance after chance? John 3:16-17 says, **For God so loved the world, that he gave his only begotten Son, that whosoever believeth in him should not perish, but have everlasting life. For God sent not his Son into the world to condemn the world; but that the world through him might be saved.** He used all of His love when He made a Calvary for us through the blood of His Son, Jesus. People may think that when God the Father created Adam maybe He used all of His love. No! Some people may think maybe the God of heaven used all of His love when He created the world. No! God used all of His love when He gave His Son, Jesus to be the sacrificial lamb for the whole world. Jesus died one time, and He's not going to die again. These lessons are encouraging and inspiring. But they're also warnings to not fall in the same state as some of the people that we have been studying. Our bible is a workbook, and we should treat it as such; write in it, make notes in it, highlight it. And if that one wears out, then just get yourself another one. I sometimes have to buy a couple of my favorite books because I write in them so much. It really depends on how the Lord is dealing with me about a certain subject. The bible says eat the word right? Psalm 105:37-45 says **He brought them forth also with silver and gold: and there was not one feeble person among their tribes.** Praise ye the Lord! Have you ever loved someone who did not love you back?

TIME AND TIME AGAIN

The children of Israel, the Lord gave them *chance after chance* to love Him with their whole heart, soul and mind. He gave them chance after chance. The Lord even displayed His miraculous power; demonstrated His love in such a great way by parting the Red Sea. He performed so many miracles. God repeatedly forgave the children of Israel, time and time again for their various transgressions against Him. However, as a result of their insurrection and disobedience, God caused them to wander aimlessly around the desert for forty years. The bible is your workbook, and you should underline the things that stand out to you. When you are studying the word of the Lord, initiate that study by asking the Holy Spirit to guide you, lead you and teach you. You gotta take time. You had to give your mind like you did when you were in school. You have to understand the way you learn. I have markers, books, and I go on the internet. When I get a certain scripture, I might go to a reference book I have, because it helps me understand how they got to this point—I need to know the history. Use history and scripture. History can tell you about the people in a certain place, during a certain time; what was going on at that time; what was the reason why the Lord moved upon them to say this or to do that.

ALL THE PEOPLE CRIED

Numbers 41:1 says, **And all the congregation lifted up their voice, and cried; and the people wept that night. And all the children of Israel murmured against Moses and against Aaron: and the whole congregation said into them, Would God that we had died in the land of Egypt!** God already told them in the previous chapter, "I'm giving you the land." The only thing they had to do was be obedient and following instructions; that was His promise to them. The Lord has promised us that He'll keep sickness away from our gates. If you get sick, you just look to the Lord that He'll heal you! The Lord said He will make provision for you;

He would look out for you; take care of you and look out for all of your tomorrows. If you do what's right according to your finances by paying the tenth you owe unto the Lord, that keeps His hands untied, and He said He'll look out for you. He'll give you a good companion if you seek the Lord for that companion. God promised to supply all of our needs according to His riches and glory by Christ Jesus. If we would only look to Him, He would direct all of our paths. In the beginning of 13, He told the children of Israel the land belonged to them. The entire congregation lifted up their voice and cried, and the people wept that night. And all the children of Israel murmured against Moses and against Aaron. The whole congregation said unto them, "Would God that we died in the land of Egypt or would God that we had died in the wilderness?" Now, this is just slavery mentality. And some of God's people are in the same state of mind today. You cried for the Lord. You had an abusive husband, and you cried out for help. "Lord please just get me away from this. Lord please. This man, he's just so controlling." Listen to me you men, those who are husbands and those of you that want to be a husband. The bible says you are supposed to love your wife as Christ loved the church, and Christ gave his life for the church. When you get married that woman is your responsibility. You gotta make sure all her needs are met, not the needs you feel like you need to be making that end up being productive for you. Somebody hear what I'm saying? Come on. Say "Amen." Say it. "Amen. Amen. Hallelujah!" Our responsibility as the woman is supposed to be to take care of our husband. You know this is what the Lord is telling us. But you know all the people, every single one of them, murmured against Aaron and against Moses. It's slavery mentality. Lord, this man is abusive to me. Lord, I'm looking for a way out. And so the Lord provides a way out for you. And maybe you have to work at McDonald's or leave that corporate job. Maybe you gotta take a different job just for your safety. Lord I want a companion. I want a companion. Maybe the Lord may move on you to look for a wife at the *Salvation* Army. Go down there to the place at the resale shop. "You know they are not making any money down there. That can't be the Lord," you might think. The Lord knows what you have and need even before you ask. Slavery mentality, slavery mentality. You can't love somebody if you haven't experienced love. You cannot do it because it's not in you. You can't give forth something to somebody that you don't know anything about. There's a lot more to this than what you see. There's more to it. God makes a man. God makes a woman. God makes a home. God makes a family. And God makes a marriage. The bible says except the Lord builds the house those that build, labor in vain. Nothing is going to happen to it. **And every one that heareth these sayings of mine, and doeth them not, shall be likened unto a foolish man, which built his house upon the sand: And the rain descended, and the floods came, and the winds blew, and beat upon that house; and it fell: and great was the fall of it** (Matthew 7:26-27) In marriage, you need divine love. Human love is not enough for those rocky roads that will come in marriage.

SIMON THE SORCERER

Simon, a sorcerer from the 8th Chapter of Acts, bewitched the people for a long time, making the people think that he was some great wonder. It's the same mentality as the children of Israel. They were used to being in slavery even though they cried for deliverance. They were used to just getting beat and making brick without all the ingredients. They were used to that for so many generations. They heard a deliverer was coming and got complacent; they got used to hearing that a deliverer was coming, but they weren't expecting him to come. They got used to the thought of a deliverer coming, but they only had mental assent; that reality never got in their hearts, sort of like some of you. You've heard me preach for fifteen years that you have to have the Holy Ghost to make the Rapture. You're like yeah, yeah, yeah, yeah, yeah, but it's not a reality. It's not a reality to you. That's slavery mentality. You cried out for Him to bring you out of darkness into the marvelous light. Jesus Christ said call upon the name of the Lord. You might be saying, "Reverend Thomas I got one for you. John 15:16 says that the Lord said I didn't choose Him but He chose me." You say, "Reverend Thomas, Reverend Thomas I got one for you. It says in John 6:44 that no man can come unto the Lord unless the spirit draws them." But you gotta have an inclination; you gotta have a desire in your heart. He will not come knocking on your door if you don't want him. No. You were in a desperate situation, and He came right on-time and made you free. Yes! Yes! Yes! And some of you were in diverse sins, practicing homosexuality, lesbianism, stealing, and thievery. Just low down, low down. Some of you were in diverse sins, but you had that slavery mentality. Now you can see. What's the problem about giving? What's the problem about increasing your prayer time? What's the problem about volunteering? What's the problem about spending all day in the church for the sake of souls? You use to spend all night out at the bar. See, it's a slavery mentality.

THE BURNING BUSH

Have you ever loved somebody that didn't love you back? The Bible let us know that an angel talked to Moses from the burning bush. An angel of the Lord spoke to Moses out of the burning bush. How long was the bush burning before he finally decided to look up there and see it? How long was the Lord after you before you had to get in a place where your life was so hard, you were so destitute, you were so desperate? The Lord has been calling. He's been calling. The children of Israel crossed the Red Sea. If I am not mistaken, they already had the cloud by day and the pillar of fire by night. Is it right somebody? Now just think about where God brought you from. But yet you complain, you mumble, you grumble, ain't thankful. It's almost like the new you and the old you are almost the same. Maybe you're back on the block. It's right here in the word. It says, you brought us out here to die. But that wasn't what they were saying when they were actually dying. That's not what they were saying! If you want to be free you'll do anything. Kind of mimics what you said right? Lord I'll do anything for you if you make me free. Lord, I'll do anything for you if I don't have AIDS. Lord, I'll do anything for you if I don't have a sexually transmitted disease. Lord, I'll do anything for you if you could get me off this porn. And now he has delivered you, yet it's just too much. Got a better job, yet you're asking for more, and it's just too much. Have you ever loved somebody that didn't love you back chance after chance after chance after chance? Numbers 14:3 says, **And wherefore hath the Lord brought us unto this land, to fall by the sword, that our wives and our children should be a prey? Was it not better for us to return into Egypt?** As soon as something happens, you want to go back to the old life. As soon as you can't get your way, you want to go back to watching those soap operas. As soon as you're challenged or your family challenges you to make a stand, you compromise, because after all, those are your kids. But what about God? Isn't He your all and all? Isn't He the God of the universe? Doesn't the earth go around on its axis at His command? Didn't He speak and the stars into existence? Come on somebody. And you talking about a human being that's probably talking about you anyway. That's just slavery mentality.

HE COULD HAVE FAILED

Did you not know that when Jesus was in the Garden of Gethsemane He could have called a legion of angels to come there? Some of you are just as dead as dead can be. That revival came, and you were on fire. You were lit a little bit. But some of you are back to your old ways, back on the internet or on that phone, back talking on the wrong conversations. That little perversion started creeping back up again. You are going to get caught. You are going to get caught unaware. Yep, thank you Lord. And they said to one another, let us make a captain and let us return to Egypt. Their only thought was let me go back. Let me go back. It's easy to do nothing. It's easy to cry wolf. It's easy to talk about not getting out of bed today. It's easy to be depressed all day and not clean up, not take care of yourself. It's easy to talk about what you're going to do, as long as you don't ever do it. It's easy to talk about fasting, as long as you don't ever do it. It's easy to talk about being committed to the Lord, as long as you don't do it. It's easy to talk about getting right, as long as you don't get right. It's easy to stay in the place you're in if it requires no effort. But the challenge comes in being better, doing better, doing what's right. The challenge comes in being the adult you always said you wanted to be. I can't wait. Now that you're grown, act like it. You always wanted to have your own castle. Now you've got it. It's a little broken down, a little patched up on a couple of ends, but that's yours. You're paying a mortgage on it. Things get broke, prop it up! That's your castle. You were disillusioned, but this is life. You wanted a baby, now you got it. And that baby has to be provided for. You have a kid, and what do you spend your time talking about? Nobody loves you. Nobody cares about you. What about your life? You should've thought about that at that time. The baby is here now. Look at this lesson about when God's people were in captivity and slavery: I want to be free Lord please make a way for me. Lord help me. And the people had heard the stories from generation to generation that a deliverer, a saviour was coming. The bible is so plain about this. Think about your life. Think about your life. When you were out in sin, those of you who are saved, you were looking for a way out. In your heart, you wanted to give up. Maybe the next day you woke up and had a new sense of hope. You just believed something was going to happen for you. I don't know how. It might have seemed like you almost got down to the floor, but some way somebody called you, somebody stopped over with encouraging words that inspired you. And the Lord touched that person to come on and get you, to get you to hold on a little while longer so He could get you right in a place so you could be delivered. But now you say you don't have time; that it's not a necessity to serve that same God—you're too busy. What you are saying is "let's make us a king." I want to go back to Egypt. To serve Christ is life. He said I am the way, the truth and the life. I'm the bread of life. Isn't that what the Lord told the woman at the well? He said if you knew who you were talking to; you wouldn't be playing them games you are playing. I'm a real man. He told her *this is real talk.*

THE PEOPLE HAD BEEN DECEIVED

Then Moses and Aaron fell on their faces before all the assembly of the congregation of the children of Israel. And Joshua the son of Nun, and Caleb the son of Jephunneh, which were of them that searched the land, rent their clothes (Numbers 14:5-6). Now, they knew something was about to jump off. Moses and Aaron knew something was getting ready to jump off; they knew it. They knew the people had been deceived; people had been seduced. You know when the Lord is bringing you through— when the Lord is delivering you that every day is not going to be a good day. Every day is not going to be a howdy howdy day. You are going to have some days that are just all right. You're going to have some days that are not so good, but at least you lived to have that day. You have to bring God with you to take you through that day. The "back-in-the-day" songwriters would say, ". . . if I never had a problem I wouldn't know God could solve them if every day was good." That's why we have so many weak children now trying to be adults. Because everything happens to them, we're running trying to get them out of it. No, let those jokers suffer so they can learn. Every time they need something we are jumping right to their command. No! You want some new shoes? When is the last time you cleaned up your room? But we are just paying for disobedience. When we were coming up we had chores before we got any money, which was very rare. They went around seeing if we did our chores. They did not just give us money and push us out of their way. Don't you know when you do that, when you assign chores and you go behind and check, you are forming character building? That's character building. And it's also character building when your child realizes that mama really does not keep her word. You told them you are going to whip them, get them! I have said that to a couple of people, and I'm going to keep my word. If you tell your kids you're coming up to that school, you better go! It'll generate more respect. It'll generate more respect for you. And so the Lord is loving saviour. God is our father. Jesus is our saviour. He doesn't give us everything we want. Where would the growth come from? Where would the love and dependence come from? Where would we have to exercise our faith and be humble and thankful and grateful? Where would that come in if we got everything we needed and everything we wanted? The Lord told Gideon he had too many people, because they will say they brought the victory and not Him. He wanted it to be an impossible situation, so when the results came out it was impossible the way they came out. But He is an impossible God. Right! Right! And you know as you go on and read the story in Numbers the 14th chapter; they just would not do what was right. And so they had to go around in the desert for forty years, although the Lord told Moses that he had forgiven the people. The people still had to suffer. Let's look at verse number 19. This is when Moses was praying that the Lord would forgive the people. **Pardon, I beseech thee, the iniquity of this people according unto the greatness of thy mercy, and as thou has forgiven this people, from Egypt even until now.**

The Lord forgave them but He still pronounced judgment. Sometimes people do something wrong to you then they say, "I said I was sorry." It's like some of these crooks that get caught. They are not sorry. They are just sorry they got caught. They are not sorry. They're supposed to be a Senator or a Congressman. They're living off the people's money. Then when they get caught, they want to seem as if they went mad like David did, acting like he was crazy. But he did that to save his life. Didn't David act like he was mad to save his life? Anybody read that? My mama used to tell us "when you get finished screaming and hollering I'm still going to whip you." You could run all around, and the Lord is the same way. When you get finished doing whatever it is, He's still going to get you. So, there's Moses praying to the Lord to please forgive his people for what they have done. Now, there's your perfect example of if you have ever loved somebody that didn't love you back. Moses could've said, "Yeah I know these people here! They're using me and they are going to make me miss my blessing! The only thing I can do is look at Canaan. I can't even. Yeah, I know I can't even go into Canaan!" Now that I think about it in retrospect, Moses is like let them too, "Go on. I'm cool. You want me to come up there?" In retrospect, he was like "its ok if I don't go. You want me to come up to the mountain? Ok Joshua. Go on boy! You deal with them people." So, Moses was praying for them in verse 18, **The Lord is longsuffering, and great mercy, forgiving iniquity and transgression, and by no means clearing the guilty.** Notice that, **visiting the iniquity of the fathers upon the children unto the third and the fourth generation.** Let me explain this verse so you can underline it and search it out for yourself. In Old Testament days, it would be often noted that the sons would have to pay for the sins of their fathers. We know in our day, since the death of Jesus, everyone is responsible for their own sins. Acts 17:30 says **And the times of this ignorance God winked at; but now commandeth all men every where to repent.**

AHAB

Remember Ahab? And the Lord said, see how even Ahab humbled himself. He said because Ahab humbled himself, he wouldn't bring destruction upon him, but his sons would have to deal with it in their lifetime (I Kings 21:29). Isn't that the same thing that also happened to Solomon? In verse 18, you have to know the history here, when we came under the grace dispensation [through the blood of Jesus, He became our grace], every man became responsible for the deeds done in his body. From the time that Jesus' blood was shed, everybody has to repent. Everybody has to repent. That's why Nicodemus snuck out one night asking the Lord what this is all about. Got to be born again. And most churches are not teaching that. How many people in hell today are thinking about that they were on their way to heaven?

PLEASE FORGIVE

Number 14:19-24 says, **Pardon, now I beseech thee, the iniquity of this people according to the greatness of thy mercy, and as thou hath**

31

forgiven this people, from Egypt even until now. And the Lord said, I have pardoned them according to thy word: But as truly as I live, all the earth shall be filled with the glory of the Lord. Because all those men which have seen my glory *Because all those men which have seen my glory,* and my miracles, which I did in Egypt and in the wilderness, have tempted me now these ten times, and have not hearkened to my voice; Surely they shall not see the land which I sware unto their fathers, neither shall any of them that provoked me see it: But my servant Caleb, because he what? **He had another spirit with him**. Caleb was different. And our young kids have to be taught to stand against the norm. There's nothing wrong with being different. There's nothing wrong with keeping your virginity until you're married. There isn't anything wrong with telling that boy to keep his hands to himself. It's the same old game, nothing new. As soon as they get what they want from you, they just pass your name all around the school. And some of you guys gotta watch out for some of these girls. They're notorious. They'll get you in the coat room and take you down. Some of these girls are ruthless. Some of you guys better keep yourself together. So, the Lord was telling Moses that yeah, *He forgave them, but they still have to pay. They still had to pay.* They wandered around in the wilderness for forty years, everyone who was twenty and above till they all died off. The Lord had to wait around. If you know anything about them going to the land of Canaan, it shouldn't have taken that long. But it ended up taking forty years because of disobedience. And you could think about that for your own life.

<u>YOU ARE NOT SAVED</u>

Have you ever loved somebody that didn't love you back chance after chance? How many chances has the Lord given you to receive the baptism in the Holy Ghost? And to not have the baptism in the Holy Ghost, you have to check if you have a real born again experience. If you say that you're saved but have no desire to receive the Holy Ghost baptism, you are not saved. How could you be? You have to really check that, because if you're really born again, you will really want the Holy Ghost and seek it. That desire not in your heart? You are probably not saved. How could you be in reality? Think about that. How can you really be saved? He saved your soul. He saved you to go on. Salvation, the baptism in the Holy Ghost, the greatness of God. The book of Acts, that's what they were about: Salvation, the baptism in the Holy Ghost, the greatness of God. Salvation, the baptism in the Holy Ghost, and the greatness of God. And when they stopped practicing that, the church was almost shutdown in the book of Acts. Amen. God even killed Ananias and Sapphira to show how pure the church must be. If you look at some of these churches today, my Lord and my God, everything is going on except honouring God. None of the people who had witnessed the appearance of God on Mount Sinai, as well as all of His other miracles on their behalf throughout the years, would not be allowed to enter the promised land on the other side of the Jordan river. In fact, anyone aged twenty or older who had grumbled and complained against God, not only would they not enter the land, but they were going to die in the desert. The leader wasn't exempt either. Even Moses, who had led them the entire way, because of anger and lack of reverence for God, was not be able to go over into Canaan.

TAKE THE ROD

Numbers 20:7-12 says, **And the Lord spake unto Moses, saying, Take the rod, and gather thou the assembly together, thou, and Aaron thy brother, and speak ye unto the rock before their eyes; and it shall give forth his water, and thou shall bring forth to them water out of the rock: so thou shalt give the congregation and their beasts drink. And Moses took the rod from before the Lord, as he commanded him. And Moses and Aaron gathered the congregation together before the rock, and he said unto them, Hear now, ye rebels; must we fetch you water out of this rock? And Moses lifted up his hand, and with his**

rod he smote the rock twice: and the water came out abundantly, and the congregation drank, and their beasts also. And the Lord spake unto Moses and Aaron, Because ye believed me not, to sanctify me in the eyes of the children of Israel, therefore ye shall not bring this congregation into the land which I have given them. This is the water of Meribah; because the children of Israel strove with the Lord, and he was sanctified in them. Now you have to think about this; you have to think about this in your life. You know in your tithes and your offering, that ten percent is holy money that you owe the Lord. You know people who live together and are not married; let them come in your house and act like they are married? Then you are not sanctifying the Lord. If you allow people to come and smoke and drink in your house, then you're not sanctifying the Lord. That's what it's all about. Maybe you know you have a child or a sibling that's a practicing homosexual or a practicing lesbian and you let them come on in like everything is good. You go to these baby showers and people not married? You're not sanctifying the Lord. It's just plain and simple. And, unlike Moses, at least he still made it to heaven. But if you're doing that in this hour, you are not going to make it to heaven. Isn't that what James 4:4 says? **Ye adulterers and adulteresses, know ye not that the friendship of the world is enmity with God? Whosoever therefore will be a friend of the world is the enemy of God.** If you don't honor the Lord on this earth and before people; if you're ashamed of Him before this wicked and perverse generation, then He will be ashamed of you before God the Father and the angels in heaven.

CUT THEM OFF!

Have you ever loved somebody that didn't love you back? Don't let anyone cause you to miss the blessings of the Lord. Cut them off; shut them up. Moses had so much on him. One moment they were grateful, the next moment they were full of complaints. One moment they were thankful, the next moment unthankful. And they were just trying to use them. You have to keep your calling and your election sure. You have to know God is calling you. God is using you. He did not ever promise us we were going to like our role. My calling is my calling. Your calling is your calling. Your calling is not the husband and the wife. You're not lumped up in this. You owe allegiance to God yourself. But you better not stop anybody else in your family that wants to serve God. You better not be in there acting a fool in that house when they are trying to listen to the sermons with your rebellious self-indifferent self; you in there turning the radio or T.V. up while they're trying to listen. I was told of a young guy in our home church who wasn't doing right and the Lord shrunk one of his legs until he got himself right then the leg grew right back out. Don't play around with that. Don't play around with that. People want to pray. Leave them alone. Let them pray. You might be getting ready to die that day, and you don't even know it. Don't be a fool. Don't do that. Be wise. Who wouldn't want their husband to pray? Who wouldn't want their husband to seek God with all this hell that's going on? What kind of fool are you? Your companion is listening to Godly teaching and you're going to turn the T.V. up. You idiot! You idiot! You wouldn't be getting anything from me but a sour look. You want to get some honey you have to be sweet.

Don't have anything to do with somebody going to hell. Don't have anything to do with somebody talking about this ministry. Don't have anything to do with somebody not making it with God. Don't have anything to do with it! Don't have anything to do with it! Don't have anything to do with it! Hands off! You leave them alone. Leave them alone. Cause God is going to get them, but you don't want him to look and see you in the path. Come on, give God praise everybody. Yes. Fortunately for many of God's decrees and rules, His grace seems to allow for a small minority of exceptions to slip by, particularly people who demonstrate unwavering faith, such as Joshua and Caleb. They were the ones who were allowed to go into the Promised Land that's recorded in Numbers 13:1-33. They were the only ones who trusted that God would protect the people upon entering the new land from the dangers that they had found there. Joshua and Caleb believed in God's promises, and they were faithful to God. Not only do you have to believe, but you have to hold on. You have to hold on. You have to hold on. Romans 1:17 says, **The just shall live by faith.** And in Hebrews 11:1 the first two words are "***now faith***." That's all you need. Don't let anybody dissuade you from serving God. Don't let anybody keep you from paying your tithes. Don't let your mama, your daddy, your companion, or anybody deter you from the goal you have to meet in God. Because when they're dead and dust, God's going to still be there. Before Abraham was, *I am,* Jesus said. Our fathers said they ate manna in the wilderness. Jesus blasted them right back and pointed out that they all died. They're trying to throw the word on the word. They were standing there talking to the word trying to throw the word on the word. He said, yeah that's good. That's good. Shut your mouth. If Abraham was really your father then you would accept me, the Lord told them. Caleb and Joshua were the only ones allowed out of that rotten group to go into the promise land from the original group. Joshua and Caleb believed in God's promises, and they were faithful to God just as they knew He would be faithful to them. They alone were allowed to enter the new land. Numbers 14:24, 30 lets us know that Joshua became the leader of the children of Israel after Moses' death. He miraculously led the people across the Jordan River during the flood stage on dry ground.

DIPPED IN THE BRIM

Have you ever loved someone who didn't love you back chance after chance? **And as they that bare the ark were come unto Jordan, and the feet of the priests that bare the ark were dipped in the brim of the water, (for Jordan overfloweth all his banks all the time of harvest,) That the waters which came down from above stood and rose up upon an heap very far from the city Adam, that is beside Zaretan: and those that came down toward the sea of the plain, even the salt sea, failed, and were cut off: and the people passed over right against Jericho. And the priests that bare the ark of the covenant of the Lord stood firm on dry ground in the midst of Jordan, and all the Israelites passed over**

on dry ground, until all the people were passed clean over Jordan (Joshua 3:15-17). That just sounds magnanimous. Shall rest in the waters of Jordan that the waters of Jordan shall—they are going to stop flowing. Not only are they going to stop flowing but they're going to rest in their place and just are heaped up. Everybody knew their place. You want God to bless you? Find your place and get in it. Find your place and get in it. You are not being blessed? Something is wrong. Something is wrong. Finances short? Something is wrong. Find your place, get in it and stay! When the water was coming in, it was parting and it was just going up in a heap. Our God is great. And the priests that bare the ark of the covenant of the Lord stood firm on dry ground in the midst of Jordan, and all the Israelites passed over on dry ground, until all the people were passed clean over Jordan. I feel like on the road to Emmaus. Didn't our hearts burn as He traveled with us and opened up the scriptures along the way? He asked why they were so sad. They said, neighbour, you must not be from around here. Have you not heard that the saviour died? Why is your countenance low? You must be a stranger from around here. You haven't heard about Jesus? You haven't heard about the Saviour? You haven't heard about God's son? They crucified him. He said, tell me more! Tell me more! And that's what we should be saying; tell me more. More of God and less of me. More of God and less of me.

MORE LOVE

Have you ever loved somebody that didn't love you back? And I'm trying to love him more and more and more. I want to love him more and more and more. The more you love him the more you'll give your finances, The more you love him the more you'll give your time. The more you love him the more you'll separate. The more you love him the more you'll sacrifice. The more you love him the bolder you'll be. The more you love him the more compassionate you'll be. The more you love him, that's the more you'll be able to take; the more you'll be able to stand. But love does it.

Love does it. Love does it. The more you love him the more you'll see the lost. The more your ears will be anointed and you can hear the Macedonia call all over the world. Isn't that what Joel said? That you'll dream dreams. It'll be in your spirit. It'll be in your heart. It'll be in our mind. You can sense that it's coming. I am not talking about imagination stuff looking in the sky. But sho-nuff. Isn't that the word that says before things spring forth I'll tell you of it? (That the secret things belong to God). And now in this final hour God is revealing His secret to the true people of God. My God, look how we were blessed tonight with these scriptures. Some of you never thought about these words. It's the power of God being manifested in our midst. Let's lift our hands up. Lift those hands up. Let's say the sinners' prayer. And everybody saying, **Oh God! Oh God! Please forgive me for sinning against you. But I have come home, never to leave you again. Oh Lord, I want to love you with my whole heart! I want to love you with all of my might and with all of my mind! And by faith in the blood, give me that love. Save my soul! Save my soul! Save my soul! Come on in Jesus!** And if you mean it, then you have that love tonight. That love, that divine love to endure. That divine love to volunteer. That divine love of faith. That divine love to wait on others. That divine love to be patient. That divine love to be kind and show compassion. That divine love to just be kind to somebody. People are suffering everywhere. And you have that love in your heart, and you don't mind. You prefer others to go before you. That's the love of Jesus. He went to the cross in our place. We should have been nailed to that cross. He looked ahead in time and he saw that we needed a saviour.

CHAPTER 3

HAVE YOU EVER LOVED SOMEONE WHO DIDN'T LOVE YOU BACK?
TEAR DOWN THEM WALLS

Joshua and Caleb believed in God's promises, and they were faithful to God just as they knew He would be faithful to them. They alone were allowed to enter into the promised land of Canaan. Joshua became the leader of the children of Israel after Moses' death. He miraculously led the people across Jordan. Joshua was in charge when the walls fell down as the people sounded their trumpets and shouted. After which they took over the city, Joshua 6:1-2 says, **Now Jericho was straitly shut up because of the children of Israel: none went out, and none came. And the Lord said unto Joshua, See, I have given into thine hand Jericho, and the king thereof, and the mighty men of valor.** Tear down them walls. The power to tear down the walls in your life can only come from God, not any other person, place, or thing. Man can't tear them down for you. Physically, you couldn't tear them down. You just have to have a heart of obedience. It does not matter where you find yourself in life. It does not matter what you have experienced. It does not matter how long you have been in a certain state. It does not matter what you're going through. If you obey God, then all of the promises of the bible belong to you. We know that all good and perfect gifts come from above. We know that all things work together for the good for those who love the Lord and are the called, according to His purpose. That's when the scripture comes in; there is now no more condemnation to those who are in Christ Jesus. Then, that scripture comes in, "**For God so loved the world.**" You know when you obey God the whole bible is for you. All the promises of God they're for you.

INTO THY HAND

Now the Lord said unto Joshua, see I have given into thy hand Jericho (Joshua 6:2). Not only did The Lord give him Jericho, but He gave him the king and the mighty men of valor. Now I want you to pay attention to this. The Lord already told Joshua that He was giving him the city of Jericho before they did one thing. Before they did anything, the Lord already told them it was theirs. But they would have to fight for it and claim it Think about the kind of faith that Joshua had to have had. He's looking at a city that's closed up. He's looking with his natural eye at things that could possibly seem impossible to him, but with an eye of faith, he knew that if God said it, it had to happen. The Lord has provided you with so much love. Love is what's going to help you get your miracle or your healing or whatever it is that you need. Love will help you to come out of that stagnant state. Love will help you to stop being a procrastinator. Love will help you to go beyond yourself. Some of you haven't even tapped into your capabilities. You haven't even tapped into your talents. You haven't even tapped into what you were born for. You haven't even tapped into the call of God for your life. And you have to think about it within yourself. If you're not where you need to be with the Lord tonight, it's your doing. I want to encourage you tonight to get on-board to answer the call of God before he takes that call away and gives it to somebody else. All of your talents, skills and abilities, if you're not going to use them give them to me. Have you ever loved somebody who didn't love you back? Tear them walls down.

And ye shall compass the city, all ye men of war, and go round about the city once. Thus shalt thou do six days (Joshua 6:3). The Lord is giving them very plain and simple instructions. Here is the thing you have to keep in your mind; the Lord is never going to ask you to do something you can't do. If He tells you to stay out of sin, He tells you to pay that tenth, if He tells you to separate, if He tells you no gossip, lying, cheating, or backbiting, He's not going to instruct you to do something that you cannot do. But the question is, do you want to do it? Let's go back to love again in the gospels. The Lord said if you love me you're going to do what? Keep my commandments. What did Jesus say oftentimes when He was alone and He was praying? He said what? I do what? Those things that please my Father.

LOVE AND SERVICE

Have you ever loved somebody who didn't love you back? And love is primarily about service. Did you know that? Love is primarily about service. It's not about self. It's about service and serving others. That's what love is all about. Having compassion, giving people the benefit of the doubt, being kind towards one another, showing sympathy, and having understanding and forgiveness. But you can't do that if you're selfish. Anytime something "comes up" you always want to see what you didn't get, how somebody treated you. But we're blessed. We are so blessed. I was at home this evening getting myself ready to come to church and was flipping through the channels. I got to this religious station that's broadcast on TV around the world. I'm sure it was being broadcast here in the city (Chicago), and I assumed that the gentleman on the platform was an authority, so-called authority, and so-called expert. And he was trying to explain the Rapture and the Tribulation Period. It was horrible. There were some men on there that were older, and they talked about what they believed in. They were taught in a seminary theology school. That's frightening. They were so far off. But here we are in this ministry getting one hundred percent of the truth. We have an opportunity to know exactly what's expected of us. We have an opportunity to know about the trinity. We have an opportunity to know about the blood. We have an opportunity to know and understand about the baptism in the Holy Ghost. We have an opportunity to not only know the word, but to handle the truth. We have an opportunity to discern the word, not to judge others, but to help ourselves. We are very blessed. When you get the truth, you are blessed! You are blessed! And one of the so-called experts that was on the program said, "Oh so if you miss the Rapture? That's ok you'll have a chance. It's going to be about three or four Raptures". That broke my heart. It's on national T.V. They had some little chart up there. I just wanted to see where they were going with it. On their chart they had the second coming of Jesus coming at the end of the Tribulation Period. Now I know that you know that the bride of Christ is not going to go into the Tribulation Period. But they said we're all going to be right here. I recently found out that one of the owners of that station had died. He has all the answers now. The Rapture is an escape for the bride. But I'm just showing you all the literature, books, CD's and tapes. We are so blessed. We don't have to worry about where we stand with God. We don't have to worry about if what I'm receiving is the truth. At least you shouldn't be. I'm preaching the same gospel that I've been preaching for nearly sixteen years. Living free, it has to be. The Lord told them something so simple to do. **And seven priests shall bear before the ark seven trumpets of rams' horns: and the seventh day ye shall compass the city seven times, and the priests shall blow with the trumpets** (Joshua 6:4). Notice this, what the Lord instructed Joshua to do? To give everybody their orders. Everybody knew what they should've been doing. And whenever there's no organization, it's a big mess. When you have a marriage where the lady is trying to be the man, you have what? You have a marriage where the man doesn't know what he should be doing. You have a marriage where the lady might make more than a man and look down upon him, making him feel bad. You don't know your place. You don't know your place. Now I'm not talking about a guy that is not doing anything, not trying to do anything. But I'm talking about two people sho-nuff trying to make that family work. You have to know your role. How do you talk to your husband? How do you talk to your wife? Tear down them walls. Tear down them walls.

PEOPLE AND THEIR TROUBLE

People have a lot of trouble with fear. People have a lot of trouble with frustration. People have a lot of trouble with a whole lot of stuff, because they just won't accept the facts. They won't face life. They won't accept the truth. The truth will take stubbornness out of you. The truth will take bitterness out of you just by accepting it. Everybody has to accept the truth; what that truth says about you. What does that truth say about you? That fear you have in your heart where does that come from? Probably from disobedience. The Lord said in Isaiah that He would keep you in perfect peace whose mind is stayed on thee. And Timothy said that the Lord has not given you a spirit of fear, but of power, love and a sound mind. And you will only keep that fear away from your gates through love, love. Loving his word, loving obedience, loving him, just loving him because he is. And that will help you.

You have to fast, pray, and study the word constantly. That's victory! You have to fast, and pray, and study, have your prayer time constantly. One week shouldn't go by without fasting. A whole day shouldn't pass without praying, calling on God, studying His word; that's where your strength comes from. That's what helps you to tear the walls down in your life. You ever noticed when you're fasting and in there with the Lord you feel strong spiritually? You don't feel better than anybody else, but you feel that when a sudden problem comes up, you can handle it. When you're not praying, you don't have any guidance, you don't have any direction, and you don't know what's going to happen to you. The devil can beat you over the head, but that word, that fasting, that prayer, it's sort of like the same hedge that was around Job. The devil had to ask the Lord for permission to remove the hedge. Some are always feeling sorry for yourself, feeling pitiful. Stop that! You're too grown for that. That doesn't look pretty, and it's not cute. Have you ever loved somebody that didn't love you back? Tear them walls down. These are things you can do with the power of the Lord. These are things so you don't have to stay evil and trifling. You can be loving, kind, and sweet. Your family might faint, but you can do better! They're so use to you growling like a bulldog. Ladies, you need to do more than smell sweet, you have to be sweet. You ever seen somebody put perfume on top of musk? Some of you act like you spiritually have on some Mitchum, but you're musty overall. Better wash your body! Put on some Mitchum,

Itchum, Pitchim, Secret, Dial, and Coast. And you know if you don't have any problems with perfume soap, like Caress, Dove and Dial. Some people use that stuff because they got sensitive skin.

In verse two, the Lord had already told Joshua these are all the things that I'm giving you. It's sort of like salvation. It's sort of like healing. It's sort of like deliverance. It's sort of like his greatness. It's sort of like salvation. And it's sort of like the baptism in the Holy Ghost. You already know these things are promised to the children of God. So, He's telling them right up front. It's yours, but notice as He goes along to giving them the orders. Now, when we first came to salvation, when some of you got saved, you loved that feeling. All your burdens were washed away. But then comes the orders, the discipline. Finding out how you fit into the whole scheme of things, not being envious and jealous of anybody else, but just glad that He saved you. Some of you, you have forgotten the diverse sins you were in. And you know what makes you forget? A lack of humility. Because if you stay humble, the Lord will keep that ever before you. Some of you were humble. Come on. You know some of you struggled with your sexuality. Come on. All kind of stuff happened to us when we were little. But with salvation, you don't even know some of the things that were going on in your body. When the Lord saved you, he healed you of that too. So, be thankful. Be humble so when you come to the Lord, and He saves you, it will be time to find your place. Where do I fit into all of this? Well, you fit in the room of preparation. You fit in the room of preparation. I want to know where you are with God. You might think, "Oh, I give so much money." I don't care anything about your money. I'm not going to have God frowning on me. Because if I do what's right, He'll send somebody way, way, way from Atlanta that was on their way somewhere and had need to stop by here and give me ten thousand dollars. Don't get caught up with money. We need money to survive, but just be careful. Don't get so hyped-up on making money. You work every single day, all the time. You have to what? Find your place. Find your place. And when you first come to the Lord, your place is in the church as much as you can be. Your place is in the prayer chamber. Your place is definitely in bible study and Sunday school. Those are the foundational classes for a new beginner. Find your place! Find your place! And little by little the Lord will move upon you to do this and do that. If you're a new convert, get active in the church! Don't just be a lay member coming doing nothing. It's too easy to sit out. Volunteer.

WALLS, WALLS, WALLS

Have you ever loved somebody that didn't love you back? Tear those walls down. Those walls of depression and procrastination. Always getting ready to do something, but you never do it! Some of you all about dead up in here compared to when we had the revival. You all looked like two separate people. Gotta keep your lamps trimmed and burning. You might have the lamp, but there is no oil in there baby. Tear those walls down! Tear those walls down! Have you ever been so determined that people will say to you, "No, you can't do it!" It just pushed you on, didn't it? Well, you have to keep that Rapture before you! He's coming for a bride without spot, wrinkle, blemish or any such thing. Now a blemish you can't even hardly see that. So everybody was in their place. He made them a promise, and then He set them up. He set them up to be victorious. He made them a promise, and then He set them up for success! He said he would never leave us, He would never forsake us. He set us up for success! He knew the blood of Jesus Christ would keep us, would heal us, it would help us. He set us up for success! But we have to fight for it! We have to fight for it. We have to be determined. We have to have divine determination. Think about how silly this must have looked to other people, them just going around these walls once a day for six days. Then here they are on the seventh day going around seven times. Man, if you look at the world, we are fanatical! If you take on the world, the lenses of the world, man, we are so strict! But if you look at the world, everything's going on, everything's accepted. But not if you take it to the word of God. It says because straight is the gate and narrow is the way that's leading unto life few there be that find it.

(Matthew 7:13-14). It says there's a way that seemeth right. It seems like we should have the rappers. It seems like we should have Christian rock. It seems like, it seems like, but it's not. It seems like, but it's not. I want you to really work on studying and correcting yourself instead of analyzing others. Why haven't you received? You're not fasting. Why? You're not in your place with God. Why? Why? Why? What's happening? What's going on with you? Why are you so easily bewitched? In Acts, the eighth chapter, Simon the sorcerer was bewitching the people often. But when the truth came, the truth came. Reverend Thomas, how do you know that was the truth? Because the people saw the miracles. They were so accustomed to being bewitched; they didn't have anything to compare it to. You don't have that excuse. You have truth and victory.

MY MOMMA WAS IN HEAVEN

My Mama died on a Friday, a service night; at three something that afternoon but that night, I was in church. She was already in heaven. If I was mad about anything, it was about how she got the victory, and I was still here. My son was killed on a Sunday night. I was in church, in my place that following service day. And believe it or not, that consistency helped me. Being in my place helped me! It gave me strength. Commit to God! Commit to doing his will! The Lord has already told you all the promises in the book are yours. Why don't you let the Lord do for you what no other power can do? Nearly seven years ago, in August, the Lord healed me of cancer. I didn't know that cancer was coming in my body. That's the second time the Lord healed me of cancer. I believe the first time was in my left breast a couple of years before that. But if I had not been in this army of the Lord, I wouldn't be alive today. Commit to something that's going to profit you. Commit to something that's going to do you good. You lying up with these men, aging your body? You're giving your whole life to these women? What are you getting out of it but a hard luck story? Time is going so fast. Make your life count for something! Make your life count for something! What's the legacy you're going to leave? What are people going to remember you for? Look at "*The War is on . . . Armageddon*"[4], written by our home church Pastor, Reverend Ernest Angley. Read it again and again! All of the prophecies, books of Revelation and Daniel, they are lined up in order in that book. You are so fortunate you don't have to worry about any false doctrine. Tear down them walls in your life. Tear down walls in your life!

Just think look how ridiculous the Israelites must have looked to the people inside those walls. Now, the people in those walls, they didn't believe those walls were coming down. People look at you. Maybe you look at your own circumstance and it's so great. You give so much power to the devil, and you keep Jesus right here on this little stool. My daughter told me she went to Croatia. She climbed up this mountain. She said they had Jesus in a statue of wood, but Mary was made of marble. I heard the scripture say that Mary was up in the upper room with everybody else. Mary was chosen because she was willing. The only one that we bow to, the only one that we pray through is in the name of our Lord and saviour Jesus Christ. **There is no other name under heaven given by men whereby we must be saved.** Acts 4:12, for that's the name of Jesus. That same stone that the builders rejected has become the cornerstone of salvation and His name is Jesus." Just think about how silly they must have looked to those people on the inside. It didn't look like they had anything to use to tear those walls down. The people in Jericho felt secure, but they had no idea what was about to happen. Just like in this world, people feel secure in the president and the government. People feel secure in their jobs. People feel secure because they have a home. All of that stuff can be taken away in a moment of time. Just ask Job. He said by the time they came and told him about his kids, he couldn't even inhale. Then, somebody was running to tell him about something else. And then, when that person left, someone else was running to tell him about something else. And, oh yeah, by the way, he

---

4   *The War is on…Armageddon*, Rev Ernest Angley, 2012, Winston Press, Akron, Ohio

had three of his so-called friends over ready to come with accusations. And when he looked around, he started breaking out with all kinds of boils and stuff all over his whole body. In the end, he stood the test. Have you ever loved somebody? Job could say yes. Jesus can say yes, Job loved him back. In the end, the Lord told those same three "friends" that they better go to His servant Job and ask him to pray to Him, because only He will hear him.

YOU CAN'T BUY LOVE

Have you loved somebody that didn't love you back? You could look at that in a very personal scenario. Don't get any rest chasing people down. You can't buy love. You can't do it. You could be better off, but you just won't let the Lord help you. He didn't hurt you. He wants to fix you. He wants to heal you. He wants to build you up. He wants to give you a new identity. That old identity, you're still dragging it around. Tear down them walls! The Lord can only make you free if you let him! Don't hold on to people, stuff, or things. You have to trust somebody. Why not the Son of God who died and rose again on the third day? What about a God who flung the stars into space, and they're still there. What about a God who set the sun to lead us by day and the moon to be light for us at night? None of them are arguing with one another. What about a God who rolled up the waters of the Red Sea? Heaped them up! And the people went over on *dry* land. What about a God that, when the prophet prayed to Him, He allowed the sun to go back in degrees. The scriptures say that Noah found grace in the eyes of the Lord. What about a God who had a servant that was so filled with his power, that when he died, they put a soldier into war to fight. The soldier came back to life, because the prophet was so anointed, even in death! What about a God who promised us of His Son's blessed return. Even though some of our family members have died in the Lord, when He comes back, He's going to bring them with Him. That's the God I choose to serve. People today, they are in the same condition. They don't know that God is about to tear down the walls, and that this time it won't be for His glory. His judgments have started and will be going forth more and more and more. God is going to settle the score with those who have rejected Him. That's something to think about. 2 Thessalonians 2:11-12 says, **And for this cause God shall send them strong delusion, that they should believe a lie: That they all might be damned who believed not the truth, but had pleasure in unrighteousness.** Even now, God is sending them strong delusions. People are rejecting the truth on a large scale. Even Pentecostal so-called preachers; they are taking their last steps toward blaspheming against the Holy Ghost. Many thousands have already sealed their doom. God will never remember anymore. He is done with them! That's really something to think about. It's something that I really take personal with my own life. No one is excluded. Don't lie to yourself about your own self. Don't be in the dark about who you are!

SELF-DECEIT

King David was so far removed from his own self-deceit. He didn't realize that Nathan was describing himself. Whatever it is, face it! Tear down them walls! Sleeping around, eating too much, not eating enough, always mad. You got to tear down them walls. In Jericho, the people in the city that were on the inside were just looking at them like "What's up with that?" But the walls did come down. Some of you have to bring those walls down so that the Lord can help you. Be determined. What was it that that Sojourner said earlier today? I was what? Too stubborn to quit. I'm going to keep on praying until I get a breakthrough. I'm going to keep on fasting till something happens. I'm going to keep on studying the word until I understand it. Lord, these are your basic instructions before leaving earth. I need to understand this. Not only am I going to come so boldly before the Lord because his word said I could, but I'm going to do my part. I'm going to set aside time. I'm not going to compete with prayer time and watching T.V. I'm going to set aside time to let the Lord know I'm serious. I'm going to stay up late and even might get up early. Man shall not live by bread alone, but by every word that proceedeth from the mouth of God. Tear them walls down, those compromising walls. Some of you are so easy to be persuaded to do wrong. That's because you don't have a real born-again experience. Just over here tarrying and tarrying and tarrying just as mean as a rattlesnake. Tarrying, tarrying, and tarrying, and oh my God, if the Lord pulled down the screen like Pinocchio, your nose would start sticking out all them lies that you be telling. Just tarrying and tarrying and tarrying and sweating, just oh my God! But you don't pray at home. The Lord said that's a hypocrite. Got to tear those walls down. The day is far spent. It's almost time to go. What are you going to tell God? And you've been in this ministry? All of those walls of disobedience, all of those walls of being opinionated. They marched around those walls seven times, but then Joshua told them to shout. So the people shouted with the priests when the priests blew the trumpets. And it came to pass when the people heard the sound of the trumpet. They shouted with a great shout. Then the wall fell flat so that the people went up into the city, every man straight before him. And they took the city (underline that), just like God had promised them in verse 2. The walls of Jericho had to come down. Notice, when we began this chapter, He started out with a promise then, He got them ready for victory. Think about yourself now. He is the Lord that healeth thee. He will never leave you. He will never forsake you. He's already telling you that.

Don't worry about what you're going to say. Don't worry about your garments. Don't worry about your life. He's going to do it all. Then He goes on to tell you to get in your place. Obey Him. He tells us to sacrifice, sacrifice before Him. Spend more time with Him. The Lord uses people to answer prayer in your life. He uses people to answer prayer. He uses people to bless you. The bible says if you love the Lord and trust the Lord, he'll even make your enemies at least be at peace with you. He said He will spread a table in the presence of your enemies. Not for you to stab them. Can I say that? You like, "I know He will, Reverend." Where they at? You got to love your enemies. Loving them is for you. Maybe you found yourself in this chapter. Tear down them walls! Tear down them walls! You still have your first love? If not, you can get it back right now. The Lord answers all your prayers? If not, come on. Come on back home, backslider; come on in sinner, while the light is still shining to show you the way. He said you've been worrying and crying, crying and worrying. And you know when you have a lot of things on your mind you just can't really pray the way you need to. Sometimes you just have to stay right there until you get a breakthrough, because the devil is already right there discouraging you. You're already feeling down, so there's not any need to pray. No, that's when you need to pray more earnestly, more fervently until that spirit lifts. Say the sinner's prayer listed below:

Oh God, Oh God please forgive me for sinning against you. But I have come home never to leave you again. Oh Lord! Help me to tear the walls down in my life! Oh Lord that part that I can do, help me oh God! And oh Lord the part that I cannot give me the strength and faith to let you do it! To let go and let God. And by the faith in the blood, save my soul. Save my soul! Come on in Jesus. Come on in Jesus. And if you meant that he has come. God bless your hearts.

Part 2

"I Am A Just God"

CHAPTER 4
EVERY CHILD NEEDS A FATHER

I was going to start out with some very important statistics. The information I am giving you is facts on fatherless kids. It is taken from *dadsforkids. com*[5]. I thought this would be important as we move on into our lesson throughout this chapter. I want to start by stating how I truly admire all of the *good* fathers in the world today; all of the families. You know a family can be just one person; it does not have to be a mother and a father—not in the conventional sense. A family can consist of a father with his children or a mother with her children; it can be older siblings raising the younger ones. The Lord is Lord of us all. He is the Lord of one person, and He is the Lord of many. Here are just a few facts I want to present. The statistics are very plain. In a study of 700 adolescents, researchers found that, compared to families with two natural parents living in the home, adolescents from single parent families have been found to engage in greater and earlier sexual activities. Fatherless children are at a dramatically greater risk of drug and alcohol abuse, mental illness, suicide, poor educational performance, teen pregnancy and criminality. Teenagers living in a single parent home are more likely to abuse alcohol at an earlier age compared to children who are reared in a two parent home. The absence of the father in the home affects the behavior of adolescents greatly and results in a greater use of alcohol and marijuana. A study of 156 victims of child sexual abuse found that the majority of those children came from disrupted or single parent homes. Only 31% of the children lived with both biological parents, although step families make up only about 10 % of all families. 27% of abused children live with either a stepfather or the mother's boyfriend. We have got to be careful. We have to be careful of who we let in our homes. This message is for all people. *Every child needs a father.*

---

[5]   Citing Website http://www.dadsforkids.org (accessed 2011).

Beverly D. Thomas

SINGLE MOTHERS

Child abuse researchers in Michigan determined that 43% of all child abuse cases are committed by single mothers. A family structure index, a composite index based on the annual rate of children involved in divorce, and the percentage of families with children present that are headed by a female is a strong predictor of suicide among young adults and adolescent white males. It is not all just the black people. This is hitting all folks. Fatherless children are at a dramatically greater risk for suicide. In a study of 146 adolescent friends, there were about 26 adolescent suicide victims, teens living in a single parent family are not only more likely to commit suicide, but are also more likely to suffer from psychological disorders when compared to teens who live in intact families. Now, this is just when the dad is not in the house. This is something that we really take for granted.

Some of the couples that I have married, had I known the way their marriages were going to turn out, I would not have married them. When I marry people, I ask them upfront if they are going to be committed to God. When they say they are going to be committed to God, then I know they are going to be committed to one another. When couples tell me they want to have a baby, I ask them, I want to know. I want to look in their faces and see their response; if they are in it *for the long haul.* If not, don't bring a child into this world. This world is too evil—too filled with hatred and such a disregard for human life to bring a child into it if one is unsaved, uncommitted and ungodly. It will not work, no matter what you do. You have to have God inside of you in order to rear children in this final hour. Some of the couples I have married have proven nothing but disappointment after disappointment. They lie right to my face. Boys who grew up in absent father homes are more likely than those with a father present to have trouble establishing appropriate sex roles and gender identity. So, if the father is not in the home, often times the boy that's in the home doesn't know how to act. That is what this article alludes to; psychiatric problems. In 1988, a study was performed on preschool children admitted

56

to New Orleans hospital as psychiatric patients. Preschool children being admitted in a psyche ward? Over a 34 month period, they found that nearly 80% of them came from homes that had no dads. Children living with an unmarried mother are more likely to be treated for emotional problems. Children reared by divorced or unmarried mothers are less cooperative and score lower on test of intelligence than children reared in intact families. Statistical analysis of the behavior and intelligence of these children reveal significant detrimental effects of living in a female headed household. Even though we try to do it all, we cannot do it all. God help us. I give fathers and father figures all of the honor and glory that is due for those men who are really trying to make an effort. There are some dads out there who are really trying to do everything they can to help with their children. Also, there are some dads that don't know any better; maybe they had no male role model in their lives and are just doing what they have been taught. Again, this message is about all **PEOPLE**. It is not just about men. I pray that as you follow along, you will understand what I am attempting to show you. I am taking you first from the natural standpoint because you can understand that, but then I am going to take you to the spiritual, where we are all intertwined. Listen to it again.

EMOTIONAL PROBLEMS

Children living with an unmarried mother are more likely to have been treated for emotional problems. The website talks about the behavior and intelligence of children who do not have an intact family. Regardless of parent education, race, and other child and family factors, 18-20 year olds were twice as likely to have poor relationships with their mothers and fathers; showing high levels of emotional distress or behavior problems. This article is saying when the father is not there [or absent], it affects the child. Children with fathers at home tend to do better at school. They are less prone to depression and are more successful in relationships. Why? They learn how to coexist. Many of our children find their roles in the roles that they see at home. And if God is not there, then what are they being taught? It's true. I am going to keep on preaching. Children from one parent families achieve less and get into trouble more than children from two parent families. Children whose parents separate are significantly more likely to engage in early sexual activity. They are more likely to abuse drugs, to experience conduct and mood disorders. This affect is especially strong for children whose parents separated when the children were five years old or younger. Compared to peers living with both biological parents, sons and daughters of divorced and separated parents exhibited significantly more conduct problems. Daughters of divorced or separated mothers show greater evidence of internalizing problems such as anxiety or depression. They have a hunger for love. Hunger for a father often afflicts boys ages one and two years old whose fathers are subtly and permanently absent. Sleep disorders, such as trouble falling asleep, nightmares, night terrors frequently begin one to three months after the father is gone from the home. Children of unmarried mothers are likely to have been treated for an emotional or behavioral problem.

In 1988, the Department of Health and Human Services found that at every income level, except the very highest level (over $50,000 per year) children living with unmarried mothers were more likely than their counterparts and two parent families to have been expelled or suspended from school or to display emotional problems and to engage in anti-social behavior. This is really something for us to think about. We better act now or pay later. Children from mother-only families have less than an ability to display gratification and poor impulse control that is, control over anger and sexual gratification. Those children also have a weaker sense of conscious or sense of what's right and wrong. ***Eighty percent of adolescents in psychiatric hospitals come from broken homes.*** Expelled—nationally 15.3% of children living with an unmarried mother and 10.7 % living with a divorced mother have been expelled or suspended from school compared to only 4.4% of children living with both parents. Kids who exhibited violent behavior at school were 11 times more likely to not have lived with their fathers and 6 times more likely to have parents who were not married. Boys from families of absent fathers are at a higher risk for violent behavior than boys from intact families. It's really something to think about, and this goes on and on and on. The website, *dadsforkids.com,* talks about the odds of kids going to college where there is only one parent versus two parents. Frankly, divorce is worse than death. We make all these commitments to one another. We are going to do this—going to do that, when the entire time, one person's heart is controlled by lust and selfishness. But we never think about the child. For 15 years neighbor, I have pastored this church. Most of the people I have counselled have issues they are dealing with that are not from adulthood. More often than not, these issues date back from "*in the day*" when they were maybe just toddlers or adolescents, maybe they were just teenagers. A lot of the trouble have to do with how many, **now-adults**, were spoken to and/or treated as children. Some have to do with incest and molestation. Yes, I am still preaching, incest, molestation and favouritism, the things that so many are grappling with as fifty year olds, forty-five year olds, thirty-five year olds. These problems, pain and dysfunctionally didn't just erupt, but grew over time. I want to tell you today that *every child needs a father*.

IN TIME PAST

Ephesians 2:11-22 says, **Wherefore remember, that ye being in time past gentiles in the flesh, who are called uncircumcision by that which is called the circumcision in the flesh made by hands; that at that time ye were without Christ, being aliens from the commonwealth of Israel and strangers from the covenants of promise, having no hope, and without God in the world: but now in Christ Jesus ye who sometimes were far off are made nigh by the blood of Christ. For he is our peace, who hath made both one, and hath broken down the middle wall of partition between us: having abolished in his flesh the enmity, even the law of commandments contained in ordinances; for to make in himself of twain one new man, so making peace; and that he might reconcile both, unto God in one body by the cross, having slain the enmity** thereby: and came and preached peace to you which were afar off, and to them that were nigh. for through him we both have access by one Spirit unto the Father. **Now therefore ye are no more strangers and foreigners, but fellowcitizens with the saints, and of the household of God; and are built upon the foundation of the apostles and prophets, Jesus Christ himself being the chief corner stone; in whom all the building fitly framed together groweth unto an holy temple in the Lord: in whom ye also are builded together for an habitation of God through the Spirit.** *Every child needs a father.* I am a child of God and so are you if you have the blood of His Son on your soul. God is our Father and Jesus is our Saviour.

IN THE NATURAL SENSE

I gave you several facts above. Maybe it was shocking to you how children act in the natural sense when a father is not present, but you should not have that excuse today, because the blood of Jesus made you nigh, *all of us* were sometimes afar off. We were adopted. Ephesians 5:30-32 says, **For we are members of his body, of his flesh, and of his bones. For this cause shall a man leave his father and mother, and shall be joined unto his wife, and they two shall be one flesh. This is a great mystery: but I speak concerning Christ and the church.** Also, look at Romans 8:15, which says **For ye have not received the spirit of bondage again to fear; but ye have received the Spirit of adoption, whereby we cry, Abba, Father.** That means that the Lord Jesus Christ himself handpicked each and every one of us, because He loved us. And Jesus instructed us to Him, our Father. So yes, every child, each and every one has a Father in Him. In Luke 15:11-12 reads, **And he said, A certain man had two sons: And the younger of them said to his father, Father, give me the portion of goods that falleth to me. And he divided unto them his living.** Now, you must think about this. This father had two sons, he loved them both. The boys both grew up and came into the knowledge that they had an inheritance. They both came into the knowledge that the Lord had promised them something. When the sons became grown it would be their possession; they would take claim of the inheritance. One of the sons decided it was his time. That son wanted to do his own thing, like some of you, who have known God but now have turned away from Him. Find yourself in this lesson. You are in here, each and every one of you. You may not be able to do anything about what happened to you in the past, but you sure can change today! If you don't like your current state of affairs, then do something about it! Maybe you are thirty, forty, fifty or sixty or even older than that and you did not get the love that you needed when you were growing up, but come on and travel with me today. We can all get what we need in this our final hour.

Neighbor, this is the greatest hour of your life because it is God's greatest hour. It might look dim now, but God is certainly moving for you. It will never get so dark that you can't find your way. There is light in the word of God! Look for it! The darkness may become so dense, but God will be there to help you purify your faith in Him. If you are hidden in the perfect divine will of the Father, ALL things will work out for your good. What the world could not do for you, God stands willing and able to perform His perfect will in your life. Jesus is our redeemer kinsman, purchasing each soul with His precious blood. If you had to purchase salvation, you will never have enough money. Billions of dollars could not buy a born-again experience. The price for our freedom was so great; it had to be a pure-blood-sacrifice to settle such a debt. Jesus purchased us with His blood, and we owe Him everything. That's all. That is the point of this lesson. That father may be the only one providing for you. What about the uncle? What about the grandfather? There are some "good" godly people, if you would but give them a chance. Everybody is not out to harm you and treat you bad. But you do have to beware of some of them. Look at the text back now in Luke 15th chapter, where the prodigal son was living in a palace with his dad. He had decided, "I am grown, I know what I need. I am ready to go. Give me my stuff!" The bible indicates that the father gave him his inheritance and he was on his way. The father did not fight his son; he didn't try to make him stay there with him. It is like coming to Christ. The Lord is not going to fight you. He offers only His best to you. The Lord does not push His will upon any of us. Jesus does not make anyone be saved; it's whosoever will. He says that if you will come, Him and His Father, through the Holy Spirit, will come and make and abode. He promised that He will never leave you. Jesus will never forsake you. The choice is yours.

HE WAS SMART

Not many days after, the younger son gathered all his stuff. He was smart. He was wise. The prodigal son had all the answers, or so he thought. Just like so many of the youth today, think they are smarter than God. The prodigal son was vain, stubborn, and arrogant. **And not many days after the younger son gathered all together, and took his journey into a far country** (Luke 15:13), not even anticipating that what he had was not going to always last. "I don't need God. I can work this out for myself. I don't need anybody to help me. I am self-made; my destiny is in my hands." But, every child needs a father. **And not many days after the younger son gathered all together, and took his journey into a far country, and there wasted his substance with riotous living. And when he had spent all, there arose a mighty famine in that land; and he began to be in want** (Luke 15:13-14). The younger son went and tried to hook-up with some other folks. Notice this in verse 15, **And he went and joined himself to a citizen of that country; and he sent him into his fields to feed swine.** Now think about this son and where he came from; compared to some, he lived in a castle. He came from a home where there was great love. The prodigal son came from a place where everything was provided for him. We are offered so much through salvation; through Christ. Christ is all we need for soul, mind and body. Jesus promised to supply all of our needs (Phil 4:19). The Lord never promised us mansions here on earth, and He never promised us an exorbitant amount of wealth, but the Lord did promise us health, joy, peace, companionship, comfort, training, and the fruits of the spirit. Jesus promised that, through His shed blood, our souls could be cleansed from all sin. He promised to be our advocate to God the Father and to be our elder brother. The Lord gave His life to be our Saviour. What more could He give? God is our Father, and Jesus is our Saviour, redeemer and elder brother.

After the prodigal son got out into the world, not anticipating the future, like some of you, he began to be in want. His father knew what was best and tried to shelter him from all of the dangers of the world, but his son wanted *what he wanted*. No doubt, the prodigal son thought, "I know better. My parents are old. They don't know what is going on in today's world. They have gotten old and out of touch." The father must have known something. He was rich and had servants. Many parents are outliving their children because of sin, sin, sin. Many of the youth today are so cocky; they do not want to listen to anybody. But hear me today, "Every Child Needs a Father." So, the prodigal is on his own, out in the cold. The picture has changed drastically from when he left his father's house. When he was in the house, he probably gave ear to his friends telling him "home is the boring place to be." Some co-workers might have made fun of him by saying he "churched too much." All he did was churching. Probably listening to his unsaved companion talking about, "You don't really love me, because you go to church too much." Here was the prodigal son with all of those opinions, and not one of those people was there with him.

FACE THE MUSIC

Have you ever noticed that? The people you listen to, when you get in trouble, where are they? They set you up and then leave you to face the music alone. Where are they? Just like the enemy. **The thief cometh not, but for to steal, and to kill, and to destroy: I am come that they might have life, and that they might have it more abundantly. I am the good shepherd: the good shepherd giveth his life for the sheep. But he that**

is an hireling, and not the shepherd, whose own the sheep are not, seeth the wolf coming, and leaveth the sheep, and fleeth: and the wolf catcheth them, and scattereth the sheep (John 10:10-12). Then, when you get yourself in a mess, they will say, "I didn't really mean it like that." Some of the situations you have gotten into, God has had a time trying to unravel for you, hasn't He? Luke 15:16 says **And he would fain have filled his belly with husks that the swine did eat.** Oh, hunger has a way of humbling you. **And no man gave unto him** (Luke 15:16). Where were we all his friends? Where were his "folks"? Where were his "boys"? Where were his "homies"? Where were his "girls"? People will only put up with you for so long, but God will put up with you for all eternity. That is the offer He is making to you. Do not be sick too long. People are such hypocrites, many of them. When you are down for a little while, they are doing it for their own glory, so they can tell people in the social club how they *had to help you*, "You poor little thing, you." They are not letting them know in a missionary way, but in a way to say, "Look at what I did." The Lord says you have your reward when you act like that. Don't be sick too long. Don't have a terminal illness or need a ride ***every*** week. Don't need somebody to turn you over day after day. Don't need someone to come see about you three days a week? That is going to really wear out. People for the most part are hypocrites. For some, they are honest-hearted and will stick with you all the way. There are others who start out with a missionary spirit but gradually dissolve into thin air.

Do you know how many times people have told me that they will never leave this ministry? Almost every one of them that said that are gone. Not only are they gone, but some left fighting, fussing, cussing and bitter. Good riddens! Gheez! So when people preface something by saying that, I am like, "ummm, they are on their way out." It's those people that are boasting the loudest. "Whoooooa! I love the Reverend. Whoaaaa!" When you look around, they will be gone. "I will never leave Reverend Thomas. If you ever need anything, you can call me." In the back of their mind, they are thinking "Just don't call me too many times. Often, people do not mean what they say and don't say what they mean. When people are discontented, or I start preaching on something that *finds them out*, I mark that person. Unless they change, they will be gone sooner or later.

WHEN YOU WAKE UP

Here is this young man, the prodigal son. Luke 15:17 says, **And when he came to himself.** He came and started thinking, "wait a minute now" in my father's house there are many mansions. In my father's house there is more food than I will ever need. The mill barrels never run low. The prodigal son had to go out into the world to realize the world had no love for him. He was fortunate. Many people go out into the world and don't make it back to God, and they die lost. They are taking that drastic turn into the world, and they are not coming back, so many of them. Listen! But the world had mercy on him, and he was able to come back. They are getting hooked-up in the wrong places at the wrong time. They are losing their lives, being in a position or somewhere they should not have been. At the funeral, people want to talk about how godly the person was, how much they loved God, and how much they were such a good person. You really have to ask yourself, why were they there? Why were they there? Who compelled them to go out at midnight? The Lord said come. Let's reason. We blame so many things on God that He has nothing to do with. God has nothing to do with death. He has nothing to do with sickness or sin, yet false doctrine will teach people that it is God's divine will for you to have cancer. Well, then you take it! You the bishop. You the evangelist. Well, then you take the rheumatoid arthritis. And let me be free! That is so foolish. They say, "It is God's will. God's going to get the glory." How is God going to get the glory out of me being twisted up, vomiting day-after-day from chemotherapy and radiation? God is not the author of sickness or death. He gives life and healing. He gives life and healing! He gives life! Every child needs a father.

Luke 15:17 talks about the hour the prodigal son *woke up*. In order for him to have went back home, the prodigal had to get some matters resolved in his heart and mind. Did you read in there that anybody made him go back? I did not read that. If you get one of those different versions of the bible, other than the King James Version, they might say the father dragged him back. You have got to watch out for those versions. Some of those versions will have a woman coming out. Too much of man in something means they have taken a lot of God out. You see, the prodigal son had to make up in his own mind and heart that he wanted to go back home. Many people are doing things because they do not have their Father's love. Everybody who did not grow up in a godly home, you grew up with something missing from your life. Some have found God and have allowed Him to now make them complete. Everyone who did not grow up in a Godly home grew up with something missing. You did not grow up intact. You started seeking it. The mind is so magnificent. When God created you, He created something marvelous and wonderful. Whether it is love, peace, affection, it is something in you. If you grew up in an ungodly home, you did not get all the ingredients. Oh no, you didn't. You can get those ingredients through God.

CHILD-LIKE FAITH

In the gospel, the Lord tells us very plainly how to get those things. We have to approach Him with child-like faith. And childlike faith is trusting and obeying. Children are so sincere. They will tell you very plainly, "Why do you have on that ugly sweater? Momma, daddy's breath is stinking! Mom, can you tell him? Daddy, did you brush your tongue?" And that is the way the Lord wants us to be with Him, to completely trust Him. For many, the trust is broken down because of bad relationships, dealing with bad folks. But the Lord can restore all that. He can give as much as you allow Him to give. The prodigal son said within him, "I've had enough of this. Let me go back to my father's house!" Some of you have gotten yourself in such bad situations. Then you start realizing, man it wasn't really that bad was it? Just complain, complain, and complain like some of our young people. They say, "Man, when I get grown, I'm going to leave home. I'm going to buy me a set of rims. My car is going to be rocking. I am going to have a lot of money. I am going to have a flat screen TV." While they are at momma's house they are doing all of this "self-prophecy." "The speakers are going to be blasting. The house is going to be rocking," so they think. Many kids are saying all that on momma's dime. Daddy is paying the electric bill. They are doing all this self-prophesying. "I am not going to ever need any money. I am not going to ever be without. I am not going to wear anything but Gucci, Aeropostale. I was hanging with the Levi's, but I am going through a transition now," until they have to get out there and start providing for them. You may have heard, "Uh, mom where's that thrift store you were telling about?" Who is this talking about the thrift store? Oh, the light is coming on. You go to visit them, and it is by candlelight. "Momma, don't turn that light on." You could never get them to eat a frozen dinner. When you open up the refrigerator the frozen dinners just start attacking you. You tried to tell them. It is just like with the Lord. He is trying to tell us that in Him we can have everything *we need*. In Him, we can be healthy, we can be strong. We can be vibrant. It doesn't matter how you talk to some people, they are not going to listen. They are going to go out there and make a mess and do their own thing.

The Lord is telling us we should be like the prodigal son today, just stop and take an inventory. Who can heal you? Who can put you back together again? Who can give you those missing parts that are missing out of your life? Another person cannot make you complete. Can I say that to you today? If you are in deceit, then you will deceive; you will hook up with someone who is deceptive. Did you know that? If you are a thief, are you going to want a thief, because you are going to want somebody to validate you—complete you? If you are whorish you are going to, no doubt, want somebody who wants an open relationship. Do you know what the translation of an open relationship is? Whorish.

THE SAME DEFECT

Every child needs a father. You have to be honest with yourself. You have to be honest with yourself. I have seen it over and over, down through these 16 years of ministry. I have seen people come to the ministry; it might be two or three of them and they both have the same defect. That same thing that was missing from the brother might be missing from the cousin. And they are in the same family. Starving for love. They don't have enough peace; cannot sit down, cannot be quiet, always running around, always running around; addicted to attention; dying for love. So, you start acting out; doing things that are detrimental. The whole problem is *you need your Father*. You need the person who can make you whole all over and that Father is Jesus Christ, your saviour. He died to be your elder brother. He willingly gave His life to save yours.

You need the person who created you. You need the person who knows more about you then anybody else. You just keep trying to validate yourself and make people believe you are somebody that you are not. *People do not care about who you are, really they don't.* They only care about what you can do for them. They don't care anything about you. It is such a rare thing to find true friends. Did you know that? Friendship now is based on what you can do for somebody and what they can do for you? When I was coming up, a friend stuck with you closer than a brother. A friend did not tell your business. They told you the truth. They did not tell you what you wanted to hear. They were like, "girl, I know you my friend, but you better cut that mess out." Some so-called friends today are only friends when they can pump you up and send you on the wrong road. That is not true friendship. Every single person that is reading this, if you did not grow up in a godly home, something is missing. There is some missing ingredient. Some of the literal stats that I read to you today from *dadforkids.com* backs up what I am telling you. Something is missing. And you just watch those children who think they know more than momma or daddy. Look at the outcome. Some kids, you try to shelter them from the things of the world, and they just run right to it. You try to watch over them. But when they get out in the streets, they are like wild animals. Some of them get into diverse sins so quick and so hard, it is amazing. This doesn't apply to all kids, and not all the adults that are acting badly came from bad homes. They just did not respond to the love that they were shown. You must respond to grow. Some kids would love to have the father and mother influence that others have. Some parents are so busy listening to what, "*they say.*" "*They say*" has destroyed many marriages. "*They say*" has caused a lot of children to leave home. "*They say*" has caused people to leave good ministries. Because of what "*they say.*" What does the Word say? A mother is somebody who cares for you, somebody who watches over you. There is nobody who is going to love you like that. A father is somebody who instructs, provides for you, watches over you, and gives you good godly discipline. I am not talking about abuse; nobody deserves that.

I thought about the parallel between my mother and my father. When we got in trouble as children, we always wanted our daddy to get us. Just a few screams, a few gasps and he was tired. But my mother, she never got tired. She came from that job at IBM. It was like she was still punching on that keyboard. It was like she was still doing data entry, and she was good at her job. It was like, "didn't I tell you?" Have you ever got a whipping and your momma is telling you to be quiet? How, can I do it? I can't shut my mouth as long as that belt is resting on my bottom? Whenever, we got in trouble we would all be praying, "Just let daddy get me." Because he was already going to be tired, he would go around in a circle for a minute, trying to converse with you. One of my sisters, she just would start screaming at the thought. By, the time my daddy got to her, he would be so tired, and sweat would be running—popping off of him. She would always get away with it. But when my momma whipped you, Whoa! It is the same thing in our lives. We need our Father. We need our heavenly Father, Jesus Christ. If your father is not present in the home, so what! If your mother is not present, so what! Stop blaming people for the way you are. Here you are thirty something years old, talking about "my mother . . .". Get a grip! Here you are forty something years old, talking about what your daddy did not do. You are grown now. You are of age. Isn't that what they said in the book of John? They got scared. My man was born blind. They immediately said, "Ask him." They came saying, "Are you his parents?" They said, "Yes." How is it that he was blind and now he is seeing? They said, "Yes, he is our child but ask him. Go ask him." Take accountability for yourself, and the Lord will be able to help you.

NOW THAT I THINK ABOUT IT

The prodigal son started thinking about, "It was not really bad at home. All I had to do was obey." But, then go on and study about the other son, not the prodigal son. You would have thought he would have been so glad that his brother was not out in the darkness anymore. You would have thought the other son, not the prodigal son, would have rejoiced when he looked up in the distance and saw his long lost brother coming back. I have had lost children out there. I know they have been out in the dark, kept me up all night. I would be praying, "Lord, Lord please, keep them safe. Watch over them. Protect them. Keep them safe." Then, to see one of them coming down the street, talking about preaching. But that one son, not the prodigal son, do you think he was glad? You think people are glad when you get yourself together? I am not talking about in the street. I am talking about in the houses of God. Everybody is not happy for you when you get yourself together and make that turn in your life. Many people like mess and thrive off confusion. They love being in your pity party. They like being your gossip buddy. They like being your party poo. Some people, all they do is instigate, keep mess going. You know when you say, "God set me free from that mess. I am not doing that no more." All of a sudden, they become your enemy. Now, the light should go on. Some of you try to call those people, and you are after them, and they are not right. The Lord delivered you. He says, "Don't go back into the bondage wherewith I have set you free". People are not happy for you in your marriage when you are getting it worked out. People are not happy for you when you come back to the Lord. You have renewed your covenant, ready, and you want to get it going. They don't care. They liked you better when you were in trouble, because that spirit agrees with the spirit that they carry, yet you say they are your friends. They are not your friends. A friend tells you the truth. A friend wants you to do well. A friend wants you to do better. A friend wants you to overcome adversity. A friend does not want you to stay down on drugs. A friend doesn't want you to be hooked-up on drugs, where all you are thinking about is your next high. A friend wants you to rise up above your circumstances. A friend wants you to rise up above your circumstances. And a friend will tell you that every child needs God, the Father.

So, the prodigal son goes back home. The father is exuberant. He is so excited. But the brother, was he not worried or concerned about his brother? Did he not worry about him and wonder how he was doing out in the street? No! The entire spotlight was on him, and he resented the fact that the brother woke up and decided to go home. It is the same way in the churches today. We are supposed to be the repair of the breach. We are supposed to be there for the widows and the orphans. We are supposed to be there for people, even though they have made a mistake in their lives. Maybe they have failed God ump-tenth times, but this particular time they decide they are going to really live for the Lord. You have those same people in the church that are like, "Umm, they are not going to be right." And it is a shame, because that is what the church was created for; to help people mend, to help people heal, to bring people back together, to reintroduce them to Christ. That is what the church is about. That is what the church is all about.

THE GOOD SHEPHERD

If you go to John 10th chapter, it says that Jesus is a good shepherd. He is not going to lead us to anything dangerous. He is going to guide us and lead us through the Holy Spirit. It tells us in John 6th chapter that it is impossible to come unto the Lord. Except His Spirit draw you. He promised He would teach us every time, as long as we make an effort to be there with Him. The Lord would help us. It is just like it is in our natural lives. When I was coming up, I had to go to a special class. I had trouble reading. But some of my own children have photographic memories. They can look at something and get it right away. There were some of my classmates that could take a test and get it right away. I was never like that. I had to study, and study and study. I learn things differently. I had to mark things down and take notes. I have to go back to the history of it. That used to intimidate me at first. And so it is with Christ. The Lord deals with each and every one of us where we are. If He dealt with me on your level, I might be lost. If He dealt with you on my level, you might be lost. He's your personal Saviour. It's like a new pair of shoes. You wear them for a while and they start forming to the configuration of your foot. That's what the Lord does with us. He takes us individually. He does not try to make me walk like you, and you walk like me. As long as we are walking, He is walking with us. As long as we are trying, he is trying with us. This is what was in one of the Pauline epistles. He says that the Lord has begun a good work. He didn't bring me this far to leave me now. I have got to keep going onward. I keep going forward. He does not want me to keep rising and going back to my father's house. He does not want me to keep on repeating that. He wants me to come to the end of myself like the prodigal son did. He wants me to be sick and tired of myself and the way that I am living. All of us have gone through something. Maybe you were molested. Maybe you were involved in incest. Maybe you did not get enough love. Maybe you were talked down upon. Maybe people said names to you. Maybe you were children of an alcoholic. Maybe your parents abused you. Maybe you did not get enough to eat, and maybe you were slow in school like I was. Maybe you had to go to them EMH, [Educable Mentally Handicapped] classes like I did. Maybe you had to go through a lot of stuff. Every child needs a father.

Even the fifty year olds, need God. Sixty year olds, they need God. Twenty-five year olds, they need God. The babies not yet born need God. These teenagers, God knows they need God. People getting married, they need God. People who have stayed married, they need God. People, who have children, need God. People whose children have gone away, they need God. What are you saying Reverent Thomas? We all need God! All of us.

THE PORTER

Jesus lets us know in John Chapter 10 that He's the porter. He said He would lead us. The Saviour will guide us. You know the greatest thing I like about this chapter? He will go before us if we accept His guidance. It's all up to us. The Lord will not force Himself upon us. Free will, that's the one thing we did not lose in the fall of man. We do not have to try to figure out everything in our lives. All we have to do is acknowledge Him as our Father and do what He tells us to do in His word.

You know if you can remember a certain time in your life. I do, I can remember when we were growing up. My mother would go to work and, every so often, she would come home with some left over lunch. I did not care what it was. It came from my momma's job, and I was glad to see her. That is all the Lord is asking of us; to be glad to spend time in His presence, to be glad to come unto His house, fellowship with His children. The Lord said to forsake not the assembling of ourselves together. But come and get strength. Come and get strength. How has the Lord moved for you since you have been these sermons? How has He lifted you up? How have you been inspired? How have you been encouraged, encouraged to change? Some of you came here and have been here battling this depression that happens during the seasons [this sermon was preached during the holiday season]. You have been feeling that pressure that you have to run out and do stuff. No, run and sit down. It's a pressure that happens around the holidays. It's an anxiety that comes with the holidays. Some people do not know how to handle it. It's a loneliness that comes with the holidays. It's a regret that comes with the holidays. For some people, they start reminiscing about their mom and dad who are dead. We start thinking about, "if I would have did this . . ." No! Stay in the *here* and *now*. That brings depression. All of that regret. I could have. I should have. I would have, but, you did not do it. You have today.

With God, all things are possible. Suicide is on the rise during the holiday season. You are sitting alone in that house, talking about how you are having eggnog with some *holiday spirits*. Alright *holiday spirits*. Spirits are catching. Then, you wake up depressed. You are taking all of these over-the-counter meds. Do you know they make you depressed? I am not going to start naming them, because they might block me on the television. Some of these over-the-counter meds are supposed to help you rest and get sleep. They alter your mind. Read the back of the bottle. Go to the internet and look those words up. What is the side effect? Some of that stuff stays in your system for days. You are sleepy for days. You wake up on the wrong train. No! Read the scriptures. Count the sheep. Some of us, we are already predisposed. Do you know what that means? Some of us are predisposed. Some of our parents are alcoholics. So, one sip and you can be sipped out. Amen. Some of our parents, they were doing more than making love when we were coming along. They were doing a little marijuana, a little coke, a little heroine. Some of us were born addicted. Some of us, we cannot play around with drugs, because that will make it easier for us to become addicts. We can become addicts quicker than those who were not exposed to drugs. So, do not play around with that stuff. Every child needs a father. You are the child. Jesus is our father. That is what I am telling you.

Just think about this outline that I have given you and about how young children are affected when a father is not in the home. Think about how you have been affected with Christ not being in your house. How have you have been acting? What are the things that you have been doing? Some of the characteristics, you have been displaying, because you have not let him in? Not because he is not available, not because he is not able, not because he does not have the power, but because you have not accepted Him.

I AM YOUR CHILD

I know I would be dead today if I hadn't allowed Him to be my father. I was in a severe depression. I was going to see a psychologist and psychiatrist. One doctor told me that the only thing they could do was cut the part of my brain out that made me depressed. But God the father, God the Son and God the Holy Ghost said "Not so!" And I just cried out to him. "Lord, I am your child. You bought me with your own blood. You let audacious men beat you. You let those people hire false witnesses against you so that I can have a good mind. You are my dad." When I had cancer, Lord, no blade touched my skin. I never had chemotherapy. I never had radiation. I just ran to my Father's house. I said, "Lord, I am your child, I am back again." One more affliction, the devil is trying to attack me again. But your word says you will keep sickness away from me. Even if the devil afflicted me, with your stripes I am made whole. I just ran to my Father. When I am lonely and don't understand, when people don't understand me, when it seems like the weight of being a pastor is so great, I just have a little talk with Jesus. I tell Him all about my troubles, and he just lets me know everything will be alright. He did not say I wouldn't go through. He said he would be with me all the way, even until the end of the world. Neighbor, God bless you! Every child needs their father. You need your daddy! Everybody needs the Lord. You need only the love that Jesus can give to you. You need that peace so that you can rest at night. You need that joy. You need that stability.

I want to pray with you, neighbor, that the Lord will move for you in a special way. I want you to know no matter what is going on in your life, I care for you. Let's pray together, me and you. We can be pen pals. You write me, and I will write you. We can move on with God together. Jesus does love you. Suicide is not the answer. Did you know suicide is murder? It is murdering oneself. Everything will be alright. Just hold on to God.

Lift those hands and let's pray:

"Oh God, In the Blood Name of Jesus, Lord. Every child needs a father, Lord. You are our father. And we say, "Our Father, today." We ask you, oh God to move for us in a special way. Those people, whoever they might be, reading this book, Lord gives them the strength and for those, who are thinking about committing suicide. Lord! Oh God, we know all demonic power must yield to the power that's in the blood. Move for them, even now! You are our Father. You bought us with your blood. You purchased us with your blood, and we are yours. Oh God! Give them the strength to hold on. Give them the hope that they need to realize you have not abandoned them. You have not left them. But, Lord you are there. If they will only cry out and say "Oh God, I need a saviour. Oh Lord, I am lost and I need to be saved." Lord, we give you, all of the honor, and all of the glory. Neighbor, remember I will be praying for you.*

What do you need today? What do you need today? Every child needs a father! It is the little things that we think don't count. They do. It is the little things. Those of you who are parents today, you have got a humongous responsibility. To show love, kids do not need stuff; they need love. We try to give them all this stuff, games and all of that. They need you. They need you to come to some of those basketball games. They need you to show up at school. They need to see that you are concerned. And touch your child, rub his head or something. Comment about your daughter's dress. You will be surprised how those things add up when they become adults. And that is the reason why some of our young kids, they are in gangs today, because it is a fake kind of love, yet it is a love. It is a family, a phony family, yet it is a family. Because, it accepts them. Did you know that? We are responsible, those of us who have children. We are responsible, that these kids get everything that they need. Believe me when I tell you. I have siblings. I have children who did not grow up with many ingredients missing. It is only by the Grace of God that I am here today. I should be dead, just by that right. But Jesus came with healing in His wing. I am glad he healed me. And he can heal you today.

CHAPTER 5
OUR LORD WILL COME

We, who are a part of the bridal company, should be encouraged each and every day that we have left. So many so-called Christians are so complacent; they believe they have such a long time to get themselves together, but our Lord will come. The Bible is right. It does not matter what people say. In 1921, the Jews began traveling back to Israel, and in May of 1948, the Jewish nation was officially established. Israel is our time clock.

THE ANTICHRIST WAS BORN

We know that the antichrist was born in the late 1960's. The forerunner of the antichrist is in a high place in government, and things are wrapping up and wrapping up fast. John the Baptist was the forerunner of Jesus Christ. Well neighbour, the antichrist, he is in the world somewhere right now at this very moment, as well as his forerunner. We have to do all that we can to make sure that we are ready when Jesus comes. This is the hour, our Lord, He will come. This is a sobering lesson, and it will help you if you allow it. It is time to check your own life today; if Jesus came back now, would you go? People are not looking for Him to come back now, that's why it's the perfect time. What an hour we are now living in. There is so much complacency, everything goes, everybody is accepted, and all religions are accepted. It is the ripe time. It is the proper time for our Lord to come.

ALMOST MIDNIGHT

Matthew 25:1-10, states that it is almost midnight, the hour in which Jesus will return for his bride, that is the bride of Christ. Jesus warned us of this midnight hour when He was here on earth. Think about the parables of the ten virgins, they really describe the second coming of our Lord and Saviour, Jesus Christ. People want to refute, dispute and debate about what the Rapture means and what its purpose is. The Rapture is the second coming of our Lord and Saviour, Jesus Christ when He will come and take His Bride. He won't come all the way down to Earth, but He will come in mid-air. And the Lord will come as a thief in the night.

Watch therefore: for ye know not what hour your Lord doth come. But know this, that if the goodman of the house had known in what watch the thief would come, he would have watched, and would not have suffered his house to be broken up. Therefore be ye also ready: for in such an hour as ye think not the Son of man cometh (Matthew 24:42-44). Neighbor, I want to assure you today our Lord will come. Matthew 25:1-10 says **Then shall the kingdom of heaven be likened unto ten virgins, which took their lamps, and went forth to meet the bridegroom. And five of them were wise, and five *were* foolish. They that *were* foolish took their lamps, and took no oil with them: But the wise took oil in their vessels with their lamps. While the bridegroom tarried, they all slumbered and slept. And at midnight there was a cry made, Behold, the bridegroom cometh; go ye out to meet him. Then all those virgins arose, and trimmed their lamps. And the foolish said unto the wise, Give us of your oil; for our lamps are gone out. But the wise answered, saying, *Not so*; lest there be not enough for us and you: but go ye rather to them that sell, and buy for yourselves. And while they went to buy, the bridegroom came; and they that were ready went in with him to the marriage: and the door was shut.** It really sounds like the Rapture to me; when that door in heaven closes behind the bride of Christ. Those left outside, those foolish virgins, they will be spewed in the

Tribulation Period. Neighbor, the tribulation winds, the foul winds of the great and horrible Tribulation Period are upon us. Think about this parable that the Lord gave us. We know that a parable tells us an earthly story with a heavenly meaning. There were five virgins. They were all pure. The Bible clearly makes it plain to us, you do not have to have the Holy Ghost to make it to heaven, but you have to have the Holy Ghost to make the Rapture. You need more power. You are going to be changed in a moment, in the twinkling of an eye. You are going to be changed from the inside out. **Now unto him that is able to do exceeding abundantly above all that we ask or think, according to the power that worketh in us** (Ephesians 3:20). I do not understand where the confusion comes in, because the Bible is very plain. The only thing you need to make it to Heaven is a pure, clean soul that has been washed and is covered with the blood of our Lord and Saviour, Jesus Christ. All you have to do is be completely obedient to the Lord. Acts 5:32 says, **And we are his witnesses of these things; and so is the Holy Ghost, whom God hath given to them that obey him.**

WATER BAPTISM

Water baptism does not bring salvation. The Bible teaches us about water baptism because we follow Christ in all things. **For even hereunto were ye called: because Christ also suffered for us, leaving us an example, that ye should follow his steps. Who did no sin, neither was guile found in his mouth** (I Peter 2:21-22). That is the reason why we only fast forty days because that's the longest Christ [our example] did. We fast, we pray and we study in the Word, because that is what the Lord did. The Bible teaches us that when all the disciples were asleep, Jesus was awake and talking to the Father. My Lord! He did not have to study the Word because John says, He was the word made flesh. And so Jesus is the word. The Bible teaches us that two cannot walk together unless they are in agreement. In agreement with what? We have got to be in agreement with the Word; that's the only way we can be in true harmony with God the Father, God the Son and

God the Holy Ghost. It is the only way we can be in true agreement in this final hour. You have to have the Baptism; you must receive Him. He is a sobering teacher. He is the Jesus revealer of the Old Testament. Jesus is in every book of the Bible from Genesis to Revelation. If you have the Baptism of the Holy Ghost, you will be changed. If you have a real born-again experience and are full of the Holy Ghost, you will be changed. There is no such thing as a cursing Christian. There is no such thing as a drinking Christian; there's no blood on that soul.

No lukewarm Christian will make it in. Revelation 3:15-16 says, **I know thy works, that thou art neither cold nor hot: I would thou wert cold or hot. So then because thou art lukewarm, and neither cold nor hot, I will spue thee out of my mouth.** We know sinners in the mouth of our Lord.

While you might have the blood of Jesus on your soul now, a continued state of lukewarmness will drive His spirit from you. **My spirit shall not always strive with man** (Genesis 6:3), While you might have the ear of God right now, but for how long? Those who are in a backslidden condition, you are not saved. That means that you have gone back on the Lord. There was something so similar about each and every one of the ten virgins. They were all pure. Five of them, at one time, had the Holy Ghost, but they grieved Him out of their lives. **And the foolish said unto the wise, Give us of your oil; for our lamps are gone out** (Matthew 25:8). They had the blood of Jesus on their souls. But neighbor, it takes more than the blood in this final hour. You need that power that will *make* you a witness. Acts 1: 8, he said that you will be witness. Who will make you a witness? It is the power that worketh in you. It is the Holy Ghost. Who is going to teach you? Who is going to instruct you? John 16:7 says that **Nevertheless I tell you the truth; It is expedient for you that I go away: for if I go not away, the Comforter will not come unto you; but if I depart, I will send him unto you** But, if I go away, I will pray to the father and he will send the Comforter. Oh God! God is our Creator. God is our Father. And Jesus is our elder brother. Jesus is our Saviour. And the Holy

Spirit, He is our Comforter. He is our guide. The Holy Spirit is our teacher of truth. Our Lord, He will come! Our Lord will come!

EAT THE WORD

Our Lord will come. You must study the word. Take no person's opinion about what the word says. Study and study over and over again. **Study to shew thyself approved unto God, a workman that needeth not to be ashamed, rightly dividing the word of truth. But shun profane *and* vain babblings: for they will increase unto more ungodliness** (2 Timothy 2:15-16). The Holy Spirit, without Him, who will help you dissect the word? The Holy Spirit, He is the one who opens up the scriptures to you and makes the word of God personal to you. The Holy Spirit is the one who will draw you closer to the Lord. You need the Holy Spirit if you plan on making the one flight out. Again, you do not only need the Holy Spirit to make it to heaven. You not only need the Holy Spirit to make the Rapture, you need the Holy Spirit to live in this present world. This world where so many people are devil possessed. There are so many backslidden leaders. There are so many backslidden churches. But the Holy Spirit, you need Him in this final hour. Who is going to get the spots out? Who is going to help you get the blemishes out of your garment? That garment is your life, neighbor. That garment is your soul. The Bible says that Jesus is coming back for a church without spot, wrinkle, blemish or any such thing. **That he might present it to himself a glorious church, not having spot, or wrinkle, or any such thing; but that it should be holy and without blemish** (Ephesians 5:27). The Holy Spirit is teaching the bride in this final hour? Is He teaching you? Do you have the fullness of the Holy Ghost? Our Lord will come. He will come. Will you be a wise virgin? Or will you be a foolish virgin? Just think about the many people today, who are sitting in churches, and they don't even know they *are not saved*. They don't even realize that they are children of the devil and children of God. A person who commits wilful sin is of the devil. I John 3:8-9 says, **He that**

committeth sin is of the devil; for the devil sinneth from the beginning. For this purpose the Son of God was manifested, that he might destroy the works of the devil Whosoever is born of God doth not commit sin; for his seed remaineth in him: and he cannot sin, because he is born of God. A person who lives in righteousness, a person who has a pure heart, belongs to the true and living God; they have His mark on them. They can say that God is their Father, and Jesus is their elder brother. But with sin and iniquity in your heart, you do not have anything to do with the kingdom of God.

5 WISE, 5 FOOLISH

Think about those five foolish virgins. While they were saved, while they had the blood of Jesus on their souls, they were still left. They still had to face the Tribulation Period. The Tribulation Period will be the worst time on earth. You cannot even put it into words what the Tribulation Period is going to be like. The Bible says no man knoweth the hour, nobody knows the day. Again, all these things are in the Word of the living God. You must study the Holy Scriptures. Will you let the Holy Spirit lead you, guide you and help you realize this is the season? This is the season for the return of our Lord and Saviour Jesus Christ. Can you fathom? Can you imagine in your mind this world going on for many more years? The next generation of our youth, they are dying at a pandemic rate. Can you imagine our kids being slaughtered the way they are being slaughtered? Can you imagine not even being able to sit on your porch? Can you imagine the health care system? Could you have imagined our space center and space program now being given into the hands of Russia? And if you know anything about prophecy, you know Russia is going to start the Battle of Armageddon. Oh my Lord! Our Lord will come.

Why were the five foolish called "foolish?" If you continue reading, it says those five foolish admitted to once having the Baptism, but they lost

Him. That meant that they had everything they needed, but something drew them away. Something got their attention. Something caused the five foolish to go into lukewarmness. James 1:8 says, **A double minded man is unstable in all his ways.** Do you think a lukewarm person is going to make it to heaven? Not so! The Bible teaches us that the Lord is married to the backslider. He is married to you, because He is waiting for you to come back. He is not partnering with you in your sins and iniquity. No! He hates the hypocrite.

The ten virgins, really sounds like the Rapture to me. Some will be ready, but most will not. Some that were once ready will forsake the Lord and turn back at the last moment. **For there shall arise false Christs, and false prophets, and shall shew great signs and wonders; insomuch that, if it were possible, they shall deceive the very elect. Behold, I have told you before Wherefore if they shall say unto you, Behold, he is in the desert; go not forth: behold, he is in the secret chambers; believe it not** (Matthew 24:24-26). It really sounds like our Lord will soon be back to get us.

Those foolish virgins, they are going to be in the Tribulation Period. You have got to think in this final hour, what is the devil's job? What is he (devil) spending so much time doing? The devil is not in a hurry. The devil he is not changing anything. The Bible tells us in the book of Ecclesiastes that there is nothing new under the sun. What worked on Adam and Eve, the devil and his demons are using the same old deceit on you. The devil's mission is to get you to doubt God's word. The devil is seeking to instil doubt into every Christian he can about the return of our Lord. Many false prophets are on the scene right now. They are saying that the Rapture won't take place, and that the second coming of Jesus is just a myth. There won't be a Rapture for them, just the Tribulation Period. False doctrine denies the power that is in the blood. False prophets can't preach 100% truth, because it is not in them. They go around "evangelizing false doctrine." So many people are in hell today because of it.

Other people, they are gathering food, storing it in quantities large enough to take them to the Tribulation Period, assuming that they are able to survive. How horrible the judgments will be during that time. There will be an underground market, where people who haven't taken the mark will buy and sell from. The born-new, Holy Spirit filled Christians need not plan for the Tribulation Period, for they won't even be in it. They have the promise of the Rapture; it's the way out that the Lord made for us. Death will reach out for us, but we will be gone! We'll be gone! We'll be gone! Those not living close to God will be swept into false doctrine in this final hour.

BLASPHEMY

Many have already blasphemed against the Holy Ghost; even preachers. It's so horrible to even think about. **Where I say unto you, All manner of sin and blasphemy shall be forgiven unto men: but the blasphemy against the Holy Ghost shall not be forgiven unto men. And whosoever speaketh a word against the Son of man, it shall be forgiven him: but whosoever speaketh against the Holy Ghost, it shall not be forgiven him, neither in this world, neither in the world to come** (Matthew 12:31-32). One great writer said, "As very man Jesus cast out devils through the power of the Holy Ghost and showed the disciples how it was to be done. Therefore doubters could speak against Him [Jesus Christ] and be forgiven; but *when they called the Holy Ghost in Jesus a devil, they blasphemed against the Holy Ghost.* This is an hour with not only a great revelation from heaven, but it is also an hour of great deceit from hell. The devil is doing everything he can to cause people to doubt the very words of Jesus. But this is the hour neighbor, our Lord will come.

1 Thessalonians 4:13-18 says, **But I would not have you to be ignorant, brethren, concerning them which are asleep, that ye sorrow not, even as others which have no hope. For if we believe that Jesus died and**

rose again, even so them also which sleep in Jesus will God bring with him. For this we say unto you by the word of the Lord, that we which are alive *and* remain unto the coming of the Lord shall not prevent them which are asleep. For the Lord himself shall descend from heaven with a shout, with the voice of the archangel, and with the trump of God: and the dead in Christ shall rise first: Then we which are alive *and* remain shall be caught up, (Sounds like the Rapture to me) together with them in the clouds, to meet the Lord in the air: and so shall we ever be with the Lord. It really sounds like the Rapture to me! That's the Rapture, neighbor.

We have to comfort ourselves and one another with the promise of Jesus' soon return, knowing that He will appear in mid-air and is coming back for us. That is something for us to think about in this final hour. Often times, I think about the city of Chicago while driving home, or I might be out in the market. I just look at all of the people that are driving by. I see all of the people with their children, and I just think about the scriptures. I think about what it is going to be like that one moment when the Rapture takes place. The Rapture will affect all people, all races and all countries. People are at such ease now. They do not have a worry in the world about their eternal lives. They do not have a care. They are driving in their vehicles. I sometimes watch the people in the vehicles. They are smiling, and some of them are watching television in the vehicles. Some of them are bobbing their heads to their favorite music. I see people on the bus. And then I look and see people with their children. I might look up and see a plane flying over. Sometimes I have to cross a bridge from one state to the next state. Sometimes the bridge goes up to let by a boat or something that is in the water. I think about in just one moment all of that is going to change. My Lord and my God! All of the small children and all of the babies will be gone. Many of the elderly, who have themselves grounded in the Lord and rooted and grounded in His word, full of the Holy Ghost, they are going to be gone. And what a world this is going to be.

I was thinking about a scripture that reminds me of the Tribulation Period; there will be so much pain and crying over the missing loved ones, but especially the children. Matthew 2:16-18 says, **Then Herod, when he saw that he was mocked of the wise men, was exceeding wroth, and sent forth, and slew all the children that were in Bethlehem, and in all the coasts thereof, from two years old and under, according to the time which he had diligently enquired of the wise men. Then was fulfilled that which was spoken by Jeremy the prophet, saying, In Rama was there a voice heard, lamentation, and weeping, and great mourning, Rachel weeping for her children, and would not be comforted, because they are not.**

You have got to think about how horrible the Tribulation Period will be. If you want to know anything about it, just study the plagues that occurred in Eqypt. **And there shall be a great cry throughout all the land of Egypt, such as there was not like it, nor shall be like it any more** (Exodus 11:6). Think about how the women cried out, during that final judgment. That final judgment was the death of the firstborn in every family. Can you hear them crying out? Can you hear the screams? Just think about how you love your child, your little baby. If they are of an age where they have not had a chance to accept the Lord, they will leave this world. Just think about the small children. Oh my Lord! Oh my God! Just think about how our elderly are being mistreated, in this final hour. Think about the way the government taxes them on everything, housing, and even how some of their own family members treat them bad. But they are just holding on. They are holding on to the horns of the altar. Think about how some children's parents are warning them over and over and over again. They are warning them, "You better get your life right son! You better live right son! Your life is going to be cut short! Son, don't do this and don't do that!" One day they are going to wake up, and mama won't be there to warn them. Mama won't be there to pray over them. Mama won't be there to cry. Because of what? Our Lord will come! So many will wake up without deceit when the Rapture takes place, but it will be too late.

Our Lord will come! Some people err when it comes to the scriptures, and if they are leaders, they cause their members to err. Some false teachers are teaching that the bride will go into the Tribulation Period. I cannot find that in the Word. People say a lot of stuff, but there is no Bible for it. There is no Bible for it. I cannot find it in the Bible anywhere that you can shack up and still make it to heaven. I can't find it in the Bible anywhere that you can have a baby out of wedlock, except you repent. I cannot see you making it into heaven. There is no scripture for it. I cannot find it anywhere in the bible where a *practicing* homosexual makes it to heaven. There is no scripture for it. There is no scripture for it!

The Bible says except you repent you shall all likewise die. I read that in the Bible. The wages of sin is death, and the gift of God is eternal life. I read that in the Bible. The soul of the father and the soul of the son, they are all to God. And the soul that sinneth, it shall die. I read that in the Bible. I read without holiness no man shall see the Lord. I read that only the pure in heart shall see God. I read, Oh my God: Be you holy for I am holy. I read that in the Bible. There is a whole lot of stuff going around. So many "fables" are out there; you must be careful. People are saying it is in the name of the Lord, but there is no scripture for it. I have not read in the Bible about a person living in adultery, a person living in fornication. I have not seen it anywhere in God's word that you can still make it to heaven. I cannot find it in the Bible about a person that is toting cocaine. I have not read it anywhere in God's word that a child of God calls themselves with an addiction, but heaven is their home. I cannot find it. There is no Bible for it! To say you are child of God, to say that Jesus is your Saviour, to acknowledge that Jesus died and gave His life for you, to acknowledge that His blood was shed to give you freedom and liberty. Not only did the Lord save you from sin, but He took all your sicknesses too. To say you are serving the Lord and you have an addiction is to say that the blood is not working. God forbid! The blood is still working today. It has not lost its power. The Bible will never lose its power. It will never lose its power. It will never lose its power. If the blood cannot do it; it cannot be done.

THE GREAT MYSTERY

1 Corinthians 15:51-52 says **Behold, I shew a mystery; We shall not all sleep, but we shall all be change. In a moment, in the twinkling of an eye, at the last trump: for the trumpet shall sound, and the dead shall be raised incorruptible, and we shall be changed.** My Lord, that sounds like the Rapture to me. That sounds like the Rapture to me. **For this corruptible must put on incorruption, and this mortal *must* put on immortality** (1 Corinthians 15:53). We who make the Rapture will not die! But when the Rapture takes place, those without spot, wrinkle, blemish or any such thing, will be changed in a moment, in the twinkling of an eye. It sounds like the Rapture to me. We will be changed! We will be changed! Our Lord will come.

So when this corruptible shall have put on incorruption, and this mortal shall have put on immortality, then shall be brought to pass saying that is written, Death is swallowed up in victory. O death, where is thy sting? O grave, where is thy victory? The sting of death *is* sin; and the strength of sin *is* the law. But thanks be to God, which giveth us the victory through our Lord Jesus Christ (1 Corinthians 15:54-57). Think about it. Those alive on planet Earth when the Rapture takes place will be changed so quickly that death will try to reach out for them, but *death won't have a chance.* Death won't have a chance at them. No sting of death. The grave will be robbed. Praise God all Mighty! Praise God all Mighty! Yes! Yes! Yes!

The Bible teaches us in the book of John, "Oh my God, don't worry about it, that if I went away, I will come back again. Acts 1:11 *Ye* **Men of Galilee, why stand ye gazing up into heaven? This same Jesus, which is taken up from you into heaven, shall so come in like manner as ye have seen him go into heaven.** Just think about that. Our Lord will come. Do you have that in your heart today? Is that a reality in your life? Or are you like the scoffers, "one of these days, one of these days"? No! No! No! The Lord's coming is more of a reality now than it has ever been. Every day that you wake up, you are getting closer to your final destination, either in heaven or in hell. Every day that you wake up you are getting closer and closer to your final destination. If you die today, you will face your judgment that day. What will your judgment be? **And as it is appointed unto men once to die, but after this the judgment** (Hebrews 9:27). Will your judgment be that you were redeemed because you have the blood of Jesus on your soul? Or will your judgment be eternal damnation? Since the flood, when the Lord went down to preach to those souls in prison, all are called to repentance. Even those souls, they were not asleep, they were in prison. They were captive. I Peter 3:18-20 says, **For Christ also hath once suffered for sins, the just for the unjust, that he might bring us to God, being put to death in the flesh, but quickened by the Spirit: By which also he went and preached unto the spirits in prison; Which sometime were disobedient, when one the longsuffering of God waited in the days of Noah, while the ark was a preparing, wherein few, that is, eight souls were saved by water.** The Lord did that because they did not have the Gospel preached to them. Jesus went down there Himself and preached the Gospel to them. Since that time, anytime a person dies, that soul goes to that place prepared for it. Our Lord will come.

I WILL RETURN

John 14:3 says, **And if I go and prepare a place for you,** I will what? I'm coming back. Our Lord will come. Our Lord will come. We are the Rapture generation. We are the Rapture generation. What will it be like when Jesus returns? What will it be like? Have you thought about it? Where will you be when the Rapture takes place? What will it be like for you? What is going to be happening in your life? Will His return find you ready to go? Will His return find your life clean and free from all sin? Oh my God! I cannot understand it. How in the world can people say that they are Christians when they have sin working in their bodies? There is no Bible for it. The book of Galatians and Romans just chop up the people who live in sin. The Bible says in Romans 1:32 **Who knowing the judgment of God, that they which commit such things are worthy of death, not only do the same, but have pleasure in them that do them.**

What an hour we now live in. **Now the Spirit speaketh expressly, that in the latter times some shall depart from the faith, giving heed to seducing spirits, and doctrines of devils; Speaking lies in hypocrisy; having their conscience seared with a hot iron; forbidding to marry, and commanding to abstain from meats, which God hath created to be received with thanksgiving of them which believe and know the truth** (I Timothy 4:1-3).

This know also, that in the last days perilous times shall come. For men shall be lovers of their own selves, covetous, boasters, proud, blasphemers, disobedient to parents, unthankful, unholy, Without natural affection, trucebreakers, false accusers, incontinent, fierce, despisers of those that are good, traitors, heady, highminded, lovers of pleasures more than lovers of God; Having a form of godliness, but denying the power thereof: from such turn away. For of this sort are they which creep into houses, and lead captive silly women laden with sins, led away with divers lust, Ever learning, and never able to come to the knowledge of the truth (2 Timothy 3:1-7).

This is the Lord's Day. This is His hour. If you are living for the Lord do not be discouraged. Look up, redemption draweth nigh. When you see all these things taking place, in the beginning of Matthew, he says these are the beginning of sorrows. He says when you see all these things taking place, do not look down. Don't be despondent. Check your garments on a daily basis; make sure you are ready to meet your Lord every moment that you have left. Our Lord will come! Our Lord will come! Our Lord will come! What a day it is going to be! What is that day going to be like for you? Will you rejoice? Will your heart skip a beat? Just think about, we have seen Jesus through the scriptures, but then we will see Him face-to-face. You won't have to lift the veil, but you have got yourself anointed in this world. You have used this life to get your life ready for eternal life. All those family members you have been labouring with, just like Lot, you won't even remember them anymore. This is the day! This is the day! This is the hour that our Lord will come. What will He find you doing? Will He find you in the vineyard? Will the Lord find you labouring for souls? Will He find you on your knees? Will Jesus find you trying to reach the very last lost soul? Oh my God! If you search the scriptures, all the prophesies about the Second Coming of the Lord have all been fulfilled with the exception of getting the final harvest in. All we have to do now is help every person around the world. We have to make sure the Gospel goes around the whole world and the Bible declares "then the end shall come." Where will that end find you? Will it find you in the whorehouse? Will it find you in the salon? Will it find you practicing homosexuality? Will it find you in abomination? Will it find you in disgrace? Oh my Lord! And Oh my God! Will it find you doing things that you shouldn't be doing? Will it find you talking back to your parents? Will it find you sneaking out at night? Will it find you with God's tithes in your pockets? Our Lord will come. Our Lord will come. Our Lord will come. What will it be like for you? What will it be like for you? Are you on fire today? Are you on fire today? Is the Holy Spirit bubbling in your heart? Are you on fire today? Do you rejoice at this message? Is this message tingling in your heart? Or is it sensational fear? Are you excited today to think that "one more" and you could be in heaven? Just think, one more step and you could be into heaven? Just one more step and you can be before the thrown? Just one more step. Think about it, when God came down in the cool of the day, Adam and Eve needed no veil; they were that holy. They were made in the true holiness and righteousness of our Lord and Saviour Jesus Christ. They could take a look right into the face of God. All of these years, we have been working our way. We have been staying separated from all that which is false. We have been yielding to the power of the Holy Ghost, those of us full of the Holy Ghost. We have been working every day to stay full. We have been checking ourselves. The Bible says judge yourself lest you will have no need for anybody else to judge you. We have been taking our lives to the Word. We have been doing what the book of James says, we have been looking in the mirror of the word. But, we have not been walking away, thinking about we don't know who we are. We have been walking away making corrections and adding the necessary missing ingredients. We have been walking away talking to God saying, "Lord it is me. I'm standing in the need of prayer." We have not been pointing our finger telling other people to take the beam out of their own eye, but we have been keeping ourselves in the mirror of God's Word saying "Lord, Oh God! Help us. Help us to be ready when you come, Lord. We know you're coming is nigh, Lord. Help us to have a seasoned tongue! Help us to have the love that we need to change! Help us to have compassion for the lost." Our Lord will come! Our Lord will come! Our Lord will come! Yes! Our Lord will come! What will it be like? What will it be like for you when Jesus comes back? What will He find you doing? Will He find you labouring for the lost? Will the Lord find you fasting and praying? Will He find you in your prayer chamber? Will He find you searching scriptures? Will our blessed Saviour find you with a forgiving heart? Will He find you full of faith? Will He find faith when He comes? What is it going to be like for you on the day that Jesus comes back to collect your soul? We are His precious jewels. We are the brightest jewels of heaven. We are the ones that He gave His life for. Will he find you with unforgiveness in your heart? You deacon! Oh my Lord! You pastor! Will He find you with another woman's number in your pocket? What will He find you doing? Will the Lord find you stealing from the church, robbing Him of the tenth? What will He find you doing? Will our precious Lamb find you making up a message, a bloodless gospel? What will He find you doing? Will He find you sounding the alarm, warning the people like in Ezekiel's day? Will Jesus find you blowing the trumpet and warning people and telling them "Wouldn't it be nice to go in the Rapture shouting God the Son is coming back?" Won't it be great to go in the Rapture?

DISTRESS

What will the day be like when Jesus returns? **And there shall be signs in the sun, and in the moon, and in the stars; and upon the earth distress of nations, with perplexity; the sea and the waves roaring; Men's hearts failing them for fear, and for looking after those things which are coming on the earth: for the powers of heaven shall be shaken. And then shall they see the Son of man coming in a cloud with power and great glory. And when these things begin to come to pass, then look up, and lift up your heads; for your redemption draweth nigh** (Luke 21:25-28). Men, they are so perplexed today. The nations are so distressed on every hand. The Lord described this time two thousand years ago. You've got to wake up to the hour in which you live. It is almost midnight. Our Lord will come. Our Lord will come. It doesn't matter what man or foe may think; it doesn't matter what the devil says. It doesn't matter, oh my God, if all fifty states legalize same sex union. It doesn't matter if they allow same sex unions in school. It doesn't matter if they teach pornography and witchcraft in one of the classes in school. It does not matter if the churches start letting everything go on in the churches, which some of them are doing just that right now. It does not matter what happens in this world. Our Lord will come. Our Lord will come. Yes!

These things that I am talking about our happening in our day. Matthew 24:3 says, **And as he sat upon the mount of Olives, the disciples came unto him privately, saying, Tell us, when shall these thing be? And what shall be the sign of thy coming, and of the end of the world? And Jesus answered and said unto them, Take heed that no man deceive you.** That is a profound statement. It's something you have to think about. You must search the scriptures for yourself. The Bible admonishes us to study to shew ourselves approved unto God a workmen that need not be ashamed. The Bible tells us about the Holy Spirit. He will teach us, lead us, and guide us into all truth. A person who does not want the truth will just read the Bible like you read a newspaper or magazine. If you have the spirit of truth, you are asking Him to shake you, fix you or whatever you need to be right. You are asking Him to anoint you. You are asking the Holy Spirit to pull out of the Word just what you need for the day. You are asking the Lord to make you. You are putting off carnality and you are getting more and more spiritual every day, desiring more of a spiritual appetite and less of a carnal one. And by that, you will want more of God's word. You are realizing what Matthew 4:4 really means when it says man shall not live by bread alone, but by every word that proceedeth out of the mouth of God. You realize that the Word is a light unto your feet. You realize that the Word is the answer; it is the direction you need in this final hour. You realize the word, in this dark-dark hour, will give you just enough light to make it to Rapture ground. While other people are talking about their theories, other people are giving their opinions, you are sneaking away. It might be in the midnight hour, but you are drawing on the power of the Lord. And you can hear the scriptures going over in your mind, **"If you draw nigh to God and he will draw nigh to you"** (James 4:8). You can hear what the Lord is telling you, no matter what it looks like. The Bible is resonating in your ears. And you hear the scriptures now coming to life. There is a way that seemeth right, but the end of that way is the way of death. You might find yourself getting discouraged, but you can hear Lot telling you to hold on, just hold a little while longer. You can hear Abraham giving you strength today as he tells you to climb up to Mount Moriah, not to sacrifice your own child, but let the sacrifice be you; soul, mind and body. You are taking yourself up to Mount Moriah. You are placing your life on the altar of sacrifice when you realize all you have is in Jesus. Then you awake, and you will start living for the very first time. Our Lord will come. Our Lord will come. Yes! Yes! Take heed that no man deceive you.

THE SPIRIT OF THE WORD

People have charisma. People know the scriptures but, they do not have discernment. People know the scriptures. They have the letter of the Word, but they do not have **the Spirit of the Word**. The Spirit of the Word is what delivers the truth of the Word. Anybody can read the Bible and give you their interpretation. It is a fearful thing in this final hour to give somebody your own theory, to give somebody your opinions. You do not prophesy in your own will. You do not speak in tongues in your own will. But the Bible says He will give us unction, when the Holy Spirit came upon us. He said that we will speak as the Spirit of the Lord came upon us, and that we will yield our tongues over to Him. That is one of the reasons why the Lord chose tongues as an initial evidence of the Baptism of the Holy Ghost. It is not the only evidence, but the initial evidence.

As you study the book of James, think about how powerful such a small member of our body is your tongue. It can start fires. It can start wars. It can ruin nations. **For in many things we offend all. If any man offend not in word, the same is a perfect man, and able also to bridle the whole body. Behold, we put bits in the horses' mouths, that they may obey us; and we turn about their whole body. Behold also the ships, which though they be so great, and are driven of fierce winds, yet are they turned about with a very small helm, whithersoever the governor listeth. Even so the tongue is a little member, and boasteth great things. Behold, how great a matter a little fire kindleth! And the tongue is a fire, a world of iniquity: so is the tongue among our members, that it defileth the whole body, and setteth on fire the course of nature; and it is set on fire of hell** (James 3:1-6). The Lord won't take your tongue; you have to yield it over to Him to be baptized. That's why so many people don't have the Baptism of the Holy Ghost. In one parable, Jesus talks about how you have to make the garment good or make the garment bad. He said you can't take new wine and pour it into an old vessel. The vessel will start leaking. We are not trying to emulate him. We have to be just like Jesus to make it up out of here. Our Lord will come! Jesus said, **Take heed that no man deceive you** (Matthew 24:4). **For many shall come in my name, saying, I am Christ; and shall deceive many. And ye shall hear of wars and rumours of wars: see that ye be not troubled; for all *these things* must come to pass, but the end**

is not yet. For nation shall rise against nation, and kingdom against kingdom: and there shall be famines, and pestilences, and earthquakes in divers places. All these *are* the beginning of sorrows. Then shall they deliver you up to be afflicted, and shall kill you: and ye shall be hated of all nations for my names sake (Matthew 24:5-9). We do not know all of the persecutions we will have to endure in this hour. Holy people of God are being killed in some nations already; missionaries and workers for God. It goes on to say, **And then shall many be offended, and shall betray one another, and shall hate one another.** And many, many, many **false prophets shall rise, and shall deceive many** (Matthew 24:10-11). Why is it that people can be so easily deceived? They are not walking in all the truth of God. Instead of looking to Jesus, they are looking to man, to personalities speaking clever words that openly contradict the word of God. Many people mock God in this final hour right in the pulpits of America. These people say they are called of God, but I heard the book of Jeremiah say, they ran but I told them that I didn't send them. He said that they dreamed a dream. It is a dream of their own imaginations. If you are deceived you can take the word of God and open up a scripture and say God told you something. But the Bible says today, whom the Son set free is free indeed. He says if you know the truth, then you will be free.

What is it to be free? It is to know the truth? And the truth is the soul that sinneth, it shall die (Ezekiel 18:4). It does not matter what people say, only holiness; you know that. It is a highway to heaven, and nothing can walk up there but the pure in heart. It does not matter if people say that you are in a cult. If you take your life with every criticism, every persecution, you take your life to the Bible. You realize you are right on track. Turn everything and everybody off—just like a dripping faucet. These people are going crazy. The harder it gets, the more you realize you must be coming to the end of the journey. You have got to tell yourself, "Our Lord will come." Our Lord will come. He won't leave me here. He did not bring me this far to leave me. He is not going to leave me down in this wicked world too much longer. He's not going to leave me to face hell that is coming. The Lord won't leave me down here to take the mark of the beast. He won't leave me down here to take the number of man, which is 666. My God won't leave me down here." The bride of Christ will not go into the Tribulation Period. But our Lord will come. Our Lord will come! For such hour you think not, the Son of man cometh. The bride is not getting ready. She is ready NOW and staying ready by fasting, praying and living in the Word of the Almighty God! The bride of Christ is doing everything that she can to win the lost. Like Lot, she is lingering, holding on to the finish. The bride knows that she doesn't have long. She can feel it in her sanctified spirit; her Master will return—He's on His way.

We don't have to worry about what's going on in this old world. Jesus will fix it when He returns. Jesus will put it all in place. He said, let that tares go on with the weeds. He said if you separate them, you might cut down some good ground. **But he said, Nay; lest while ye gather up the tares, ye root up also the wheat with them. Let both grow together until the harvest: and in the time of harvest I will say to the reapers, Gather ye together first the tares, and bind them in bundles to burn them: but gather the wheat into my barn** (Matthew 13:29-30). Know that when Jesus comes for us He will set everything in order. We know he is going to wipe away the tears; All of the tears from all of the persecutions from everything we have been through; how we have been mistreated, the injustices some have faced. He will take all of that when Jesus returns. No need for violence or vengeance. Our Lord will come. We know He is going to set it all in order. All the tugging and pulling on our family; we have been on our knees praying for God to change their hearts. We know that when He comes, He is going to wipe all our tears away. And we are going to go up into heaven, and we won't remember them any longer. There will be no more tears, no more sorrow, and no more sickness. Oh what a happy day that will be. When I see my dear mother, she will be young and happy; she will be so beautiful. We are going to party for seven long years. We are going to be served by John the Baptist. No doubt, Paul is going to come by me and sit by me at the table, along with all those who have been martyred: Stephen, the first martyr, he is going to tell me how good it feels to be into heaven. He has already been there, my Lord and my God, for so many years. And then we are going to sit down with Jesus the Christ, and we are going to tell him all that's on our hearts. He will pull back the curtain of time and reveal to us just what we did for the kingdom. Oh, what a happy day that will be. We won't remember loved ones who didn't live for God. We are going to tell him how good it is that we kept on going, and that we did not faint because we knew we would reap. We didn't faint, but we just kept on going. We just kept the scriptures going on in our mind that our Lord will come. We knew that the Lord wouldn't put more on us than we could bear. We will know we had to go this way because of some little lamb, because He did it. In the book of John, it talks about how he leads us. He does not put us in the pasture by ourselves, but he goes before us, so we know the way we are traveling. If we keep our hands in the nail driven hands of the Lord, then we will know that every step we make he has already made before us. We know, oh Lord, that he will be our guide, even unto death. We know that everything we need, we can find it in the Lord. Our Lord will come. Our Lord will come. Yes! Yes!

WAKE UP!

What is the Lord going to find you doing? What is He going to find you doing? Some of you, nothing moves you. Nothing moves you. Nothing changes your heart, but that Tribulation Period will wake you up. There used to be a time when we were affected by babies getting killed. We used to be affected by divorce. Divorce is worse than death. We used to be affected by paedophiles and people doing stuff to children. We use to be affected by people losing their jobs. But these reality shows, I just believe the antichrist is involved in all of this. These reality shows desensitize you to violence, sex and drugs; they desensitize you to raw porn. There you are watching two men—two homosexuals in the nude having intercourse, and that don't turn your stomach and make you sick? You're addicted to porn, but yet you say you are on your way to heaven—there's no Bible for it. Don't be deceived. Wake up while you still have time. Reality TV desensitizes you to disrespect your parents and not have a reverence for God. Some of these cartoons show kids talking back to their parents; it's something else. It is all in the plan of the devil. We used to be alarmed when people failed God, but now it is so common to so many people in the church. They know their leader is not living right. They know that their leader smokes, drinks, curses, fornicates, commits adultery, and takes them to casino. And they are still hollering, "pastor." The Bible warns us that we must serve the creator and not the creature. Paul said, follow me only as I follow Christ. If you are married to a man, the Bible tells us you should follow your husband *only* as he follows Christ. But if that man is not living right, you do not owe him a thing. The song says, "I pledge allegiance to the Lamb." I pledge allegiance to the Lamb. Your first priority is to the Lord. Amen.

LIES, LIES AND MORE LIES

1Timothy 4:1-3 says, **Now the Spirit speaketh expressly, that in the latter times some shall depart for the faith, giving heed to seducing spirits, and doctrines of devils; Speaking lies in hypocrisy; having their conscience seared with a hot iron. Forbidding to marry, *and commanding* to abstain from meats, which God hath created to be received with thanksgiving of them which believe and know the truth.** People are calling these women their wives; they are shacked up with them, but they are not married to them. That is not your wife. That is your whore. It is in the scriptures. **Flee fornication. Every sin that a man doeth is without the body; but he that committeth fornication sinneth against his own body. What? Knew ye not that your body is the temple of the Holy Ghost which is in you, which ye have of God, and ye are not your own? For ye are bought with a price: therefore glorify God in your body, and in your spirit, which are God's** (I Corinthians 6:18-20). **The soul that sinneth, it shall die** (Ezekiel 18:4).

There is no other name under heaven given among men where we must be saved. Nicodemus sought Jesus at night. Jesus plainly told him about a born-again experience, telling him "Nicodemus, you got to be born again." I do not understand how people can preach and say that you can commit sin and still go to heaven. How? The Bible says that Lucifer was cast out because iniquity was found in him. When what? Iniquity was found in him. Sin was found in him. But you are going to heaven? I cannot understand it. Church after church after church preaches that, "Nobody can live free from sin." Think about what that is saying. "I am a sinner saved by grace." You are saying you are still a sinner, but then you are not saved! He says, grow in the grace and the knowledge of our Lord and Saviour Jesus Christ. You've got to come out of disgrace in order to grow into grace. Our Lord will come.

If you are sinning, the devil is your daddy. I John 3:8-9 says, **For this purpose the Son of God was manifest that he might destroy the works of the devil.** I John says, if I said, if I was never a sinner, then I am a liar. Do you know what people use that scripture for? To stay in sin. They say, "Well, the bible plainly says, if I say I am not a sinner." It says if you have *never* sinned. He says, but if I confess my sins, He is faithful and just to cleanse me from all my sins. He says I have fellowship with him, and the blood of Jesus will cleanse me of all my sins. I do not know what people are preaching, but if this mess is going on in your church, you better run for your soul. The Bible says that the fire [hell] is not quenched. The worm [your soul] dieth not (Mark 9:44). You are not going to ever die; the real you, the eternal you. It doesn't matter what people are telling you. You are not going to ever die. You are not going to ever die. I have seen people so tormented from cancer. I have seen them so tortured from AIDS. But, when they die, that is just the beginning of wherever they are. You can make it to Heaven with AIDS. You can make it to Heaven with cancer. But *you can't make it to Heaven with sin*. Our Lord will come.

And Jesus, on His third appearance, will no longer be the Lamb. He is going to be the Lion of the tribe of Judah. Where will you run? Where will you hide? Where will you go? Where will you hide? What will you say? What will you do? There won't be a hiding place. Pastor and evangelist, you are going to the lake of fire for deceiving God's people, prophesying over people without even being saved yourself. You are telling people it is okay. They are coming with a broken heart, which is supposed to be an opportunity for you to lead them to the cross. Woe, Oh Son of Man! Woe, Woe, Woe to you who have scattered the flock of the Lord. How valuable is one soul? It is worth all of heaven. How Heaven must have cried when Jesus was on the cross? Yet some leaders and preachers say people cannot live free from sin. God is not with you in the whore den. He is not with you in the salon. He is not with you when you are watching porn. That is false doctrine. The Bible says in Matthew 24th chapter, many, many, many false Christ is going to come saying, "I'm Christ, look at me." That is the doctrines of devils. I am going to read something to you out of one of our "Giant"[6] little books.

TWO WILL BE SLEEP, ONE WILL BE TAKEN

We are talking about how our Lord will come. I just want you to listen. "It is the day of the Rapture." Just listen. Our Lord will come. Now just imagine, many people going to sleep on a Sunday night beside their loved ones. Maybe some of them went to sleep cussing, fussing and complaining, but they awake on Monday morning to discover their companions or their children have vanished into thin air taking nothing with them. Nearly every home in the city, nearly every home in the state, nearly every home in the country, nearly every home in the Midwest, nearly every home in the world will be affected either directly or indirectly. All of the babies and the small children will be gone; not one will be left. In some homes, the

---

[6]   *Giant Little Books* are produced and written by Reverend Ernest Angley, Ernest Angley's Grace Cathedral, Winston Press, Akron, Ohio.

husband will have vanished, and the wife will still be there. In other houses, the wife will be taken and the husband will be left. The city is going to be turned into utter chaos. Drivers will suddenly vanish from their cars. Thousands of accidents will turn every road into a parking lot. Trains will be left without engineers, and they will have ploughed through forests and neighbourhoods. Airplanes will have missing pilots and will crash to the ground. Just think, the scene is going to be the same all over the world. The inhabitants of the Earth will be dumbfounded. It's going to be mass hysteria. People will be frantically searching for missing loved ones, but they will not find them. Breaking news bulletins will dominate the airways. Dazed and confused, newscasters will announce the unbelievable story. "Like magic, thousands of people have vanished from the face of the Earth around 6'oclock this morning." Not law enforcement officers, the President, or even the FBI can explain the greatest mystery to ever take place in the history of mankind. What could have possibly happened in the universe? What could have possibly happened in the universe to cause so many people to disappear without warning, leaving behind no trace or clues to their whereabouts? So many people are filled with questions, while others are coming up with thousands of speculations and bizarre stories and theories as to what happened to all of these people. Only yesterday, some of them sat in their churches hearing the story, hearing the testimonies about people being saved and the blood of Jesus on their soul. Only yesterday, they were pricked in their hearts to go down to the altar and give their souls to the Lord, but they said, "Next time." Next time never came, neighbor.

Our Lord will come. In the moment, in the twinkling of an eye he is going to come. We are going to be caught away to live with the Lord forever. Neighbor, not one sin, not one sin. Galatians 5th Chapter and the whole book of Romans talk, in great detail, about sin. Not one sin is going to ever enter Heaven. It is not going to happen. If you are sinning today, you are not a child of the Lord. If you can speak in tongues whenever you get ready, you don't have the Baptism of the Holy Ghost. Salvation has nothing to do with water baptism. Water baptism is just symbolic, if you give your heart to the Lord. Confess with your mouth and believe in your heart that Jesus is the Son of the living God. Confess, "Lord, I am lost, and I need a Saviour." We get baptized because we follow Christ in all things. But neighbor, if you never make it to the water, and your soul has been changed, I will see you one of these days. You and I will sit and talk as the endless ages roll. The Tribulation Period is going to be the worst catastrophe ever known to mankind throughout the whole word. Neighbor, I want you to know I care about you. I love you.

Our Lord will come. Our Lord will come. You know this is the perfect time and the perfect season. People are on the beaches, driving in their cars, flying in their planes, talking about their money and got their stuff. People are depressed and oppressed. The suicide rate is up. This is the hour. People are living such degraded lives. It is the right time for Jesus to return, neighbor.

Change your life. Make a vow to the Lord that you are going to live closer to him than you ever have. You young people separate, separate from all that is false. You parents be parents to your children. Do what is right. I will see you in heaven one of these days. I am looking forward to seeing my momma. I miss her so much, but I know I will see her again.

Why don't you lift your hands and ask the Lord to come into your hearts today, wherever you may be. I want you to say with your whole hearts today: ***Oh God! Oh God! Oh God! Please forgive me for sinning against you, but I have come home. And Lord, I do believe you are the Son of the Living God. Oh Lord, I do believe that since you shed your Blood every person must live free from sin. Oh Lord, by Faith and the Blood, I accept that Blood on my soul. Save my soul! Save my soul! Save my soul! Come on in Jesus! Come on in Jesus! And now that I have you in my heart. And now that I know you are in my soul. I am going to work until you return.*** God Bless you neighbor.

CHAPTER 6
CAN A SAVED PERSON BE LOST?

There are so many today that are living in sin. Some of them are preachers. Some of them are evangelists. Some of them are singing in the choir. Some of them are passing out the holy sacrament of the Lord. And they are not saved. Can a saved person be lost? Think about when you do not live free from sin; you do not worship the true and living God. Some people believe a whole lot of stuff. In this final hour, you either live free from sin or you are living in the bondage of sin. It is as simple as that. You are either free from all sin, or you are living in the bondage of sin. Ask yourself, "Which way does the bible endorse?" Certainly, you know the answer. But the devil however, he is so cunning. He is so manipulative. He has caused man to take the holy scriptures of God, the voice of God, and twist it around into all kinds of falsehoods that have deceived people. Many declare, in this final hour, in churches all over the whole world, that they are on their way to heaven when, in fact, they are going straight to hell.

JUST BECAUSE

Can a saved person be lost? Can a saved person be lost? Just because you knew the Lord once in your lifetime, that does not mean you are still saved today. **The blessing of the Lord, it maketh rich, and he addeth no sorrow with it** (Proverbs 10:22). God's greatest gift to mankind was that of salvation. But salvation is based on condition. It is based on condition. Think about the Garden of Eden. What did He tell them? In Genesis 2nd Chapter verses 16 and 17, the Lord made it so plain. But when you do not know the truth of God; when you do not study the bible; when you don't have the Holy Spirit to teach you and to train you, the enemy is right there. Do you know that the enemy uses the Bible to condone sin? The enemy uses the Bible for people to go on and curse and fornicate and shack-up. The enemy uses the Bible and twists the truth of the Lord to make people feel comfortable in sin. The light still shines, and I am so excited that we can bring to you that light, which is the truth that is in God's word. It is the truth that is in God's word. I believe in "once saved, always saved." I believe that a person can be saved one time and be saved for the rest of their life, if that person does not commit any sin. "Once saved, always saved," it could be a logical belief, if you understand what that means. A person can be saved and always saved, if they are saved from the time that they accept the Lord Jesus in their heart, they do not commit any wilful sin until they die. Then, they are once saved, always saved. I believe that. But it is not what most people believe today.

ONCE SAVED ALWAYS SAVED

People believe that once they give their hearts to the Lord that they cannot fail God, they cannot go away from the truth of God. Some people believe that once they are saved, they can do anything they want to do and still call heaven their home. Neighbor that is the doctrine of devils. It is not Bible. It is not biblical. It is not found anywhere in the word of God. In Eden, there was a man and woman that were made in the image of God. People want to come up against me, so to speak, saying that everybody was born in the image of God. No neighbor! No neighbor! You do not know your Bible. When you go to the Bible, you will see that Adam was made in the image of God. He was made in the likeness of God. And the Lord, God the Father, God the Son, and God the Holy Ghost, they put Adam to sleep. They took one of his ribs, and they made woman. The Bible says that when Adam woke up, he knew that was his wife. He knew, oh my Lord, that she was made for him and that they were supposed to be one. But then Adam failed and went to the tree and ate that fruit that the Lord told him not of. Nobody since that moment has been born in the image of God. It took the blood of Jesus. It took him being slaughtered on the cross. It took the crucifixion. Oh my God! Isaiah said that if we did not know it was Christ, we would not have known him by the way they beat him, the way that they slaughtered him. "Oh, Lord and Oh God!" It took that blood that was shed on the cross; it brought us into the image of God. Nobody on planet Earth today is born in the image of God. The psalmist said, in the 51st Psalm verse five, **Behold, I was shapen in iniquity; and in sin did my mother conceive me.** Oh my Lord, and oh my God, it is so plain. I do not understand it. I do understand however, that people want a doctrine that makes them feel comfortable in sin, but you are not going to get to heaven in the end. Why live a life of deceit and then, at the end, go to hell when you do not have to, when you can live free from sin? You can live in the riches of God's grace. You can live in the healings and blessings. You can live in the fruit that is flowing from the truth of God. You can love the bible and love walking in holiness and trueness. Just like Adam and Eve did before they failed God. Before they failed God, they would have never been sick. They did not need tear ducts. They did not need a digestive system. They did not have to worry about acid reflux, and all these cancers and things. Oh my Lord, people are blaming God for sickness, but sickness came from the fall of Adam, the Adamic nature. Sickness does not come from God, but when you do not know the Bible, that is what you might think. The Lord is about healing, health and life. That does not mean that the Lord cannot strike you with a disease. That does not mean that He will not strike you with a disease. Sickness does not come from God. The Lord is about life. He is about you living. The Bible says He wants you to **prosper even as your soul prospers.** He **says every good and perfect gift comes from above.** He let us know that if anything is too hard for you, show Him. He says **healing is the children's bread.** He promised to keep us in perfect peace. He promised that when people forsake us He will take us up. He said he will lead us and guide us. He said He will never leave us. He said that if He sent us into a valley, He would go with us. But when you do not know the truth of the Gospel, you err. Think about that. In Eden, you find a man and a woman made in the image of God. It did not stop there. When they sinned against God, what happened? They were cast out. This is so simple. I do not understand why people cannot get it. When they were in the Garden of Eden obeying the Lord and doing everything He asked them to do, it was good. But when they sinned, they were cast out. Adam and Eve sinned against God. They were cast out of the Garden of Eden. But you can curse and smoke and do all kind of manner of things, and you are going to heaven? Then, you have got to apologize to Adam! No apology is needed, because **the soul that sinneth, it shall die** (Ezekiel 18:4). Can a saved person be lost?

LIVE FOREVER

Think about Adam and Eve; they were wonderfully made. Their bodies were completely healthy. They were to have lived forever, just like God the Father, God the Son and God the Holy Ghost without one speck of hate or disobedience, without tears, no sorrows or heartaches. However, when man sinned, he found that his eternal life in paradise was conditional. The Lord, in fact had let Adam and Eve know from the very beginning that **of every tree of the garden thou mayest freely eat: But of the tree of knowledge of good and evil, thou shalt not eat of it: for in the day that thou eatest thereof thou shalt surely die** (Genesis 2:16-17). What is so spooky about that? It is transparent. He says He is giving you all of these things but this one, thou shall not. It is foolish of us to think we can commit sin; we can go against the laws of God and still get to His heaven. It is ridiculous to believe. When you curse, you blaspheme the name of the Almighty God. Smoking marijuana and smoking cigarettes, the government already told you that cigarettes give you cancer. People say we are teaching a strange doctrine. I beg to differ. I beg to differ.

Adam and Eve would have never been sick. They would have never had to earn their food by the sweat of their brow. They would have never seen one dead loved one. Never had been separated from those they loved. No, they were beautiful in every way. They were pure in their thinking and pure in their actions and God would come down daily to walk and to talk with them. As much as a family in heaven is a part of God, they were a part of God's family. They were on their way to live forever in the grace of God, possessing everything they could have ever longed for. Adam and Eve, they did not need banks. They did not need security. All that they needed was freely given to them. Think about that! They were never meant to have not one worry and not one sorrow. But when the man and the woman God created fell from grace, they lost everything. They lost everything. They lost everything. And so I ask you again today, can a saved person be lost?

SINNER SAVED BY GRACE?

People say, "I am a sinner saved by grace." What you are really saying is, "Yes, I am a sinner and because Jesus died, I can do all the sinning I want. And I have that grace I can keep going back to." But it is not biblical. Jesus died for all of your past sins. He did not die for you to keep on sinning. This is baffling me. I do not understand the logic of it. Jesus died for all of your sins. In Paul's writing it says Jesus died for the whole wide world once. He said Adam brought down the whole wide world, and Jesus brought up the whole wide world. Can a saved person be lost? People are chewing tobacco, and smoking cigarettes and marijuana, and sleeping around. Someone is sleeping around with someone who is not their husband. How can they be saved? Saved from what? Sin is not a fault. It is sin. You might have things to work on in your character or your attitude, but you do not work on getting away from sin. You stop sinning. You cannot be saved and a sinner at the same time. It is impossible. It is not biblical. That same serpent that worked in the Garden of Eden, he is still here today. In Genesis 3:4, it says, **And the serpent said unto the woman, Ye shall not sure die.** And it is the same today. What is so sad is that the serpent talk is coming right from the pulpits of God's churches here in America. They are telling people that God understands. They are saying, "It is alright to sin. All you have to do is repent." That is trampling the blood of Jesus underfoot. That makes no sense. If you could not live free from sin, the Lord would not ask you to do something that you cannot do. In yourself? No! But through the power that is in the blood, the freedom from all sin is there. You have got to think about what God said about sin. He really meant it. The Bible warns us about how some people twist the word of God. The Lord says, the soul that sinneth, it shall die. That is what he means. That is exactly what he means. But that old serpent talk, think about how that old serpent talk is still alive and on planet Earth today. It is telling preachers, priests, evangelists and teachers, and people on the mother's board, those who do communion, those in the choir, "You won't really die. No one can live free from sin. God didn't really mean that when he said it." Oh, you better not today. That what God has said is what he means, and what he means is what he says.

GET OUT!

Can a saved person live free from sin? Genesis 3:24 says, **So he drove the man; and he placed at the east of the Garden of Eden Cherubims, and a flaming sword which turned every way, to keep the way of the tree of life**. God put angels by the garden and a flaming sword and turned in every direction to make it possible for man and woman in their sinful ways not to get back into Eden. They could have lived forever. So, if you cannot live free from sin, why did he cast Adam and Eve out for? You can do anything you want to do and still call out to God? My Lord and my God! Why did he put Adam out? Why didn't he just forgive them and let them keep going on in sin? No! The Lord put that illustration in the Bible to let us know that there is some sin He does not forgive. He wants us to know emphatically that when He tells us not do not do something, do not do it.

What is deceiving a lot of people is that we are in the grace dispensation. Because we have the blood, because we have the Holy Spirit, because we have the anointing of God, they believe that we can just keep on sinning.

Do not let that deceive you. Whatever you sow, you are going to reap in this final hour. God is still the same. That is really something to think about.

Can a saved be person be lost? 1 Corinthians 6:9-10 says, **Know ye not that the unrighteous shall not inherit the kingdom of God?** See, this is all in the Word of God. So, why do people call me and write me as if I wrote the Bible? No, the King James Bible was written in 1611, I was not here yet. **Know ye not that the unrighteous shall not inherit the kingdom of God? Be not deceived: neither fornicators, nor idolaters, nor adulterers, nor effeminate, nor abusers of themselves with mankind, nor thieves, nor covetous, nor drunkards** (I Corinthians 6:9-10). There goes the people that go to the lounges; the social drinkers. You know the holidays are around. They have the cocktails around. **Nor drunkards, nor revilers, nor extortioners, shall inherit the kingdom of God (vs. 10)**. Many think that even though they are disobedient, they are still a child of God, because *they were once saved.* They were once saved. They were once saved. Once you go and wilfully sin against the blood, you are no longer saved. Salvation is based on condition. Even people who are devil possessed will tell you they are saved. No one is going to get into heaven unless that one is sinless through the blood and the pure Word of God. The Bible lets us know that the word "Jesus Christ" was made flesh and dwelled among us, and we beheld His glory. The Glory as of the only begotten of the Father, full of grace and full of truth. Jesus was the living word and He speaks, **I am the door, by me if any man enter in, he shall be saved** (John 10:9). Does that mean you are going to live in Jesus? His word abides in you, and you are going to still curse? You are going to still tell lies? You are not saved. The blood of Jesus is not on your soul. It is not, if you have unforgiveness in your heart? No way! If you are sleeping around with somebody that is not your husband, you are not saved.

A SOCIAL DRINK

People want to debate with me about having a social drink. You are drinking for the purpose of what, to get drunk? Drinking leads to adultery and fornication. You either want to fight, or you want to have sex. One or the two, you are ready to humbug or you are ready to sleep around. You are talking about how you get warm all over, but once you are in hell, you will be hot for all time and eternity. Think about that hotness. Can a saved person be lost? Jesus makes it so plain. But people have been spewed with this vomit for so many years, believing that God just accepts anything. He does not.

The Beatitudes, in Matthew 5, lets you know that only the pure in heart shall see God. So, if you are pure in heart, do you curse? No! Do you lie? No! Do you still steal? Do you cheat? Do you misuse people? Do you participate in same sex unions? No! It is not biblical. It is not in the Bible. The Lord made a man to co-habitat with a woman in marriage. That was it. The Lord loves the homosexual, He loves the lesbian, and they can be free. The Lord loves them. The Lord looks upon the practice of homosexuality and lesbianism just like he looks upon any other sin, such as the liar, the thief, and the whore-monger. Same-sex union is not the divine will of the Lord. It is not. There is no Bible for it. There is no Bible for it. There is no Bible that endorses it. There is no Bible that uplifts it. Not the Bible printed in 1611. There are a lot of versions of bibles out there now. They are taking out the blood. They are taking out the righteousness. They are taking out the fact that Mary was a virgin. She was a virgin. People have ripped out there altars at the church. They do not want people kneeling down to pray. Where is the mourning bench? Where is the mother's board that pulled the young women aside and told them to keep their virginity to their wedding night? These young kids now, the young girls and boys now are having intercourse as young as 10 and 11 years old. 10 and 11 years old? It is alarming. It is alarming. In John 10:9 it says, **I am the door by me if any man enter in, he shall be saved, and shall go in and out, and find**

pasture. Jesus is our door into heaven, but we can only go through that door into heaven if we are without sin. This is so plain. I do not understand it. Where is the confusion coming in? No sin, no particle of sin. Not one grain of sin is going to get into heaven. And if that sin is in you, you are not going to heaven. It is not something we have to go and research, it is obvious. There is no scripture that teaches or even hints that the doctrine of "once saved, always saved" is valid. Nowhere in the Bible does it say that. Galatians 5:16 says, **This I say then, Walk in the Spirit and ye shall not fulfil the lust of the flesh.** That is what the bible says. So, what do you do with these scriptures when people endorse false doctrine? Those who endorse that people cannot make it to heaven sinless? What do you do with the scriptures? What do you do with the Word? What do you do with the scriptures like Galatians 5:17-18? **For the flesh lusteth against the Spirit, and the Spirit against the flesh; and these are contrary the one to the other: so that ye cannot do the things that ye would. But, if ye be led by the Spirit, ye are not under the law.** After you receive salvation, you are no longer under the law of the Old Testament. You are under the sinless, Jesus, love law; the sinless love law of Jesus. He says my sheep know my voice. They will not follow the voice of a stranger, the voice of sin, the voice of doubt, the voice of fear, frustration and unbelief. There are so many voices now. There are so many doctrines, so many denominations, and so many interpretations of the Bible. Jesus did not endorse any of it. He endorsed living free from sin, it has to be. That is the only denomination that Jesus endorsed. Holiness is not a denomination; it is a way of life. It is a way of life. It is a way of life.

ALL LIARS

It really breaks my heart that people are going to church every day and dying, lost without the Lord Jesus Christ on their side. They believe they are on their way to heaven. And you are lying about their social security. You are lying about your unemployment. You are not going to heaven.

That is a lie. People are lying on their applications for jobs about how they can do this and do that. No! No liars are going to heaven. If you are committing adultery of the heart, the only thing you are missing is an opportunity that you can sleep with somebody. There is no blood on your soul. No blood. No blood at all. Luke says that Jesus went after the lost. He left all of His sheep there, and he went after the lost. But it was a lost one found. People think once you are saved, you cannot go astray. No! A sheep is lost until it is found. Did you hear me? A sheep is lost until it is found. **And he (meaning Jesus), spake this parable unto them saying, What man of you, having an hundred sheep, if he lose one of them, doth not leave the ninety and nine in the wilderness, and go after that which is lost, until he find it? And when he hath found it, he layeth it on his shoulders rejoicing. And when he cometh home, he calleth together his friends and neighbors, saying unto them, Rejoice with me; for I have found my sheep which was lost. I say unto you, that likewise joy shall be in heaven over one sinner that repenteth, more than over ninety and nine just persons which need no repentance** (Luke 15:3-7). Jesus is clearly saying here that His sheep, if they have gone astray, must repent if they are to come back into His fold.

CAN YOU SIN AND MAKE IT IN

Can a saved person be lost is my question? Can you sin, do degrading things, be evil and mean, spew out curse words, gamble and still be in the fold of Jesus? No! No! Absolutely not! Absolutely not! Think about that. Can a saved person be lost? It is something for us to think about.

My sister wrote a wonderful song about living free from sin and I love it!

Living free, it has to be

God winked at ignorance, but He's callin all to repentance.

Don't you tell a lie, cause the soul that sinneth, it shall die

Living free, it has to be

Walk in the spirit, and you won't fall for lust

You won't see Jesus, if you cuss

Living free, it has to be[7]

In I John 1:10, it says, **If we say that we have not sinned, we make him a liar, and his word is not in us.** John very clearly makes this statement, because we were **ALL** born sinners, and we **ALL** need a Saviour, not for us to keep on sinning. *So, if you say that you are not a sinner, then you are lying to Jesus.* No! That is not what he is saying. He is saying, if we say we have not *sinned.* That is past tense. If I was never a sinner, then I am a liar. But we were all shaped in iniquity and born in sin. You don't stay in sin. People will use this scripture to justify staying in sin. Just like in John 8:39, he says, **They answered and said unto him,** (which is Jesus)**, Abraham is our father. Jesus saith unto them. If ye were Abraham's children, ye would do the works of Abraham.** What was Abraham's work? Just. **But now ye seek to kill me, a man that hath told you the truth** (vs. 40). People hate truth. They hate the truth. They don't mind the rapping. They don't mind the skits. They don't mind the plays. But don't start talking about living free from sin. "Oh what kind of Gospel is that?" It is the Gospel of Jesus Christ. It is the Gospel He gave His life for. Multitudes are dying, lost on a daily basis, being reassured within their own hearts, but they don't have Jesus. They don't have Jesus. Jesus did not let these people get by claiming that Abraham was their father. He denied that they were the true children of Abraham. They were not doing the works of Abraham. If we are God's children, we do the works of God, not the devil. The people who claim to be the children of God and continue in sin, they are doing the works

---

[7]   Bridget Johnson-Welch, *Living Free*, 2013, Chicago, IL

of the devil. It is impossible to be a child of God if you sin. Can a saved person be lost? Yes, indeed!

John 8:42-43 says, **Jesus said unto them, If God were your Father, ye would love me: for I proceeded forth and came from God; neither came I of myself, but he sent me. Why do ye not understand my speech? even because ye cannot hear my word.** The word was made flesh. The word was speaking. Now, this is powerful. Some people think that we preach strong at our church, but Jesus really preached strong. He said, I am telling you the truth. Why can't you get it? You have to have a heart to hear the truth. People can talk to you all day long; it will never get in if you don't have a heart to receive the truth. I had a person tell me one time about living free from sin. They said, "Well, you know nobody can live free from sin. We all make mistakes." I said "But brother, a sin is not a mistake." No! Wilful sin is a sin that is premeditated. It is planned out. You know you are going to lie before you do it. You have been sitting in church all day thinking about what woman you are going to sleep with and fornicate with. You already know you are going to do it. The Bible says the Lord don't tempt no man. But a man is tempted when he is drawn away by his own lust and enticed. We have to stop lying on God. The works of the flesh, sin does not come to you. You go to sin. That serpent did not come to Eve. Eve sought the serpent out. We do not know for how many years. We don't know how long she played around with him, until he got her. The Lord told her, "Thou shall not." And she brought that deceit back to her husband. Her husband, for a moment, was confused because he saw her physically still alive, but spiritually she was dead. She was dead. She was dead. We just have to face things.

YOUR FATHER, THE DEVIL

In John 8:44, Jesus told His accusers just who they were. **You are of your father the devil, and the lusts of your father ye will do. He was**

a murderer from the beginning, and abode not in the truth, because there is no truth in him. When he speaketh a lie, he speaketh of his own: for he is a liar, and the father of it. Your father is the one that you are going to act just like. How about that one? Your father is the one you are going to act like. Now, the devil is a liar from the beginning. If you commit sin, then the devil is your father. Think of people who are in hell today who believe they were going to heaven. Think about that. That just blows my mind. There are people who believed they were going to heaven, but they went to hell. Are you going to be one of them? He said, **because strait is the gate, and narrow is the way, which leadeth unto life, and few there be that find it** (Matthew 7:14). God says He will not change; He will not change His mind. The Lord will not compromise with sin. The Bible lets us know, which some people take out of context that the Lord will not look upon sin. That does not mean He cannot see you whoring and committing adultery. It means He won't reason with sin, He won't excuse sin, He won't continue to pardon unrepentant sin. That is what that scripture means. That does not mean He cannot see you with the shade down over your girlfriend's house while you are married to someone else. That is not what it means. It means He will never excuse sin. No! You have got to be Godly sorrow about what you did. And that takes humility to recognize your faults that you are lost and need a Saviour. People will write or call and say, "What is this that she is talking about? I never heard this before." No, you need to get your Bible and study. Nobody can live free from sin? What kind of doctrine is that? What did Jesus die for? Why did He give Himself over to the hands of audacious men? Why? Why was His life a sacrifice? Why did His blood need to be shed? Why did the Romans soldiers stick the sword in His side? Why did the Jews kill him? So that you can be free!

You've got to live free from sin if you are going to God's heaven. There is no if, ands, or buts, about it. These pastors and leaders are being exposed. And the people in the congregation are just covering up and letting them back in. Don't you know your soul at risk? I would not even sponsor a lying preacher. Some of you know your pastor is a whore, yet you keep on giving them your hard-earned money. The devil really makes idiots. You just keep on supporting them. "Well, you know, we are going to get better. God is helping us!" Yeah, God might be helping you to get better in some things, but not sin. The Lord does not mean for you to stay there and work out your own soul salvation with fear and trembling. That is not what that means. It does not mean to labor with your brother. He wants you to labor in righteousness and true holiness. He wants you to labor in being spotless and right before God. When you talk about being perfect they say, "Oh my God, that is ridiculous. Nobody can be perfect!" You are right! I cannot be perfect within myself, but I can be perfect in His love and His grace. I can be perfect in His love and His grace. You are always going to look at me or whoever you might be with, or your kids, and find some fault within them you do not like. Am I perfect in the ways of the Lord? That blood makes me perfect when I draw on it. Yes! Yes!

Think about how many people died today thinking that everybody sins. Everybody sins. Everybody has sinned. But not everybody is sinning. Some of them have been born new. Everybody has sinned. Not everybody is sinning. Many have been born new. The Bible tells us to be holy. Hebrews 12:14 says, **Follow peace with all men, and holiness, without no man shall see the Lord**. What do you do with these scriptures? What do you do with the scripture that says **the soul that sinneth, it shall die** (Ezekiel 18:4)? What do you with the scripture that says **the blood of Jesus Christ his Son cleanses us from all sin** (1 John 1:7)? What do you do with the scripture that says, **ye shall be holy, for I am holy** (Leviticus 11:45)? What do we do with those scriptures that say, without holiness no man shall see the Lord? What do we do with those scriptures, the lust of the flesh in Galatian 5th Chapter? What do we do with those scriptures in the midst of God's people? God meant what He said, and He said what He meant. Living free from sin, it has to be. It has to be that way, or you are not going to God's heaven. He says here in John 8:45, **because I tell you the truth, ye believe me not**. It is just the way some people are. They will hear this message and say, "What in the world is she talking about?" It is because they have been in that world of false doctrine so long. That vomit has covered them so long, until when they hear the truth of God, they feel as if that is strange. Yes, it is strange if you have been living in darkness all of your life. When that light starts shining, oh my Lord and oh my God, it is like being down in the dungeon. And when they bring you out to the light, it burns your eyes. As long as you stay in the sun, you get used to it, and you begin to welcome it. This is nice. When you've been in the darkness for so long, then hear the truth, it is like, "What kind of mess is this?" But it is the truth. You have been in a mess so long, until you hear the truth, you can't comprehend it. Stay out in the sun and let it warm you up, and you will come to love it. Yes! John 8:45-47 says, **because I tell you the truth, ye believe me not. Which of you convinceth me of sin? And if I say the truth, why do ye not believe me? He that is of heareth God's words** (this is powerful) **ye therefore hear them not, because ye are not of God.** It is just that simple. When you have one sin in your heart, your soul is dead. How about that one? If you are born again, and then go back into sin, you are no longer a child of God. Hear me today! If you are born again, and go back into sin, you are no longer saved. That blood is no longer on your soul. If you die, you are going to hell. A dead soul cannot enter into heaven. Ezekiel 18:20, **the soul that sinneth, it shall die.** Can a saved person be lost? The answer is absolutely.

HE THAT SINS

John 3:8 says, **He that committeth sin is of the devil; for the devil sinneth from the beginning. For this purpose the Son of God was manifested, that he might destroy the works of the devil.** If you could not live free from sin, what was the purpose of Jesus' coming? Why did he shed His blood; for you to keep on sinning? No! Absolutely not! Absolutely not! Absolutely not! Are you going to heaven whoring? Are you going to heaven being a liar? Are you going to heaven, yet you are mistreating folks?

Come on, you have got to let the light come on into your mind. What type of heaven would that be? It would be no different than Earth. No! No! No! You have got to live free from all sin. No sin, not one particle is going to enter into heaven. Everyone who commits wilful sin belongs to the devil. I do not care if you are a bishop. I do not care if you are an evangelist, an elder, an apostle; if you are sinning, you belong to the devil. The son of God was sent to Earth where people could see Him, where they could talk to him, and He could talk to them. He came for one purpose; to destroy the works of the devil.

Can a saved person be lost? Yes! Look at this person that was saved in Acts 1:16. Acts gives us an account of a follower of Jesus who fell into the hands of the devil and went to hell. Now notice this, he was a follower. Once he was walking with Jesus, then he did not. Acts 1:16-17, *Judas, which was guide to them that took Jesus. For he was numbered with us, and had obtained part of this ministry.* At one time, Judas was handling the power of God. Jesus had let Judas handle His power. He (Judas) was casting out devils and doing all kinds of stuff. In the next moment, he was not saved anymore. He was not saved. One moment he was saved, and the next moment he wasn't. Again, that is Act 1:16-17, **Judas was guide to them that took Jesus. For he was numbered with us**. At one time, he was one of the disciples. **And he obtained part of this ministry** (Acts 1:17). He had the grace of God. He used the power of God. It says**, Now this man purchased a field with the reward of iniquity; and falling headlong, (Judas committed suicide) he burst asunder in the midst, and all his bowels gushed out. And it was known unto all the dwellers at Jerusalem; insomuch as that field is called in their proper tongue, Aceldama, that is to say, The field of blood. For it is written in the book of Psalms, Let his habitation be desolate, and let no man dwell therein: and his bishoprick let another take** (Acts 1:18-20). So they were saying, Judas fell away from God, rise up somebody else Lord. Let the church roll on. One moment he had the power of God and was a believer. One moment he had the power of God and was saved. The next moment, he was without God, lost and on his way to hell. You might be saved right now, but if you commit wilful sin, that blood leaves your soul. You no longer belong to God. No! Absolutely not! It is so tragic for a person to die lost and to go to hell, especially one who was once so close to God that he was numbered with the disciples of Jesus. Think about that. Keep that in your mind.

The Bible says, and then he, Jesus, called His twelve disciples together and gave them power and authority over all devils and to cure diseases. Judas at one time had the power of God. No, it is not true that Jesus was always a devil. He had the power of God. But, then he fell by transgression. It says by transgression he fell. He fell from grace. To fall from grace you first have to be in grace. Amen. Acts 1:25 says, **Judas by transgression fell, that he might go to his own place**. Can a saved person be lost? Yes! Yes! The disciples were choosing a man to take Judas' place. They just went right on. Think about that. He failed God, and they got somebody else. Peter had already said that Judas was numbered with them. In other words, he was like them. At one time, Judas was a part of them. He had the same power. Judas had the same ministry. Nevertheless, **Judas fell by transgression, that he might go to his own place** (Acts 1:25). Each person chooses his own place, either heaven or hell. Devil possession made Judas go mad, and he committed suicide by hanging himself. It is so incredible that Judas once had the power of God, but he failed by transgression. So many ministers today, they started on fire. They started out preaching the truth. God was moving and helping them. Then they started worrying about the numbers. They started worrying about what people thought. They started worrying about people leaving the church. They started compromising.

A LOST WAY

Can a believer, can a person that was once saved lose their way? Absolutely! Absolutely! Absolutely! Can a person in one moment be in the Grace of

God, then again not be in His grace anymore? Absolutely! Absolutely! Romans 8:13 says, let us know that **For if ye live after the flesh, ye shall die.** That is something for us to think about. Our salvation is a precious fragile gift based on condition. One moment you can have eternal life; the next moment, it may not be promised to you anymore. Salvation is based on condition. Paul told them in Galatians that he was dealing with sin in such a marvelous way. He said in Galatians 3:1 says, **O foolish Galatians, who hath bewitched you.** Who put this devilish spell on you to make you think that you can sit in the houses of God with sin in your heart and still go to heaven? Who has bewitched you? He said in another book of Galatians, you ran well when you were living for God but who did hinder you? I marvel that you turn so quickly away from the truth. People are so deceived. This is such a deceivable age, he says, if you continue in His word. Isn't that what he said in the book of John? If you stay grounded in faith, if you stay grounded in truth, then you are my disciples. He says if any man, any woman, any boy, any girl be in Christ, they are new. They are a new creature. Can a saved person be lost? Yes! Yes! Not one sin is going to be in heaven. You think about the mighty king David, he backslid. He was a mighty king. Psalms 31:9-10 says, **Have mercy upon me, O Lord, for I am in trouble: mine eyes is consumed with grief, yea, my soul and my belly. For my life is spent with grief, and my years with sighing: my strength faileth because of mine iniquity** (my sins) **and my bones are consumed.** David was so afraid God would never take him back. He was so afraid that God would never take him back. It takes true repentance to have a born again experience. It says, **For Godly sorrow worketh repentance** (2 Corinthians 7:10), meaning you are truly sorry, not just saying, "I'm sorry." You must be truly sorry.

Can a saved person be lost? Yes! David went on in Psalms 31:22, David was afraid God would never take him back. He says here, **for I said in my haste, I am cut off from before thine eyes; nevertheless thou heardest the voice of my supplications when I cried unto thee.** You have got to cry out to God to be free. You have got to get that sin out of your heart.

It is so foolish for us to think we can just go on and do what we are going to do, and God is going to accept this stuff in our hands. No! No! It is not the will of the Lord! No! No! No! No! And God places pastors, leaders and watchmen to warn the sinners, to let people know that they are on a slippery slope. He said that if the watchman did not warn the wicked, that the sinner would die. Then the watchman would be responsible for the blood of those whom he failed to warn. Our mission is to warn people in this final hour. Read what the Lord told Ezekiel. Son of man, I have made thee a watchman unto the house of Israel. Therefore, hear the word at my mouth and give them warning from me. When I say unto the wicked, thou shall surely die and thou givest him not warning, nor speaketh to warn the wicked from his wicked way to save his life. The gospel is to warn people that they may save their lives from a terrible and awesome God who is not going to accept any sin. The purpose of a pastor or leader is to guide you on good pasture, good clean pasture, holy pasture, sinless pasture, a pasture where God dwells. Yes! And a lot of people believe that you cannot live free from sin from the pulpit. They are taught to blaspheme God's name. People preach right in the pulpits cursing. Right in the pulpit, curse words right from the pulpit. They go right down in the church and have a beer and light their cigarette. He says, thou givest him not warning, nor speaketh to warn the wicked from his wicked way to save his life. The wicked man shall die in his iniquity. But, his blood will I require at thy hand. But, yet if you warn the wicked and if he turn not from his wickedness, nor from his wicked way. He shall die from his iniquity but you have delivered your soul. That is what our responsibility is. It is our responsibility to warn people, but it is up to them what they are going to do. Most people are not going to heed this lesson. Most people are not going to turn away. They like living in sin. They enjoy it. They are intoxicated by the works of the devil. They are intoxicated by this whole world. This world is going to hell.

A NARROW WAY

Jesus said **for this people heart is waxed gross, and their ears are dull of hearing, and their eyes, they have closed; lest at anytime they shall see with their eyes, and hear with their ears and should understand with their heart and should be converted, and I should heal them** (Matthew 13:15). People are deaf to God's word, because they want to be deaf. People are blind to God's word, because they want to be blind. The Bible says **because strait is the gate, and narrow is the way, which leadeth unto life, and few there be that find it** (Matthew 7:14). No matter what happens, neighbor, you have got to be the one that makes it. And remember, no matter what you are going through, I am praying for you. Neighbor remember, **with God all things are possible** (Matthew 19:26). Living free from sin, it has to be neighbor. It has to be. You get your Bible, and you pray out to the Lord, "Lord in the Name of Jesus I come." You might have been going to this church ten to twenty, forty, fifty years. Thank God for the light that still shines. What is that light? **It is the truth that is in God's word!**

CHAPTER 7
TODAY YOU LOVE ME

Maybe it's your companion, or children, maybe people at work, but sometimes you just feel like "Man, my wife really loves me today," or, "My husband really loves me today!" And then sometimes you are like "Does anybody love me? I don't even think they like me today!"

TWO RIVALS

Think about that from the standpoint of your relationship with the Lord. Has the Lord asked you recently, "Oh, today you love me?" I want to share a little story with you. There were two magicians; one was driving the other one crazy with jealousy. They are rival stage magicians in London at the end of the 19th century. They were obsessed with creating the best stage illusions; they had to outdo each other. They engaged in competitive showmanship with tragic results. Don't forget about what the title of our lesson is—Today You Love Me. I'll call the one guy Jim, because this was based on a real movie. I'll call the other Bill. Jim is obsessed with some of the magic tricks that Bill can do. As the story goes on, Jim has a wife name Ruthie. Well, once Jim's wife, Ruthie, was in the magic trick. You know these magic tricks when they put a person in a box full of water, and then when the assistant removes the cover, the person in the box has escaped. On this particular day, the trick didn't work. It must have been the way the rope was tied, which did not allow Ruthie to get out and escape. Well, Bill was in charge of Jim's wife; putting that rope on her and making sure she could get out of the water. Somehow, some way Ruthie died, and this is how the hatred between these two men started. All of his life, Jim blamed Bill for his wife's death; he was always looking for a way to get back at him.

As time passes, Bill marries and has a child, and Jim becomes more and more obsessed and bitter. They both attend each other's shows, trying to discover how the other one did the tricks. There's this real, real super trick that Bill did; other novice magicians would go to see if they can steal tricks and ideas. Don't forget, Jim blames Bill for his wife's death. As time goes on, Jim has discovered a way to clone himself, but it's very, very dangerous. The man who owned the machine told Jim to stay away from it. One time, they started the machine, and it turned all the lights out in many cities. That constant need to be better, to outdo the other person, kept them both going at each other. Bill also found out a way that he could produce a double of himself, and it just drove Jim nuts. As the story progresses, it is discovered that Bill has a twin that his wife did not know about. Bill would use his twin for the show, and they both would take turns being with Ruthie, Bill's wife. Ruthie had no idea who she was sleeping with at any given time, but did state when Bill's brother was with her, "Oh, today you love me". Because both of the twins were spending time with her, Ruthie could tell the difference between the one that loved her and the one that didn't. That's what I'm telling you today.

GOD KNOWS

God knows if you love Him or you don't. Ruthie didn't have it all figured out, but she recognized love. The constant change from being loved and not being loved was so strong until one day when she hung herself. Some days, when the brother was there, she knew he loved her just by the way he treated her, and the love that he showed her. Then, when her husband, Bill, would come, she would say, what? You don't love me today?" She didn't know there were two men, but the love was different, and she could tell. So, the Lord says to you, "Today you love me."

Beverly D. Thomas

IF YOU LOVE ME

Genesis 29:1-5 says, **Then Jacob went on his journey, and came into the land of a people of the East. And he looked, and behold a well in the field, and, lo, there were three flocks of sheep lying by it: for out of that well they watered the flocks: and a great stone was upon the well's mouth. And thither were all the flocks gathered: And they rolled the stone from the well's mouth and watered the sheep, and put the stone again upon the well's mouth in his place. And Jacob said unto them, My brethren, when be ye? And they said, Of Haran are we. And he said unto them, know ye Laban the son of Nahor? And they said, We know him.** This is Jacob making his way to Laban's house. You know he was in that treachery with his mother. She said if you love me do what I say and he paid for it for the rest of his life and so did she (verses. 6-8) **He said unto them, Is he well? And they said, He is well: And, behold, Rachel his daughter cometh with the sheep. And he said, Lo, it is yet high day, neither is it time that the cattle should be gathered together: water ye the sheep, and go and feed them. And they said, We cannot, until all the flocks be gathered together, and till they roll the stone from the well's mouth; then we water the sheep.** They had a plan just like God has a plan for you. **And while he yet spake with them, Rachel came with her father's sheep: for she kept them. And it came to pass, when Jacob saw Rachel the daughter of Laban his mother's brother, and the sheep of Laban his mother's brother, that Jacob went near, and rolled the stone from the well's mouth, and watered the flock of Laban his mother's brother. And Jacob kissed Rachel, and lifted up his voice, and wept** (verses 9-11).

Now, I think Jacob loved her at that very moment. Go on and read and study all of the deceit and everything that took place in his life. Other people are affected by our actions; what we do, what we say, and how we carry ourselves. This is not just our own thing for us to do any kind of way we want. You have to think about somebody who comes to the ministry.

126

Maybe the Lord has been working on that person for a long time and finally they begin to respond. God's time is not our time, but everything has to be done the way He says. Jacob kissed Rachel, and he loved her immediately, but immediately she was not given to him. Genesis 29:16 says, **And Laban had two daughters: the name of the elder was Leah, and the name of the younger was Rachel.** Jacob knew the history; he knew the order of things. Jacob knew the protocol. What made him think that Laban was going to step out of tradition for him? You know God's requirements. You know the tenth is holy unto the Lord. No prayer, no power; little prayer, little power. You know that! So why should you expect to be able to stand against one of the greatest tests in your life when you're not ready? Jacob had been raised with the knowledge and the wisdom of how protocol goes in terms of order. The older sister got married first. Why would he think that Laban would care that much about him to change that and shame his family? Tradition? Laban was a ruthless businessman in his dealings, but God used him to punish Jacob. Deceit means defeat. Jacob ran and went to another place. Come on, you have to think about this. Is anybody swaying you or influencing you against being faithful to God? You better get away from them. This is deep, but you gotta take it. They used lies and deceit. So Laban told Jacob all these lies; he was a good worker, and Laban knew he loved Rachel. Laban used that information for his benefit against Jacob. Yes he did.

YOU TALK TOO MUCH

People have knowledge about you that they use against you for their benefit. Some of you talk too much and put information into the enemies hands. Some of you are scared of your own shadow, talking about fighting devils. Come on. We are about to go into the woods, so to speak. But without the Holy Ghost, you are not going anywhere; you are going to eventually fall on your face. It's just mental assent. It never really drops into your heart, because if it really permeated in your heart, you would have the

Holy Ghost or be earnestly seeking Him. Amen Reverend Thomas! If it was real. What have you spent your time thinking about this week? That'll tell you. That'll tell you. People say, "Reverend Thomas, I love you." I'm leery of when people in the congregation tell me that now, because almost every person that has told me that is gone from this ministry. People didn't have to pull them out; baby, they ran out! Talk is cheap. Love is an action word.

Love is a word that motivates you to prove yourself. God is weighing you on His scales every day on how much you say you love Him. Is He asking you like He asked Peter? Peter do you love me? Then feed my sheep. But you can't feed his sheep when you're feeding yourself or self-indulged. Today you love me. Laban makes Jacob a false promise. People have made you false promises too, if you would just go ahead and admit it. "I love you." That's a lie! "You the best thing I ever had." Lie! And because you don't know who you are, you figure you must be what they say about you. But know who you are first! Don't lie to yourself about yourself. How in the world can you tell if something's false? You have to first know the truth about the matter. That's the only way you can tell when something is wrong. You can't measure wrong against wrong. You measure with the truth. But if you don't have the truth, you're going to come up short every time. Laban got Jacob. Rachel, poor heartbroken girl, she's seeing all of this. And then bless God, there is Leah. Didn't do anything wrong. She was the one that was fertile. But what did she say? Genesis 29:23 **And it came to pass in the evening, that he took Leah his daughter, and brought her to him; and he went into unto her** (verses. 25-26) **And it came to pass, that in the morning, behold, it was Leah:** Lord have mercy! **and he said to Laban, What is this thou hast done unto me: did not I serve with thee for Rachel? Wherefore then hast thou beguiled me? And Laban said, it must not be so done in our country, to give the younger before the firstborn.** Oh my Lord. How would you feel, waking up to that reality? God used Laban to punish Jacob for part in the deceit he sought out against his father with his mother. She paid too.

A BALL OF CONFUSION

Now, there you are, in a place you shouldn't be. That music gets you warm all over. You weren't even trying to see any light. You're just in a daze—in a fog—a ball of confusion. Don't know where you're going or which way; you're just totally, totally inebriated with lust. But you claim you love God. The Bible says, how can you love God whom you never seen? You know the people at the white throne judgment are not going to see the face of God. How in the world can you say you love God? How can you say you love God who you've never seen? And your co-worker, because they don't smell as sweet as you do, you treat them with disrespect? **Then shall he say also unto them on the left hand, Depart from me, ye cursed, into everlasting fire, prepared for the devil as his angels: For I was an hungred, and ye gave me no meat: I was thirsty, and ye gave me no drink: I was a stranger, and ye took me not in: naked, and ye clothed me not: sick, and in prison, and ye visited me not. Then shall they also answer him, saying, Lord, when saw we thee an hungred, or athirst, or a stranger, or naked, or sick, or in prison, and did not minister unto thee? Then shall he answer them, saying, Verily I say unto you, Inasmuch as ye did it not to one of the least of these, ye did it not to me. And these shall go away into everlasting punishment: but the righteous into life eternal.** (Matthew 25:41-46) What do you mean? I didn't give you water and I didn't treat you right? What you do to the least of these; what you don't do for them is the same way you treat me. But today you love me. Today.

Jacob went in unto who he thought was Rachel, but *in the morning* he discovered he had been tricked. There was no way to repair it. There was no way. You know what the funny thing about it is: I believe in my heart Leah really loved Jacob. Jacob went on and worked another how many years for Rachel? Now, here he is with his heart's desire, and a wife he didn't plan on. He found everything he wanted, everything he needed in Rachel, and then there was Leah. God made Leah fruitful and Rachel was barren. The Lord is not to be mocked. He has a way of bringing you to your knees. Galatians

6:7-8 says **Be not deceived; God is not mocked: for whatsoever a man soweth, that shall he also reap. For he that soweth to his flesh shall of the flesh reap corruption; but he that soweth to the Spirit shall of the Spirit reap life everlasting.**

WHEN REALITY SETTLES IN

Jacob had to look into Rachel's face day in and day out. When the reality sets in of what you've done, the choices you've made, it will knock the wind out of you. Leah gave Jacob children, but Rachel was barren for a long time, yet he still loved her. See how life is? See how life can get you if you don't do right? That's what I'm talking about. You're not getting away with anything! Genesis 29:31 says, **And when the Lord saw that Leah was hated.** "Hate" is a powerful, strong word. It wasn't Leah's fault. Her father, Laban, was the one in deceit and made her part of his deceit. Today, these kids that are six, seven years old try to tell you what they're not going to do. When we were coming up, you better not even look like a thought was trying to form in your mind that was derogatory. You better have waited until you got in that room, and then you wanted to turn the lights out because you didn't want your thought to reflect on the wall. Because your mama could reach through that keyhole and choke you! Not today. While I was growing up, I learned to keep my opinions to myself. Where do you think I learned to keep a straight face when things be going on in this church? I learned it at home, because I knew when my mama said something to me I didn't like, she would keep looking at my face, "trying to see what I'm doing with it," is what she said. I wasn't about to get chopped down. My mama knew karate. Did I tell you? She knew kung-Fu. She knew all those other techniques. My momma was in that movie, what's that movie when they fly across? Yes, The Matrix! Yup, did y'all see her?

Today's kids talk back to you, hit you. Hit my mama? My mama been in heaven for over two years, and I still can't process the thought of hitting her, talking back to her, treating her bad in any way. I think a rock will come flying from Heaven and hit me while I'm walking down the street somewhere. But that's why a lot of people don't respect God, because they treat God like they treat their folks. So many have grown up in deceit; they had no respect for their parents so, likewise, they have no respect for their Creator. Many have failed to realize that God is not their friend or sibling, He's God. He's God!

NOW HE WILL LOVE ME

Genesis 29:32 says, **And Leah conceived, and bare a son, and she called his name Reuben: for she said, Surely the Lord hath looked upon my affliction.** What was she looking for? **Now therefore my husband will love me,** but Jacob never did come to love her like she wanted. **And she conceived again, and bare a son; and said, Because the Lord hath head that I was hated, he hath therefore give me this son also: and she called his name Simeon** (vs. 33). Think how God must feel. Some days you love Him; some days you don't. Some days you pray; some days you don't. Some days you love His word, some days you don't. Some days He's your all-in-all; some days you don't even want to see the Bible. Yup, some days the services, ooh you just can't wait to be in church, but then some days you're trying to figure out what time you're going to get out. That's something to think about in this hour we're living in.

Genesis 29:34 says, **And she conceived again, and bare a son; and said, Now this time my husband will be joined unto me, because I have born him three sons: therefore was his name called Levi.** After the birth of this son, Jacob still failed to love Leah as she had hoped. **And she conceived again,** just having baby after baby. Bless her heart. **And bare a son: and she said, Now will I praise the Lord: therefore she called his name Judah; and left bearing** (vs. 35). She stopped having kids. Did you

131

notice, she stopped looking for love from her husband and was just grateful to God. Yes! Yes! Yes!

Today you love me. I hope this is encouraging you to think about the love of the Lord. Sometimes we think love is just sunshine, going to the beach. No, love is during those hard days and your ability to endure.

HE CAN'T SEE HIMSELF

King David was so deceived that he couldn't even see himself when Nathan was running it down to him. The Lord would have done anything for him, just like He will do anything for you. He loves you with an unending love. That's what he was telling him! Nathan was rehearsing in his ear how the Lord had moved people out of the way. Why? Because He loved him. He had given him great victories. Why? Because David loved God. All the Lord wanted from David was faithfulness, consistency and total obedience. So, Nathan was describing David to himself, but he didn't even recognize that that was him. Today you love me. So Nathan goes on. And listen to this part right here. Second Samuel 12:7says, **And Nathan said to David, Thou art the man.** Nathan was describing David's sins to his face, but he couldn't see himself. He was deceived about who he thought he really was. Has that ever happened to you? People are talking to you, confronting you about an issue, and you just stand there plain-faced as day and can't even see yourself. *Self-deceit is the worst deceit.* You know, when some studies have been about things you may hate about somebody else, they just may be what you hate about yourself. "I hate that your waist is so tiny. You just flaunting yourself." Well, maybe you need to do some push-ups. It's easy to find the flaws and faults of others when the biggest problem is yourself. Life is hard, and people are going through so much, so very much. You don't know what people are going through in life. You don't know what people are enduring. I just believe in my heart, for the most, people are just doing what they can do. That's it. 2 Samuel 12:7-8 says, And Nathan said to David, **Thou art the man. Thus saith the Lord God of Israel.** Isn't that something when you get in trouble, and people start back to your mind the entire setup. Most times, when you've been found out, you just want them to shut up, don't you? But they don't! When God gets you, you know why He's getting you and what it's for. **Thus saith the Lord God of Israel, I anointed thee king over Israel, and I delivered thee out of the hand of Saul; And I gave thee thy master's house, and thy master's wives** (verses7-8). God is challenging us. Seems like the less some had, the more dependable they were. The less you had, the more faithful you were to the Lord, because you didn't know where the next meal, coat, or shelter was coming from. Nowadays, we have so much. Something for us to think about—money hungry; money hungry—that's the "golden calf" spirit. Not going to pay your tithes because you have to pay a bill. Whereas I remember back in the day you paid your tithes, because you didn't have the money to pay the bills. Today you love me. Finally, the Lord says, **And I gave thee thy master's house, and thy master's wives into thy bosom, and gave thee the house of Israel and of Judah; and if that had been too little, I would moreover have given unto thee such and such things** (verse 8). The Lord is not concerned about money or stuff. He wants total obedience. Sometimes you're happy, you're glad to be here. Sometimes you get yourself ready. You've been praying, and you're just on point. Then some days you come here just off the chain. Mad, angry, tired, sleepy then you go home and eat and stay up all night doing nothing. You spend more time investing in yourself than your memory verses. The Lord's going to make a way. There are people waiting to hear these messages that you're hearing and reading. They are waiting. They are waiting. They're waiting to be made well, but they don't know. We must shine the light before it is too late. What's the light neighbor? *It's the truth that's in God's word.* Yes! Yes! God did not spare my life just for my congregation. This ministry reaches far beyond these walls. It's up to you if you're still going to be here when it gets going. It's up to you. Love is an action word. It provokes you to give; give your finances, your time, and it provokes you to volunteer; to do something without being asked or paid for it—you see it needs to be done, and you volunteer.

LOVEST THOU ME?

John the 21:15 says, **So when they had dined, Jesus saith to Simon Peter, Simon, son of Jonas, lovest thou me more than these?** Do you love me above all the stuff you have? Do you love me above all the possessions? Do you love me above wealth? **He saith to him, Yea, Lord; thou knowest that I love thee. He saith unto him, Feed my lambs.** Keep my storehouse filled up. **He said unto him again the second time, Simon, son of Jonas, lovest thou me? He saith unto him, yea, Lord; thou knowest that I love thee. He said unto him feed my sheep. He saith unto him the third time, Simon, son of Jonas, lovest thou me? Peter was grieved because he said unto him the third time, Lovest thou me? And he said unto him, Lord, thou knowest all things; thou knowest that I love thee. Jesus saith unto him, Feed my sheep** (verses 15-17). What caused Peter to get mad? Must have been something the Lord was saying—was touching him right on the nerve. He said unto him, yea Lord thou knowest that I love thee. Fill your name in the place of Peter's. Lovest thou me? Then feed my sheep. Let's get this work done.

Prayer is not when you feel like it; it is because you're supposed to pray. Coming to church is not when you feel like it; it's your obligation and your responsibility. Paying your tithes is not something you want to do; it's something you owe. All of us can love the Lord more. We can do more. **And I want everybody saying oh God! Please forgive me for sinning against you. But I have come never to leave you again. Oh Lord, I do love you. Oh Lord, I do love you. Help me oh God. Give me the strength I need Lord to go all the way to the end. And by faith in the blood, save my soul! Oh God, save me Lord! And if you mean it, you have Him today.**

Part 3

". . . Hast Thou Not Glorified"

CHAPTER 8
WHEN LOVE TURNS TO HATE

Love *is* strong as death (Song of Solomon 8:6).

Love: a profoundly tender, passionate affection for another person. A feeling of warm personal attachment or deep affection, as for a parent, child, or friend.[8]

Hate: to feel intense dislike, or extreme aversion or hostility. To be unwilling.[9]

Think about children, your best friend, or even your own companion that you believe God gave you. Can you remember the love you had on your wedding day; the love you shared with one another? The Bible says, **A woman when she is in travail hath sorrow, because her hour is come: but as soon as she is delivered of the child, she remembereth no more the anguish, for joy that a man is born into the world** (St. John 16:21). All the pain felt by that mother is diminished by the fact that she has brought a baby into the world. Parenting. For a parent to hate his or her child, how awful that must be. We know that the Bible teaches us that if you do not give your child(ren) godly discipline, you will eventually hate them. **He that spareth his rod hateth his son: but he that loveth him chasteneth him betimes** (Proverbs 13:24).

The feeling that I am talking about today is sort of like when you do all you can for your child(ren), yet they just keep on kicking you. That spirit of ingratitude has taken them over. Arrogance and disobedience just ooze

---

8   Dictionary.com
9   Dictionary.com

Beverly D. Thomas

from them. That's what I mean. Now, keep in mind, I believe it takes a whole lot for a parent to dislike a child, and we know in God's eyes that you cannot hate them. But you can get to the place where you don't want them around you; you've decided that "enough is enough." You cut the ties, and they are no longer welcomed in your home. *That hurt is so deep.* The wound appears so massive, because those you have loved the most, tend to hurt you the most. Did you know that?

NINE MONTHS

You carried that child for nine long months. Maybe you developed a pregnancy-related disease, like gestational diabetes or some other disease directly related to pregnancy—just because you were pregnant. Then, you breastfeed the child and carry the child along. You nurture the child, but then to have that same child grow up and give you nothing but trouble, refusing to be a thriving adult—not because he or she cannot, but they simply WILL NOT do anything for or with themselves. You think about how maybe you had trouble conceiving that child, you are thinking about this on your worst days, your hardest day. Even the father is a witness to all that the mother has to endure in order to bring forth life. In some cases, the mother literally gives her physical life so that child can be born. Or you may have had a child who suffered with a physical limitation or learning disability, and it tears at you. It tears and rips at your heart, because you have become involved in the possible discrimination that comes with handicaps and the like; learning disabilities—you are now the burden barer for your children. All out discrimination—you share this with them all the while they are growing up, attempting to "come into their own." And for them, after all of this, when they are grown and have overcome all these difficulties, they kick you aside and act as if you had nothing to do with their development; nothing to do with them becoming who they are; forgetting all of the sacrifices you chose to make on their behalf; all of the occasions of going without so they could have. That hurts.

Have You Ever Loved Someone Who Didn't Love You Back?

If you somehow can understand what I'm saying, then you have a glimpse into the mind of God for His people and how they have treated Him and His Son and His precious Holy Spirit.

GOD SO LOVED

John 3:16-17 says, **For God so loved the world, that he gave his only begotten Son, that whosoever believeth in him should not perish, but have everlasting life. For God sent not his Son into the world to condemn the world; but that the world through him might be saved.** We were all born needing a Saviour. There's no question about that. David makes it very clear in Psalm 51:5 when he says, **Behold, I was shapen in iniquity; and in sin did my mother conceive me.** We all need somebody to sacrifice themselves so that we can live. Just like we, as parents, give 18 sometimes, 20 years of our lives, trying to mold and build character, what we hope to be a thriving, independent adult. It's a painful, sometimes very disappointing situation when that doesn't happen.

Rev 1:7 says, **Behold, he cometh with clouds; and <u>every</u> eye shall see him, and they also which pierced him: and all kindreds of the earth shall wail because of him.** This is when Jesus will come the third time, and the Bible teaches us that every person will see Him. No doubt, He will be suspended in air for days or even weeks. Every eye shall see Him. When the Lord comes to fight in the Battle of Armageddon it won't be a comforting sight. The Lord will have the most furious look that man has ever seen. No one will have ever looked so terrible as the *Lion of the Tribe of Judah*, the Son of God, when He comes in judgment. His eyes will be like fire, and Jesus will descend, not in love, but with furry. All the hate that the Godhead has felt for sin these thousands of years will be poured forth. All the judgment of destruction that God has held back in His great love will be poured out. It is the love of the Saviour, the Lamb that is holding back the judgments that this world rightly deserves. It is His love that woke us

139

up this morning. His love is the reason why we have been provided for all this time; the reason we have experienced a reasonable portion of health and strength, because of love. But when that love is turned to *hate*, watch out.

Woe. Woe to the inhabitants of the Earth. Even the angels will be screaming. Where will you be when the sun refuses to shine; when the moon turns into blood, and the stars of heaven begin to fall? Where will you be when men and women, boys and girls run from the rocks and the mountains, crying for them—the rocks and mountains to please fall on them. There will be no hiding place for those who have rejected His love.

When you think about the great price, it says, "For God so loved." Now, in that love is everything that you need, and to constantly reject that precious love will turn that love into hate in your life. Many could have had love, but they didn't want it. Just think, today you can have His love through this message. You can have His love; you can have forgiveness. Whether you realize it or not, this is a great love call. Hear the Lord calling to you today. This is a message of great warning. Today, some of you are not ready to meet the Lord, are you? You have been taught what will happen after the Rapture takes place and the great winds of Tribulation move in, yet some still sit in ease. All I can say is "Awake, awake thou that sleepeth while there is yet time."

Look around you lukewarmer. Sinner man, what do you see? Many stand against God. They blaspheme His name no matter what the Lord does, just like that parent I talked about earlier. They want no part of God the Father, God the Son or God the Holy Ghost, seeking instead their fornication, thievery, devil worship, witchcraft, sins. No value is placed on the soul, and on and on they go in their sins, some divers. They die without calling out to God for forgiveness. Men's hearts are growing harder and harder toward God. Things won't get better because the spirit of the antichrist is changing the behavior of people more and more, influencing the actions of the government. How many people are really living holy and free from all sin? When I talk to people about living free from sin, it seems like we are speaking a totally different language; a language that they have never heard before. It is embedded in God's word—the soul that sinneth, it shall die. When I start talking to people about salvation, particularly among most Christians, I lose them; so many of them have no idea of what I am talking about. They look at me as if I am in a cult; as if I am teaching through the spirit of fanaticism, yet through God's word. He said the soul that sinneth, it shall die. Not one liar, not one thief, not one curse word, not one fornicator is going to enter into Heaven. And when I preach that, I am looked upon as if I am preaching some strange new doctrine, but it's the doctrine of Jesus Christ. It always has been. How many are looking for Jesus to come? How many?

LET US

Genesis 1:26-27. It says, **And God said, Let us make man in our image, after our likeness: and let them have dominion over the fish of the sea, and over the fowl of the air, and over the cattle, and over all the earth, and over every creeping thing that creepeth upon the earth. So God created man in his own image, in the image of God created he him; male and female created he them.**

This isn't something that was just thrown together. The reason why I am taking time to go through Genesis is because sometimes we don't appreciate what we have; we don't know the price that was paid so that we could have it. It's just like one of the great civil rights activists, Rosa Parks. She sparked the Civil Rights Movement. Martin Luther King, Jr. came after. His message came forth as a result of Rosa Parks' refusal to continue riding in the back of the bus. You have heard the speeches, many of you, on the news and on the radio; you've heard the many accolades—many well know dignitaries in our state and in our nation proclaiming they are where they are because of the stand that Rosa Parks' took. Basically, what they were saying was that Rosa Parks paved the way for them in one way or another. That's all I am telling you. Someone paved the way. Somebody was killed. Someone was assassinated. Jesus was brutally murdered for our freedom. Sometimes we can't appreciate what has been given to us, because we don't know the history; we don't know the price—the truth that was made possible for us—how people had to die—most of the disciples were martyred so we can enjoy such a rich gospel. When is the last time you read *"Foxes Book of Martyrs?"* It's all there. You should read it from time to time. Also, *"The Cost of Discipleship."*

When Love Turns To Hate

Adam knew God; this is how much wisdom and knowledge was imputed to Adam. Adam knew God took a part of him to make a woman. He knew that from the moment he woke up. God explained it. God loves His children, and He wants them to understand things that are important for them to know. He teaches us step-by-step about His work. The Bible is our workbook; a workbook of God, showing us the things He has done and why. It is a wonderful love book of God's love for mankind. Would Adam and Eve had children had they stayed in the Garden? Evidently, the Lord planned for them to have children, but the childbirth would have been painless.

Genesis 2:18 says, **And the Lord God said, It is not good that the man should be alone; I will make him an help meet for him.** What love God has for mankind. He knows what you need. He knows your heart's desire and wants to meet every need that you allow Him, *according to His divine will.* Genesis 2:19 says, **And out of the ground the Lord God formed every beast of the field, and every fowl of the air; and brought them unto Adam to see what he would call them: and whatsoever Adam called every living creature, that was the name thereof.** The Lord created them and brought them to Adam. Whatever he named them, they are still named that way today. What love. What trust the Lord had in Adam. **But for Adam there was not found an help meet for him. And the Lord God caused a deep sleep to fall upon Adam, and he slept: and he took one of his ribs, and closed up the flesh instead thereof; And the rib, which the Lord God had taken from man, made he a woman,** [that's how close God the Father intended for married couples to be; complete unity] **and brought her unto the man. And Adam said, This is now bone of my bones, and flesh of my flesh: she shall be called Woman, because she was taken out of Man. Therefore shall a man leave his father and his mother, and shall cleave unto his wife: and they shall be one flesh** (Genesis 2:20-24). When Eve came forth, she was not a stranger to Adam, because she came forth from him. What love the Father has bestowed upon the human race. That's how intimate, how intertwined God expects man and woman, in marriage, to be. He wants them to have great love for one another; great companionship. *And the rib, which the Lord God had taken from man, made he a woman, and brought her unto the man* (vs. 22). What love.

HISTORY AND THE GOSPEL

We must study and study to understand the price that was paid for us. In that, we will appreciate how great our God is. You must study history along with scripture. History plays a very, very important role in scripture. No one scripture stands alone. Remember this.

You were born at the right time. You were born to serve the true and living God. Look back at your past to see how His miraculous hand moved for you again and again to bring you to this point in your life. Your life means much to God and to the kingdom of heaven. The enemy, no doubt, tried to kill you many times throughout your life, but God stayed the hand of death so that you could serve Him in this last and final hour. Danger after danger, He watched over you; kept His hand on your life. For what? For this hour; for you to choose Him as your personal Saviour. And after all of that, to reject that love by saying, "This is not for me. I don't want to do Your will." That love will turn to hate, to not have God on your side.

Genesis 3:6 says, **And when the woman saw that the tree was good for food, and that it was pleasant to the eyes, and a tree to be desired to make one wise, she took of the fruit thereof, and did eat, and gave also unto her husband with her; and he did eat.** Now God the Father and God the Son would come down in the form of a man and walk and talk with the man and the woman that they had made. *Adam and Eve could look right into the face of God!* Remember, the trinity helped to make the first man in perfection. Adam and Eve were just like them. The Father and the Son thoroughly enjoyed the fellowship they had with their perfect man and woman in Eden. Think about what great love that was. God and His Son would go down to walk, talk and embrace the man and woman they had created. But when sin entered, that fellowship was broken. No longer could they go down to visit because man and woman, because they had become so very ugly before God with sin, disobedience and ungodliness. How people can even imagine going to God's heaven with sin baffles my mind, when the scriptures plainly show that Adam and Eve **LOST EVERYTHING** because of sin! Adam and Eve were ultimately responsible for their actions, and so are you. God gave the commandment, and they paid for disobeying that single commandment. The price was death. Don't you agree that if Adam and Eve had truly repented and made reconciliation with God, it would have been noted in His word? But it is nowhere to be mentioned. There's no mention of the faith chapter. Why? Because they failed God and didn't have an opportunity to get back with Him.

BLASPHEMY AGAINST THE HOLY GHOST

There is a sin for which there is no forgiveness. Matthew 12:31-32 says, **Wherefore I say unto you, All manner of sin and blasphemy shall be**

forgiven unto me: but the blasphemy against the Holy Ghost shall not be forgiven unto men. And whosoever speaketh a word against the Son of man, it shall be forgiven him: but whosoever speaketh against the Holy Ghost, it shall not be forgiven him, neither in this world, neither in the world to come. I am convinced that Adam and Eve blasphemed against the Holy Ghost, and we will never see them in heaven.

The world as a whole is starving for love, and some of you have discovered that the price gets higher and higher. At some point, you have to reason with yourself and ask, "Is it worth it?" Some of you are still paying, wondering, "Will I ever get finished paying?" Some have babies and get married, thinking that will complete them, but what you end up with is a broken-down marriage ending in single parenthood; a shipwreck. You are supposed to marry for love; anything else will fail. The Bible declares that Love is as strong as death. Love will cover a multitude of sins [faults]. That's why you need divine love in marriage. Human love is not enough. Many marriages have tried it and ended in failure. Don't deceive yourself about who you are. So many people live their entire lives in deceit only to die deceived. You need love. You need to be loved. You need to accept love—real love. God is your source of strength not another human being.

And they heard the voice of the Lord God walking in the garden in the cool of the day: and Adam and his wife hid themselves from the presence of the Lord God amongst the trees of the garden. And the Lord God called unto Adam, and said unto him, Where art thou? And he said, I heard thy voice in the garden, and I was afraid, because I was naked: and I hid myself (Genesis 3:8-10). Adam and Eve lost EVERYTHING. In many of the pulpits, homes, jobs, schools, people make light of the consequence of failure; the consequence of sin. Some make light of the consequence of failing God. All we have to do is go to God's word. It's all there and it's very, very plain. Some never made it back from failing God; they blasphemed, while others barely made it back. Those who were able to return from such a failure, never became what God had originally planned for them. How disappointing. Our kids need to be taught. It must be explained to them the price that was paid for redemption. Christ's death purchased our redemption, our freedom, so that, while you are in a world filled with sin and degradation, you can still have Eden on the inside and live completely free from all sin. Sin is bondage, but Christ offers grace and freedom from all sin.

WHEN LOVE TURNS TO HATE

Genesis 3:9-12 says, **And the Lord God called unto Adam, and said unto him, Where art thou? And He said, I heard thy voice in the garden, and I was afraid, because I was naked; and I hid myself. And he said, Who told thee that thou wast naked? Hast thou eaten of the tree, whereof I commanded thee that thou shouldest not eat? And the man said, The woman whom thou gavest to be with me, she gave me of the tree, and I did eat.** God will not ask you to do anything that you cannot do. He will provide a way and give you the strength to carry out His will. James 1:13-16 says, **Let no man say when he is tempted, I am tempted of God: for God cannot be tempted with evil, neither tempteth he any man: But every man is tempted, when he is drawn away of his own lust, and enticed. Then when lust hath conceived, it bringeth forth sin: and sin, when it is finished, bringeth forth death. Do not err, my beloved brethren.**

God says what He means, and He means what He says. Those of us in leadership positions, this means you, must stand on the word of God. We can't compromise at all. Do you let your kids shack-up under your roof? Do you endorse same-sex relationships? God loves all people, hates the hypocrite, and He will not endorse sin in any way at all. Do you go to a baby shower when the people are not married? Do you attend weddings where the people have been shacked up?

He says in verse 11-12, **And he said, Who told thee that thou was naked? Hast thou eaten of the tree, whereof I commanded thee that thou shouldest not eat? And the man said, The woman who thou gavest me, she gave me of the tree and I did eat.** Now starts the blame game. It's everybody else's fault . . . but mine. **And the Lord God said unto the woman, What is this that thou hast done? And the woman said, The serpent beguiled me, and I did eat** (vs. 13). For many, it's just a vicious, repetitive cycle. It's always the other fella.

Many say, "Now, if my daddy would have . . . ," but he didn't. "If my momma wouldn't have . . . ," but she did. Stop blaming everybody else. Grow up and learn how to face life, and facing life is simply facing facts [truths] about yourself. **When I was a child, I spake as a child, I understood as a child, I thought as a child: but when I became a man, I put away childish things** (I Corinthians 13:11). Each and every person who grew up in a home without God was victimized by the devil. Now that that is settled, let's move on into the newness of life. Christ came so that we no longer had to live in the bondage of sin, sickness and the past. John 8:31-32,36 says, **If ye continue in my word, then are ye my disciples indeed; And ye shall know the truth, and the truth shall make you free. If the Son therefore shall make you free, ye shall be free indeed.** You don't have to stay in the shape that you are in. I always say, "If you don't like the way your life is going, change it!" God will help you and give you the grace to move forward. Are you bold enough and brave enough to let God help you, right now, right this very moment? Then let's go.

BACK FROM THE EDGE

Mental illness is the worst illness in the world to me. God gave me a great, great miracle for my mind. I went to a Psychologist and Psychiatrists. Nothing could help me, but the blood of Jesus. Why, one doctor told me plainly, "All we can do is take out the part of your brain that makes you depressed!" I thought, "Oh God, even as depressed as I am, I know that ain't right" Haha. God moved, and He set me free, and I still have that miracle [His miracle] working in my mind. One songwriter put it so wonderfully.

I was in the darkness, I was out in the cold

Seemed nothing could heal this, this hole in my soul

You reached out your arms to me, held out your heart to me

Pulled me back from the edge, thought I'd reached the end

When I was drowning, when I was so confused

You, oh you, you pulled me through

I was in the shadows, lost, nothing left to lose

You, oh you, you pulled me through[10]

Did you know that that is the first place that God begins to deal with you, is your mind? If He can't reach the mind, He can't reach you. Once, on one of our recent trips to our home church, *Ernest Angley's Grace Cathedral* in Akron, Ohio, I witnessed this first-hand. We had travelled there for one of the Friday miracle services. There were two separate experiences that I witnessed. One lady got on the stage and was asking for prayer for her brother who suffers with schizophrenia. The man of God asked her, notice this, **before** her brother was in that state, "Did he serve God?" The sister, with tears running down her face said, "He once knew God, but went back and no longer serves Him." The pastor said, "Oh, what a horrible thing". We are talking about the mind.

---

[10]   Jennifer Hudson—*You Pulled Me Through*, Diane Warren, writer

During that same service, another lady approached the man of God for her mother who was suffering with Alzheimer's Disease. Again, the pastor wanted to know where the person stood with God *before* this happened to her mind. He asked her, "Did she [your mother] serve God before this?" Her heart-breaking response was, "No." All that was left for the pastor to say was, "Well, let's pray that she gets saved." Chills ran down my back. Serve God now. You don't know what's going to happen to you in the future; you don't know about tomorrow, because you have never been into tomorrow. When tomorrow gets here for us, it will be our "today!"

And the Lord God said unto the woman, What is that that thou hast done? And the woman said, The serpent beguiled me, and I did eat (Genesis 3:13). The woman brought the deception home. You have to face this. When Eve was created and appeared on the scene, all was in order; she didn't want for anything. We have everything we need in Christ; He is our sufficiency. **But my God shall supply all your need according to his riches in glory by Christ Jesus** (Philippians 4:19). Eve let the devil deceive her, and she had to pay for it. She had to live with that decision for the rest of natural life and probably eternity too, because we don't read anywhere in God's word of her or Adam reconciling with God. There's no Bible for it.

God told her that in sorrow, she would bring forth children into the world. God did not intend for childbirth to be painful, but the process became part of the curse. Bugs and insects did not infect Eden. They too were a part of the curse. Not until the fall did the bugs and insects come into being. Can you see Adam and Eve with a fly swatter? That came after the curse; after the fall of Adam. In Eden, everything was beautiful; everything was calm.

Even with all that man had done, God was already preparing a way for us to get back to God. Listen to the Lord talk to the serpent when he says, **And the Lord God said unto the serpent, Because thou hast done this, thou art cursed above all cattle, and above every beast of the field; upon thy**

belly shalt thou go, and dust shalt thou eat all the days of thy life: And I will put enmity between thee and the woman, and between thy seed and her seed; it shall bruise thy head, and thou shalt bruise his heel (Genesis 3:14-15). God was making a way for the redemption of mankind.

Here, the Lord is talking to the devil. He is talking about the crucifixion. Already, the Lord has a plan in place to redeem mankind. Can you see it? At the very instance that man failed, God had a plan to draw us back to Himself. God did not know that Adam was going to fail Him. Remember, He's God! He can choose to know something or choose not to know. God is God. He did not know that Adam was going to fail Him. When you come to Calvary and sincerely repent for your sins, the Lord *does not look* into your future to see if you are going to fail Him. What kind of Savior would that be? He trusted man. Remember, God came down in the cool of the day. Adam looked directly into His face. Adam was not in the cleft of the rock like Moses was; he saw God face-to-face. When Adam failed, that communication and fellowship no longer existed. God hates sin. He hates sin.

Here in verses 14 and 15 the Lord was talking about the crucifixion. Christ was nailed to the cross; those heels were bruised just like God said. God reveals His mysteries, if we would but yield to Him. Even though the woman has introduced man to the devil and brought the deception home to her husband, Adam, Christ yet used the woman to bring liberation to the whole world. It was a woman that brought the deception to Adam, but even in all of that God's great love didn't leave it that way. He allowed a woman to bring the Savior of the whole world into this world. What love. What love. But when that love is rejected, cast down and frowned upon, it will turn to hate!

A CHILD OF THE HOLY GHOST

Matthew 1:18-20 says, **Now the birth of Jesus Christ was on this wise: When as his mother Mary was espoused to Joseph, before they came** together, she was found with child of the Holy Ghost. Then Joseph her husband, being a just man, and not willing to make her a public example, was minded to put her away privily. But while he thought on these things, behold, the angel of the Lord appeared unto him in a dream, saying, Joseph, thou son of David, fear not to take unto thee Mary thy wife: for that which is conceived in her is of the Holy Ghost. That was our way make; a bridge had been made in the form of Jesus Christ. His blood would be the reconciliation needed for man. When the wise men looked upon the face of Jesus in the manger, that was God's way for man to be reconciled to Himself, but it would cost heaven all that it had, which was Jesus Christ. For God to pay such a price and for that love to be rejected, what will be your judgment? Oh the amazement of man when he falls into the hands of an angry God.

And she shall bring forth a son, and thou shalt call his name Jesus: for he shall save his people from their sins. Now all this was done, that it might be fulfilled which was spoken of the Lord by the prophet, saying, Behold, a virgin shall be with child, and shall bring forth a son, and they shall call his name Emmanuel, which being interpreted is, God with us. Then Joseph being raised from sleep did as the angel of the Lord had bidden him, and took unto him his wife: And knew her not til she had brought forth her firstborn son: and he called his name Jesus (Genesis 3:22-24). Adam was the head of the human race and he sold us out to the devil. God had put everything under Adam's dominion. What do you think would have happened to Eve had she been the only one to eat of the forbidden fruit? Possibly God would have destroyed Eve and given Adam another help mate. Although the Bible doesn't tell us that God would have destroyed Eve had she sinned alone, I would like to believe He would have just given him another beautiful Eve, as long as Adam would have kept himself pure, clean and holy. But the curse came when he [Adam] partook of what was given to him. You can't do anything about the thoughts that flood your mind, but when you bring them into you, now they are yours. Sin can be around you all day long, but you will not be held responsible until you embrace it and accept it as your own. That's the one thing we did not lose in the fall of man, free will.

Genesis 3:22-24 says, **And the Lord God said, Behold, the man is become as one of us, to know good and evil: and now, lest he put forth his hand, and take also of the tree of life, and eat, and live for ever: Therefore the Lord God sent him forth from the garden of Eden, to till the ground from whence he was taken.** Now, the ground that the Lord used to bring forth man, man would have to go out and work with his own hands to make provisions. Once, it all had been given to him, but not anymore. **So he drove out the man; and he placed at the east of the garden of Eden Cherubims, and a flaming sword which turned every way to keep the way of the tree of life.** How many times do you think Adam went back to the garden hoping, wishing, and praying that God might change His mind. Remember that.

YOUR APPOINTMENT

From the hour you are born, you have an appointment with death. Only those taken by way of Rapture will escape the destruction and torture that awaits many in the Tribulation Period. Man's life span on earth, it's very short. Life after death, either in heaven or hell, is eternal, lasting forever and ever. Why do you think the Lord allowed the devil in the garden? He wanted Adam and Eve to choose His way, because they loved Him, not because they were forced to love Him. He wanted to be "their" choice.

God did not want man to be a mechanical being. Adam and Eve were made free moral agents with just as much choice between good and evil and we have today. In the fall, Adam and Eve lost everything but their free choice. Free choice has never been taken away from mankind by God. We will have it until the day we die.

CHAPTER 9
WHEN LOVE TURNS TO HATE
THE LOVE OF GOD

Sometimes we can take God's love for granted. We are living in the grace dispensation. Had we been under the law, we would have all been killed. I think sometimes as being a parent rearing children, we don't know how good we have it. We don't know the sacrifices that have been made for us to enjoy the luxuries that we have. A TV, DVD player, while they may be inexpensive now, they had to evolve over time. Do you remember one of the first cell phones? They were quite the thing; very, very heavy. It was more of a weapon than anything else, but things changed and evolved into small pieces of equipment as we see them today.

I want us to look at the love of God and examine how much He really loves us. And with that same degree of love, His feelings can and will turn to hate. I was just thinking to myself that, like little children, sometimes we don't value what we have, because we lack the knowledge of what has been paid for what we have.

I HAVE CALLED AND CALLED

What if the Lord said to you, *I have called and called unto you. I have told you to flee my wrath and judgment and for a moment only the fear of God comes upon you and rests upon you, but darkness is closing in on you more and more. If your eyes could be opened and you could see the minsters of Lucifer, saith the Lord, you would cry in terror this day, cause the demons stand by to destroy you.*

The enemy has come to kill, steal and destroy us. We must have discipline in our services, because we want lives to be changed when they leave church; we want them to experience God. We don't provide entertainment, but an experience with the true and living God. If the devil can keep you away from life-changing services, such as the ones we have in our church, then he has a very good chance to "get you." The enemy sends demons, like angels minister to those who are the heirs of salvation, demons are assigned to you, to rob you, to tempt you, to get you to doubt God's word about the end of this world; to get you to doubt God's word about what He has said will happen to those who reject such love. If the enemy can get you to doubt that this is the final hour; if he can get you to doubt that we are end-time-folks, he has you. The enemy has you. He has you, and you will fail God. Just like God has a plan for your life, the devil has a plan for your life as well. Wake up!

According to the book of Jeremiah, from the time you are born, God has a plan for your life, if you will accept it, but so has the devil. **Then the word of the Lord came unto me, saying, Before I formed thee in the belly I knew thee; and before thou camest forth out of the womb I sanctified thee, and I ordained thee a prophet unto the nations** (Jeremiah 1:4-5). The devil will never, never give up on you. The devil is very patient, masterful and oh so organized. He has an organized army standing by, and the devil punishes his army when they don't succeed at getting you to fail the almighty God. The devil uses your personality and your weaknesses to attack you.

What if the Lord spoke these word to you, *. . . you will cry and in terror because the demons stand by to destroy you. They have been assigned to you. Their [the demons] mission is to defeat you, to destroy your faith and to feel you with doubt.* God has called and called and called. The Gospels let us know that everyone is being called in this final hour, but only a few will rise up and be chosen. Will you be one of the chosen ones? Only you can answer this. Just think about God's voice growing fainter as you continue to reject His love call. You won't even recognize His voice, if you continue on this path.

Oh, you will cry unto me. You will cry and cry and cry but I won't hear you, saith the Lord. My ears will be close to your voice and My eyes will not behold you in your distress. I will never look at you through eyes of love again. That is how God is looking through us today, through eyes of love. But when that amazing love turns to hate . . . wow, wow, wow.

God is pleading, begging each sinner man, woman, boy and girl to turn back while there is yet time. Turn back while God is still calling. Turn back while it is still daylight in your life. Turn back while God is still near. Turn back now while the Holy Spirit is drawing on you! John 6:44 says, **No man can come to me, except the Father which hath sent me draw him: and I will raise him up at the last day.** The Lord knows how terrible hell is going to be for you. He knows that once you enter the mouth of hell, you will never, never get out. Once you are in hell, there is no getting out. That's it! You don't know what lays ahead for you—but God knows. God knows all. Some of you are so gullible, so weak, and so selfish you can't see that your destiny contains destruction. Mark 9:44 **Where their worm** [soul] **dieth not, and the fire** [fire of hell] **is not quenched.** Some people are so filled with fulfilling the lust of the flesh. This is such a pleasure-seeking age. The Lord is pleading with every person to go away and sin no more unless a worse thing come upon them. **For all that is in the world, the lust of the flesh, and the lust of the eyes, and the pride of life, is not of the Father, but is of the world** (I John 2:16). The Lord, the God of this universe is trying to get people to simply save their own lives. Save your own life. Save your soul. Save your own life. You, some few of you, have no clue what awaits you. Just think of God saying, *I will never look at you through eyes of love again. And when you come before Me, you will come before an angry God.* Oh, the amazement of man when he stands an angry God.

155

CHAPTER 10

WHEN LOVE TURNS TO HATE
THE TRIAL AND THE MURDER
OF JESUS CHRIST

When love turns to hate. I thought about how Heaven cried that day when Jesus was crucified. I thought about the Angels and about God, who gave His only begotten Son so we could be here today. I thought about that day in the Gospels where it says that the sun refused to shine, and that it was so dark that day that surely, God was crying. And I know millions of Angels cried that day. For what? For me. For me to have redemption. I thought about how the Lord, as we are going to study, was betrayed by audacious men, yet some of those men ate bread with him; one even dipped his bread in His cup, but he betrayed Him.

Paul talked about it in the book of Acts; about how the aprons that came from his body were illuminated with the Power of God. And that is it. We don't have anything great here. So the prayer cloth is used with your Faith. You can get whatever you need. The power of God has been so great in our services. You have not had a need for any man to lay a hand on you. All you have had to do was to yield and talk to God; just have a little talk. And where God is honoured, there will be manifestations of His Power, of His Greatness. Matthew 26:36-38, says **Then cometh Jesus with them unto a place called Gethsemane, and saith unto the disciples, Sit ye here, while I go and pray yonder. And he took with him Peter and the two sons of Zebedee, and began to be sorrowful and very heavy. Then said he unto them, My soul is exceeding sorrowful, even unto death: tarry ye here, and watch with me.** Jesus was not asking them to do anything great. Jesus was the Son of God. Remember, He was human, as well as divine. The Lord was the son of man born of a woman, which made Him the Son of Man. He was the Son of God because God is His father. But, even in His human state, Jesus was not asking them to die in His place. He was not asking them to assume His role; the Lord just wanted a little fellowship, because He knew His time was near. He knew it was time for Him to pay the debt for the whole human race. Matthew 26:39-40 says, **And he went a little farther, and fell on his face, and prayed, saying, O my Father, if it be possible, let this cup pass from me: nevertheless not as I will, but as thou wilt. And he cometh unto the disciples, and findeth them asleep, and saith unto Peter, What could ye not watch with me one hour?** And all the time, Jesus wanted Peter, in particular, to come into the knowledge of what His mission was, the Lord had such hope, He had such great aspirations for Peter. Jesus wanted them to just understand, yet they still could not get it. That can be so frustrating as a parent. It can be frustrating as a leader. You spend so much time training, you spend so much time nurturing and supporting, you spend so much time teaching and encouraging people to come along, yet in your greatest time of need you find them asleep, not adhering to the things of God. But Christ in His human form said, if there is any way to pass this bitter cup to someone else, but in the divine form He said nevertheless. **What, could ye not watch with me one hour? Watch and pray, that ye enter not into temptation: the spirit indeed is willing, but the flesh is weak. He went away again the second time, and prayed, saying, O my Father, if this cup may not pass away from me, except I drink it, thy will be done. And he came and found them asleep again: for their eyes were heavy** (Matthew 26:40-43).

WHY ARE YOU SO SLEEPY?

Many Christians are sleep to this final hour, so complacent and living a life of ease. They are so *intoxicated* on the things of this world. This is such a pleasure-seeking age. The Rapture is so far away for so many of

God's children. The great Tribulation Period and the signs of the end are everywhere. As we look around, we can see that the sea is raging, we see that the storms of life are raging. Many of God's people, they are asleep. Their eyes are very heavy. Many of them have fallen back into a lukewarm condition. Many of them have reverted, living in a backslidden state. As the bible says, as a dog returns unto his vomit. Many people have gone away, and now they have been taken over by seducing devils. Oh my God, they are asleep. This is the greatest hour for the human race. You are talking about getting to the point of your life, you are in the prime of your life. You are in the prime of your life. But here is Jesus, and their eyes were so heavy. Matthew 26:43-46 says, **And he came and found them asleep again: for their eyes were heavy. And he left them, and went away again, and prayed the third time, saying the same words. Then cometh he to his disciples, and saith unto them, Sleep on now, and take your rest: behold, the hour is at hand, and the Son of man is betrayed into the hands of sinners. Rise, let us be going: behold, he is at hand that doth betray me.** Now, Jesus had very well accepted that His hour had come. If you study the scriptures, John 18 chapter, Jesus was and often time when he performed miracles and did different things, often times He would tell them not to tell people about their miracles, not to tell different ones who had healed them, not to tell different ones of His identity because His hour had not come. Jesus knew that His hour had come.

WHOM SEEK YE?

John 18:1 says, **When Jesus had spoken these words, he went forth with his disciples over the brook Cedron, where was a garden, into the which he entered, and his disciples.** Jesus was going into the garden of Gethsemane to pray in this verse. In John 18:2, Jesus is done praying. He has told them arise let's go pray and then He meets Judas. **And Judas also, which betrayed him, knew the place: for Jesus ofttimes resorted thither with his disciples. Judas then, having received a band of men** and officers from the chief priest and Pharisees, cometh thither with lanterns and torches and weapons. Jesus therefore, knowing all things that should come upon him, went forth, and said unto them, Whom seek ye (John 18:2-4)? Who are you looking for? They answered him, Jesus of Nazareth. Jesus saith unto them, I am he. And Judas also, which betrayed him, stood with them (John 18:5). The enemy among us. And soon then as he had said unto them, I am he, they went backward, and fell to the ground (John 18:6). Now Jesus had to repress, He had to suppress His divinity. At that time, so much power came out in His voice. They were but just flesh. They fell down under the power of God that was in the Lord's voice; they couldn't stand under that mighty blood voice. He had to subject Himself. He had to repress divinity and be quiet, because they could not stand under the power of God. He said who are you looking for? When love turns to hate.

Now, you would think something should have illuminated in their head by now, but they were asleep in their minds. They were asleep to the hour. They were asleep to the love. They were asleep to the reality of why Jesus had come to Earth. Then asked he them again, Whom seek ye? And they said, Jesus of Nazareth. Jesus answered, I have told you that I am he: if therefore ye seek me, let these go their way: (John 18:7-8). Jesus, in all his infinite wisdom and knowledge, dared not risk the lives of others. He says, they do not have anything to do with this. It is me you seek, let them go. Notice how smooth of an operator He was. Even in the midst of persecutions and everything that was going on around Him, He was still in control; always remained in control. The Lord never got away from His mission. He was never distracted from His mission. Jesus started, and He finished. He had come to Earth to fulfil a mission, then, He would give His life's blood; be murdered; be killed; be lied on by audacious men. The Lord knew from the very beginning that He would walk among men, and they would try to make Him their king. He knew from the very beginning that He would feed people, and they would follow Him to use Him, to get what they could from Him. John 6:26 says, **Jesus answered them and** said, Verily, verily, I say unto you, Ye seek me, not because you saw the miracles, but because you did eat the loaves, and were filled. The Bible tells **For we have not an high priest which cannot be touched with the feeling of our infirmities; but was in all points tempted like as we are, yet without sin** (Hebrews 4:15). **There hath no temptation taken you but such as is common to man: but God is faithful, who will not suffer you to be tempted above that ye are able; but will with the temptation also make a way to escape, that ye may be able to bear it** (I Corinthians 10:13). The Lord never lost sight of His mission. We have help, if we would just yield. **For there is one God, and one mediator between God and men, the man Christ Jesus** (I Timothy 2:5) Jesus is our mediator. He was inflicted. He endured. He knows what it is like to have a headache. He knows what it is like to have people reject you and push you aside. Why? Because of love. Isaiah puts it best, **For he shall grow up before him as a tender plant, and as a root out of a dry ground: he hath no form nor comeliness; and when we shall see him, there is no beauty that we should desire him. He is despised and rejected of men; a man of sorrows, and acquainted with grief: and we hid as it were our faces from him; he was despised, and we esteemed him not. Surely he hath borne our griefs, and carried our sorrows: yet we did esteem him stricken, smitten of God, and afflicted. But he was wounded for our transgressions, he was bruised for our iniquities: the chastisement of our peace was upon him; and with his strips we are healed** (Isaiah 53:3-5). Oh, how He loved you so much, but when that love, the deepness of it, is rejected, it will be woe, woe, woe. How vast it is. How humungous it is. It is so deep, deeper than any well. Can you imagine, can you fathom, that love being turned to hate against you?

Jesus answered, I have told you that I am he: if therefore ye seek me, let these go their way: That the saying might be fulfilled, which he spake, Of them which thou gavest me have I lost none. Then Simon Peter having a sword drew it, and smote the high priest's servant and cut off his right ear. The servants name was Malchus. Then said Jesus

unto Peter, Put up thy sword into the sheath: the cup which my Father hath given me, shall I not drink it? (John 18:8-11). Can we give such an answer? Can you live with the hand that has been dealt you, so to speak? Or are you unlike Jesus? Are you blaming everybody for the predicament you are in? Are you still running around asking why were you born and blaming *everybody else* because this happened to you or that happened? Listen, bad things happen to good people. Good people file for bankruptcy. Good people lose their homes. Good people get evicted. Good people suffer with diseases. Good people have family and friends turn against them. But will you? Can you, like Jesus say, shall I not drink the cup that has been given to me? He already settled it in the garden of Gethsemane. He already settled it.

GETHSEMANE

Think about this when Jesus went into the garden of Gethsemane, He knew all things were coming upon Him. Think about that glorious scene before Jesus went to the garden of Gethsemane, just coming from that wonderful dinner in the upper room. In just a moment of time, His life changed. It had only been about two hours, some Historians say, from the time of the last supper until Jesus was in Gethsemane, and Judas appeared to betray Him. Judas had handled His power, even though people may say that Judas was a devil. No, Judas handled the power of God; he once had the gifts of healing. But he did not keep his mission. Judas failed to keep his mission before him. Judas betrays his best friend. Jesus had to have been his best friend to use His power the way he did. Think about this, Judas was not forced to betray him. No. He was not forced to betray him. He personally chose to betray Christ. And this treacherous act fulfilled prophecy. God did not cause Judas to sin. Judas chose sin. The hour for which Christ was born had come. He had been down on the Earth for thirty something years. But Jesus knew, as He exited out of the garden of Gethsemane, that His most trying hours were just ahead, yet He thought about us. What about you today? There was no other way. There would be no way for you to have a healthy body; to be renewed in your mind; to be strengthened; to endure this hour; to be able to fight against your enemy and the arch enemy of God. The Lord knew there would be no other way. Somebody had to be murdered—to die for the whole world. So, Jesus yielded Himself to be killed. Philippians 2:7-8 says, **But made himself of no reputation, and took upon him the form of a servant, and was made in the likeness of men: And being found in fashion as a man, he humbled himself, and became obedient unto death, even the death of the cross.** They are going to take him from hall to hall. Why? Because of love. That love for you was the same amount of love that the Lord had, and He yielded. He is going to remember that when you do not accept His love.

And there is Peter being trifling as ever. There is Peter being up and down, in and out. Sound familiar? Up and down, in and out, up and down, in and out. He could never stay on the right road. All of us today, we have a mission. We have a path that is laid out for our feet. Some only want Christ when the sun is shining. but see Him there in the garden of Gethsemane. Historians say that in the garden of Gethsemane there were many exits. But He chose to endure affliction. He endured. The Lord chose to endure hardship as a good soldier. He knew He had to fulfil His mission and would not fail. Some people are always looking for a way to escape problems, to escape trials; always looking for a way out of hardship. Life is not like that. Peter said Christ was our example. He started out for something, and He completed His mission. If He did it, then we are expected to do it with His love help. The Lord is not asking you to do anymore. Jesus is not going to ask you to do something that is impossible for you to do. Sixteen, seventeen, eighteen years old . . . you can remain a virgin until your wedding night. He is not going to ask you to do something that is impossible. To ask you to come out from among them and be ye separate. If you could not do it, He would not ask you. The word says "Let God be truth and every man a liar." So, if you could not go to Gethsemane, if you could not go to your own Golgotha hill, if you could not go to Calvary, why is it in the Bible?

Think about Jesus as He stood there when the soldiers came to accuse him. He was not surprised when they came. He heard the soldiers marching and coming in like a gang. He stepped forward to meet them. Under His mighty voice, they fell. They were slain under the power of His blood voice. The Lord had to suppress that feeling. He had to suppress that authority that was in Him, yield Himself to their control, and go away with them. This was the Lord's crowning point in life. Have you thought about that? This was His crowning point in life, fulfilling the purpose for which He was born. **He that committeth sin is of the devil; for the devil sinneth from the beginning. For this purpose the Son of God was manifested, that he might destroy the works of the devil. Whosoever is born of God doth not commit sin; for his seed remaineth in him: and he cannot sin, because he is born of God** (I John 3:8-9). Going to heal people, that was magnificent. Raising people from the dead, that was magnificent. Sort of like how you getting a college degree is magnificent, or owning a home or condo, owning a car, splendid. But you have come into the hour for which you were born or nothing else will matter. Being used by the Lord; this is the high point of your hour. Becoming a great soul winner; this is the high point of your life. This is the prime. This is the crème de la crème of your life. The path forward, should you choose to accept it, will be covered with rocks and thistles. There are wolves out in the forest watching your every move, tongues licking out to get you. There are demons assigned to you, yet it is the greatest time of your life, because our mission is almost done.

CAIAPHAS

John 18:12 says, **Then the band and the captain and officers of the Jews took Jesus, and bound him, And led him away to Annas first; for he was father in law to Caiaphas, which was the high priest that same**

year. Now Caiaphas was he, which gave counsel to the Jews that it was expedient that one man should die for all people. And Simon Peter followed Jesus, and so did another disciple: that disciple was known unto the high priest, and went in with Jesus into the palace of the high priest. But Peter stood at the door without. Then went out that other disciple, which was known unto the high priest, and spake unto her that kept the door, and brought in Peter. Then saith the damsel that kept the door unto Peter, Art not though also one of this man's disciples? He saith, I am not (John 18:12-17). All of a sudden Peter was ashamed of his mission. All of a sudden, he did not really want to be what he was born to be. All of a sudden, all of those stories and everything that Jesus tried to prepare him for held no meaning. All of a sudden, Peter was rejecting it. "No, it cannot go down like this. This cannot be what Jesus was talking about when He said He put me out there like a sheep among wolves. This cannot be what He was talking about when He said the daughter was going to deliver up the mother and the son was going to betray the father. This cannot be what the Lord was talking about. This is not what I thought." But this was Peter's mission. And suddenly, Peter decided he did not want it; it was too much. **He saith, I am not. And the servants and the officers stood there, who had made a fire of coals; for it was cold: and they warmed themselves: and Peter stood with them, and warmed himself. The high priest then asked Jesus of his disciples, and of his doctrine. Jesus answered him, I spake openly to the world; I ever taught in the synagogue, and in the temple, whither the Jews always resort; and in secret have I said nothing. Why askest thou me? ask them which heard me, what I have said unto them: behold, they know what I said** (John 18:17-21). They were trying to perpetrate Jesus. They were trying to portray Him as somebody who did something in secret. They were trying to allude to the fact that the Lord had some secret thing going on. Jesus said, "No. Ask those people who I taught. They will tell you of My doctrine." He was wondering, even though Jesus knew the answer, He challenged them to think. "Why are you coming at me now? Why did you try to get me secretly? Why did you try to come take me in the open?

What have I done?" They killed an innocent man, but they are going to pay. **And when he had thus spoken, one of the officers which stood by struck Jesus with the palm of his hand, saying, Answerest thou the high priest so? Jesus answered him, If I have spoken evil, bare witness of the evil: but if well, why smites thou me** (John 18:22-23)**?** He said I am on My mission, but you are beating Me because of truth. Watch it. You are striking Me because of truth. You want to kill Me because of truth. And you think your life is going to be easy, and everybody is going to love you and care about you? Stop being so naïve and gullible. This is your example right here. **If the world hates you, ye know that it hated me before it hated you. If ye were of the world, the world would love his own? But because ye are not of the world, but I have chosen you out of the world, therefore the world hateth you. Remember the word that I said unto you, The servant is not greater than his lord. If they have persecuted me, they will also persecute you; if they have kept my saying, they will keep your also. But all these things will they do unto you for my name's sake, because they know not him that sent me. If I had not come and spoken unto them, they had not had sin: but now they have no cloke for their sin. He that hateth me hateth my Father also. If I had not done among them the works which none other man did, they had not had sin: but now have they both seen and hated both me and my Father. But this cometh to pass, that the word might be fulfilled that is written in their law, They hated me without a cause** (John 15:18-25). They slapped Jesus because He was the truth. People hate truth; they can't handle it. The Lord allowed Himself to be murdered because of the truth. Because of the truth. Because of truth. When love turns to hate.

TRUTH CAUSES TROUBLE

Truth has always caused problems. It has always divided families. It has always separated. Truth divides church members. Many churches today are without truth; they teach a *bloodless gospel*. The truth brings a division. It cuts them. They do not want to yield to truth. **Behold, I send you forth as sheep in the midst of wolves: be ye therefore wise as serpents, and harmless as doves. But beware of men: for they will deliver you up to the councils, and they will scourge you in their synagogues; And ye shall be brought before governors and kings for my sake, for a testimony against them and the Gentiles** (Matthew 10:16-18). Matthew goes on to let us know, **And the brother shall deliver up the brother to death, and the father the child: and the children shall rise up against their parents, and cause them to be put to death. And ye shall be hated of all men for my name's sake: but he that endureth to the end shall be saved** (Matthew 10:21-22). Be ready. Stay ready.

Now Annas had sent him bound unto Caiaphas the high priest (John 18:24). Here they are shifting responsibility. Nobody really wants to make the final decision about the murder of Jesus Christ, but they were *all* responsible. Now, the Lord is on trial. **And Simon Peter stood and warmed himself. They said therefore him, Art not thou also one of his disciples? He denied it and said, I am not. One of the servants of the high priests, being his kinsmen whose ear Peter cut off, saith, Did not I see thee in the garden with him? Peter then denied again: and immediately the cock crew. Then led they Jesus from Caiaphas unto the hall of judgment: and it was early; and they themselves went not into the judgment hall, lest they should be defiled; but that they might eat the passover** (John 18:25-28). Still trying to be Holy. They did not see anything wrong with that they were doing. They led Jesus from Judgment hall to judgment hall. And then they went and sat down to eat. Just like Joseph's brothers in the book of Genesis. They threw him in the pit, and then they sat down to eat. It is just like people that come to service. They might say the sinner's prayer, but, they are not really repenting with Godly sorrow. Then, they go away and fornicate and commit whoredom. They go away and sit down to sin. We have Holy Communion in this church, and I know people who come up to take Holy Communion are sinful, that they have degradation working in them. They are warned before each communion service that if they have sin in them, don't do it! They are immoral. They are no different than the people who led Jesus to the hall of judgment. No different. But when loves turns to hate, you are damning your own soul. When you take Holy Communion, and there is a lie in you, it is hypocrisy and deceit. You are coming up for Holy Communion because you are putting on a front. You do not want people to know you are not righteous. They might whisper, "Why are you not taking Holy Communion?" But you prefer to damn your soul because of what people think. It is not about what people think. It is what God knows about you. That's what you will be judged by.

WASH YOUR HANDS

So, the enemy dare not go in because they had the Passover. When love turns to hate. Again, in John 18:28 it says, **Then led they Jesus from Caiaphas unto the hall of judgment: and it was early; and they themselves went not into the judgment hall, lest they should be defiled; but that they might eat the passover.** They still wanted to go in. If you know anything about the custom of that day, they had to wash their hands, probably all the way passed the elbow, then sit down and say all these vain prayers that are not full of nothing, that do not mean anything. It will damn souls to hell too.

Pilate then went out unto them and said, What accusation bring you against this man? They answered and said unto him, If he were not a malefactor, we would not have delivered him up unto thee. Then said Pilate unto them, Take ye him, and judge him according to your law (John 18:29-31). Now, Pilate really did not want to have anything to do with this. But Pilate was a leader in the community, and everybody was watching him for a response. Pilate's wife had a dream, and she warned him through God not to have anything to do with this man. Leave him alone. But Pilate was concerned about his reputation. He was concerned about what people would think of him as a leader. He had people under him that were following him. He had to make a good appearance. Just like some of you, worried about what people say. But when it is all said and done, it won't mean a thing. It does not mean one thing. **Then said Pilate unto them, Take ye him, and judge him according to your law** (John 18:31). Pilate is telling them, take him back where you come from. Why are you bringing Him here? They wanted to kill Jesus, but they did not want to be the one to say crucify Him. They wanted to be like some of you today; the blame game. Just like Adam, "That woman you gave me". Nobody forces you to sin. You are a free moral agent. You did not lose that when Adam fell. You can live for Christ if you choose. Momma cannot keep you from serving God. Daddy cannot keep you from serving God. Your companion cannot keep you from serving God. Why? It is whosoever will. But too many are into the blame game. They wanted Jesus dead. Nobody wanted to be the one to say, "I did it." We look over in these third world countries where they are blowing people up everywhere, they are so proud to say, "I did that." I am the one that did that. The blame game: you may have orchestrated it, but subliminally, you put somebody else in the front, and others put their name on it. You really were the one responsible. When love turns to hate. Plotting, scheming, conniving, that is what they were doing, but they did not want anybody to know that the idea originated with them.

TALKING, TALKING, TALKING

Sometimes in counselling, when I or one of the ministers here is listening to people, they are talking, talking, talking, and talking. Finally, you find out they have been talking to somebody else. So, they are coming to counselling with somebody else's ideas. They are coming to counselling with somebody else's view of their problem to one of us. Why come to us then? Do not bring us that garbage. You come for yourself. Do not come to counselling with what *somebody told you*. Do not be such a fool. You come to church reading the gospel. God is blessing you. He is uplifting you. He is opening up your mind to His mysteries. *Then there you go, weak and gullible, go to discuss what you got in the services to a sinner. How can they help you? I have not heard such a thing like that. Fasting! That means you are not eating. That cannot be of God. They only had to fast. Your pastor must not know that scripture about it says that the disciples of John, they fasted. What do you have to fast for? Jesus paid it all. Does she know that song? Write it down for her. Fasting! No, "Jesus has already overcome. There is nothing else for us to do. Our redemption has been paid for. Our redemption has been purchased. What is she talking about?"* Live free from sin, that's what we are talking about, have been talking about, and will continue talking about until the day Jesus comes for us. Hallelujah!. *We are but flesh.* You better run. Don't let people pollute your spirit with such as that. You'll spend days and weeks getting deflead. "You better get away from that church. You come back more confused than ever. You were already in a weak state." Now, here you come back, want to take me in the office and rehearse with me somebody else's ideas. You dummy. That is a dumb-dumb. What is in between your two ears? What is that instrument sitting on your neck? A brain, use it. Use it. Some people are in an identity crisis. Thank God, Jesus knew who He was. He knew from day one, and He knows today who He is. And when you do not know who you are, and you do not know where you are going, you can be persuaded with every wind of doctrine. You can be talked out of your marriage. You can be talked into running away from home. You can be talked into leaving the church. You can be talked into leaving God. You can be talked into robbing a bank. You can be talked into shooting somebody, kidnapping somebody, killing somebody. But, in the end, you are the one who has to answer for what you did. Think for yourself. Make your own decisions. Be your own person. Be what God created you to be. Come out of the shadows of sin. Come out of the shadows of hypocrisy. Amen. Be who God made you to be. He made you to be somebody. Stop running around here acting like someone who was an accident. Now, we know that God does not make any accidents, and that your birth was perfectly planned for you to be here in this hour. But some of you walk around acting like you evolved from monkeys. Some of you walk around acting like your birth was an accident. It contradicts the word of God according to Jeremiah chapter 1 and other chapters, and Genesis. It contradicts the word.

JUDGE HIM

He said, take him back to your own town. John 18:31, **Then said Pilate unto them, Take ye him, and judge him according to your law. The Jews therefore said unto him, It is not lawful for us to put any man to death.** They just want their hands clean. They do not want to have no part of Jesus' death. **That the saying of Jesus might be fulfilled, which he spake, signifying what death he should die. Then Pilate entered into the judgment hall again, and called Jesus, and said unto him, Art thou the King of the Jews? Jesus answered him, Sayest thou this thing of thyself, or did others tell it thee of me** (John 18:32-34)? Look at what he is saying. Are you listening to others? Or are you making your own decision? That is what Jesus is saying. He said, Sayest thou this thing of thyself, or did others tell it thee of me? Do you know this for yourself, or is this something you heard? Pilate comes on. He put Pilate on trial. Who do you say I am? Who do you say I am? **Pilate answered, Am I a Jew? Thine own nation and the chief priests have delivered thee unto me; what hast thou done? Jesus answered, My kingdom is not of this world: if my kingdom were of this world, then would my servants fight, that I should not be delivered to the Jews: but now is my kingdom not from hence. Pilate therefore said unto him, Art thou a king then? Jesus answered, Thou sayest that I am a king. To this end was I born, and for this cause came I into the world, that I should bear witness unto the truth. Every one that is of the truth heareth my voice. Pilate saith unto him, What is truth? And when he had said this, he went out again unto the Jews, and saith unto them, I find in him no fault at all** (John 18:35-38). Get this man away from me, Pilate was trying to convey. I cannot be a part of this mess. Jesus had hit Pilate where it hurt. He had hit him where it hurt. Pilate came rushing in telling Jesus, "Wait a minute. Your own nation, your own people are trying to condemn you." Jesus was like, "Them are not my folks. I am now coming into My hour. Do not let them fool you. Those are not My people. If those were my people, they would hear My voice. But, it is obvious, they are not My people. I am now coming into My hour," Jesus was telling Pilate. He said "What is truth?" He said "Pilate, what is truth"? There he goes, back again. Now, you want to know who is in the judgment hall, Pilate or Jesus? Pilate surmised and said within himself, "I find in him no fault, get Him away from me?" He was probably remembering the dream of his wife, "Have nothing to do with this innocent man." That is what the Lord is warning you today. Have nothing to do with the innocent shedding of His blood. Have nothing to do with it. Run away from it in every form, in every fashion, every appearance, in every shape. Run away from it, as pornography is presented on your computer and on your TV. The Lord says run away from innocent blood. Run away. When you hear this Gospel, you are responsible for the shedding of innocent blood to save a whole world. When you engage in gossip, Jesus is telling you, "You better run for your soul". Now, that is the time to run.

When love turns to hate. John 18:39-40,19:1 says, **But ye have a custom, that I should release unto you one at the passover: will ye therefore that I release unto you the King of the Jews? Then cried they all again, saying, Not this man, but Barabbas.** *Barabbas was a robber.* **Then Pilate therefore took Jesus, and scourged him**. This means he whipped Jesus with a Roman scourge. Now, they are slapping him, beating him. Keep this picture in your mind, because if we are not serving God with our whole heart and mind, we are no different. Then, all that love He used to save you is going to be equal in hate. Again in verse 40, **Then cried they all again, saying, Not this man, but Barabbas.** Remember, Barabbas was a robber.

Then Pilate therefore took Jesus, and scourged him. And the soldiers platted a crown of thorns, and put it on his head, and they put on him

a purple robe (John 19:1-2). They were mocking him. And said, Hail, King of the Jews: and they smote him with their hands. Pilate therefore, went forth again, and saith unto them, Behold, I bring him forth to you, that ye may know that I find no fault in him. Pilate was trying to leave with a clear conscience. He doing everything he can. But Pilate was subjected to them because they put him into office. The scripture had to be fulfilled, But he was subjected to them, because they voted him in. Pilate was doing all he could. He did not want to be responsible, yet *he was responsible*. He did not want to be the cause of it, yet he was. We are **all** responsible once that blood is introduced to us; all of us. All of us are responsible. You are responsible for this message. When love turns to hate. You are responsible for fulfilling the mission God has given to you; the reason why He did not allow you to fall into a drought; the reason why He allowed your mom to continue to hold you, even when they said against all odds she could not have another child, that her womb could not even hold you was for God's glory. You are responsible. You are responsible for fulfilling your mission to God; when you hear the truth, you then become responsible for it. You owe Him you to say the least. To say the least. The trial and murder of Jesus Christ.

The Lord loves you. John 19:5 states, **Then came Jesus forth, wearing the crown of thorns, and the purple robe. And Pilate saith unto them, Behold the man! When the chief priests therefore and officers saw him, they cried out, saying, Crucify him, crucify him. Pilate saith unto them, Take ye him, and crucify him: for I find no fault in him. The Jews answered him, We have a law, and by our law he ought to die, because he made himself the Son of God. When Pilate therefore heard that saying, he was the more afraid** (John 19:5-8). Pilate was feeling the fear of God in his heart, just like you have felt at times. It said he became *more* afraid. **And went again into the judgment hall, and saith unto Jesus, Whence art thou? But Jesus gave him no answer. Then saith Pilate unto him, Speakest thou not unto me? knowest thou not that I have the power to crucify thee, and have power to release thee? Jesus answered,**

Thou couldest have no power at all against me, except it were given thee from above: therefore he that delivered me unto thee hath the greater sin. And from thenceforth Pilate sought to release him: (Pilot was trying all he could). **but the Jews cried out, saying, If thou let this man go, thou art not Caesar's friend:** (And Pilate knew that meant you are going to die). **whosever maketh himself a king speaketh against Caesar. When Pilate therefore heard that saying, he brought Jesus forth, and sat down in the judgment seat in a place that is called the Pavement, but in the Hebrew, Gabbatha. And it was the preparation of the passover, and about the sixth hour: and he saith unto the Jews, Behold your King! But they cried out, Away with him, away with him, crucify him** (John: 19:9-15). We do not want Him. This is Jesus the Christ.

ADULTERY AND THE PRESIDENT

We will vote somebody in we know is crooked. We had a president nearly impeached for adultery, but he remained president of the United States of America. You see stuff and just turn your heads, like it is not even happening. Then, when a righteous one comes, someone with the power of God preaching, people seduced by the devil will line up with the enemy to have that one destroyed. You better watch yourself. You better be careful with the words you say. You do not know who belongs to God, and you do not know how close that person is to God, and how God favours that person, and how He looks out for that person and stands by them. The Lord stands by His own. Let you not be that example He uses to show others that He is real, that He is really real. You keep your mouth off people. You keep your hands to yourself. Mind your own business. You do not hook up with any evilness. I do not care if that person is in the pastor's family, let them drown alone. Do not be hooked up with them. Be not deceived. Search the scriptures. The Lord had children killed for talking against his servant and speaking against the Holy Ghost. Those children blasphemed. This is a serious hour. This is a dangerous hour to not belong to the family of God. Search the scriptures, for in them you think you have eternal life. If you're with somebody and they start mouthing off, run. Let them talk to you from a distance. You will look back, and the house might be blown up. This is the hour the Lord is manifesting His glory. He is opening up the eyes of people for them to see who His servants are, and who does not belong to Him. Do not be counted among them. All those people, Korah caused them to rise up. And Moses told them, "I am not doing this on my own. But, tomorrow God will show you which one of us belong to him." And they are still in hell today. They are still in hell today. They are in hell right now as you are reading this, and they will never be free. As the endless ages roll, they will still be there. Yes, do not hook up with anybody saying anything, passing little seeds of deceit. It is a wonder one of your legs is not shorter than the other, or one of your kids is not afflicted. But it is love. Love! It is love. It is going to take that to shape us. We have a magnificent ministry and, even with all that God is doing in this Jesus ministry, a few have allowed themselves to be so easily seduced; so easily persuaded. One day they are of God, but as soon as I say something they don't like, I am not called of God. When you go away from God's people, that's when the voices come back. If you do not even yield to the spirit of fasting and praying, that is when the torment comes back. Oh my God, when you give ear to that which is wrong, you open up your mind to what you were delivered from in the past; you open up your mind to seducing spirits. Oh my God, homicidal thoughts, and lesbianism thoughts, and thoughts of homosexuality arising up and being a paedophile again; the return to the **practice** of these hideous acts. Thoughts you can't control, but when you "practice" such degrading acts, then it becomes sin. Yes, God can uncover you today. With love, He did not bring forth this teaching to judge you, but to help you and heal you. Jesus loves you and He needs you. He came to open up your eyes today. Do not be Judas Iscariot. Be John the Revelator, who came back to the cross on that horrible date, even though all others had failed the Lord. John came back. He became Mary's, the mother of Jesus, son. But then love turns to hate.

PLACE OF A SKULL

Then delivered he him therefore unto them to be crucified. And they took Jesus, and led him away. And he bearing his cross went forth into a place called the place of a skull, which is called in the Hebrew Golgotha (John 19:16-17). Now the Lord did all this for every one of us. Everything that happened to Him, He allowed it. They did not force one thing upon Jesus Christ. Sometimes when we are long suffering, and we do not lash out, people think we are weak, but take a lesson. Take a lesson. Take a lesson. You young people do not have to be a follower. You can be a leader. If you stand up, God will stand with you.

And he bearing his cross went forth into a place called the place of a skull, which is called in the Hebrew Golgotha: Where they crucified him, and two other with him, on either side one, and Jesus in the midst. And Pilate wrote a title, and put it on the cross. And the writing was, JESUS OF NAZARETH THE KING OF THE JEWS (John 19:17-19). Pilate did not know it, but Jesus is the King of the Jews. **This title then read many of the Jews: for the place where Jesus was crucified was nigh to the city: and it was written in Hebrew, and Greek, and Latin. Then said the chief priest of the Jews to Pilate, Write not, The King of the Jews; but that he said, I am King of the Jews.** *Pilate answered, What I have written I have written.* **Then the soldiers, when they had crucified Jesus, took his garments, and made four parts, to every soldier a part; and also his coat: now the coat was without seam, woven from the top throughout. They said therefore among themselves, Let us not rent it, but cast lots for it, whose it shall be: that the scripture might be fulfilled, which saith, They parted my raiment among them, and for my vesture they did cast lots. These things therefore the soldiers did. Now there stood by the cross of Jesus his mother** (think he is still on his mission), **and his mother's sister, Mary the wife of Cleophas, and Mary Magdalene. When Jesus therefore saw his mother, and the disciple standing by, whom he loved, he saith unto his mother, Woman, behold**

thy son! Then saith he to the disciple, Behold thy mother! And from that hour that disciple took her unto his own home. After this, Jesus knowing that all things were now accomplished (John 19:17-28). Look, He had the victory. Jesus' hair was matted to His head. That crown was pressed into His innocent skull. Oh my God, His feet, the nail, He could feel the anguish of the nail being pierced through His foot and through His hands, the whips, and the ligaments that were ripped out of His back. But Jesus looked ahead. His mission was now fulfilled. No matter what it looked like to the world. He was looking up. He knew, Lord, you always hear Me. Jesus always sought to please His Father. And to a lost and dying world, it seemed like He had degraded Himself, but it was His greatest hour, and that became our great hour. For in that hour, the church was born. When they pierced His side, we began to live, and now we can live for all eternity. When the side of the Lord was opened and blood and water poured forth, they drew the line for excuse making and wilful sin. If you go and read the chapter, He looked ahead and said, **It is finished** (John 19:30). The Lord knew His mission was fulfilled. Oh my God, it did not look like it naturally, because the blood was coming down on His face, and His hair was matted together. Later, they tried to give Him vinegar to drink to quicken His death, but He said, "I am too far now. The scriptures must be fulfilled. I am too close to finishing My mission. I am not going to allow you to get Me to hurry up, but I am going at the speed of my Father, because I am going back home. I am going back home". You can just hear Him in a high priestly prayer. Bring me back to where I am. He had such reality. He remembered what it was like to stand at the right-hand of God. There He is talking to the Holy Ghost, and the entire heavenly host. Jesus remembers how they were singing the chorus of Holy, Holy, Holy, Holy, Holy. And He saw the cherubims and the seraphims. I can imagine Him talking to Michael, God's chief commander; the archangel, and Gabriel, who came to announce His arrival. He remembered that, and His heart leaped with joy. No longer was the Lord focused on His bruises. No longer was He focused on the persecutions. Jesus realized that His mission to save my life, to save your life, to save humanity was almost completed. It is almost done. I am almost back to glory. I am almost back to my Father. No matter what it looked like, to the world, the precious lamb looked weak. He looked like He was full of degradation. Jesus looked like the world had won. But, oh my God, they were casting lots. They wanted to finish Him off, but they had no control of what was going on. It was the Father's will to bruise Him. It was the Father's will in perfect action, perfect submission, perfect humility.

When they pierced the Lord in His side, out came redemption for the whole lost world. We were the lost boys, the lost girls, until then, but out came my redemption. When they lifted Him up, just think about how horrible the crucifixion was. The crucifixion was the worst death. The Romans reserved crucifixions for criminals and slaves. But He was my slave; He worked. The Lord was *a solider of love*. Love held Him on that cross. Jesus allowed Himself to be beaten. He allowed Himself to be subjected to man, that I could live, be free; that you could be free. You hear this redemption story. It is the story of your life. And oh, the cross, it was usually a pole fixed in the ground with an attached cross bar. Jesus had to carry His own cross. But oh, when they lifted Him up. Jesus! Oh, when they lifted Him up. It says said Golgotha was not too far from the city limits. The people could look from miles around. They could see the Lamb of God there on the cross. Read the letters of Isaiah. Did they think about what Christ said? If you lift Me up, I will be able to draw all men. And there He is, His hair is so matted, and the crown of thorns pressing His head. He looked so shameful. And Isaiah said, oh my God that we esteemed Him not. He was stricken. Because the Lord was smitten by his stripes I am healed today. By His stripes I am healed today. The world looks at a pitiful Christ. They looked at Him and felt so sorry for the Lord. They slapped Him and beat Him. They pushed Him from side-to-side. And somebody said, He *saved others but He cannot save Himself*. On that shameful cross, He was saving me. He was redeeming you—all of us—right up there. And oh, oh, He began to cry out to His Father, **Father, why have you forsaken Me?** But the Father loved me so much. The Father loved you so much. Do not you know? He would have destroyed humanity if He did not yield to love, but when that love turns to hate. Jesus was unaware that the Father would not be there to help Him on the cross. Have you ever thought about it? The love of God. God could not look at His Son, because He saw you. Did you not know what that scripture meant? He said, Father, Father, Father, why have you forsaken me? But love looked at you. And when Jesus was up there crying, and they had beat Him, and it seemed like He had taken His last breath, God was looking at me. He knew it was the only way I could be redeemed. He knew that it was the only way you could have new life. There was no other way out of whoredom for you. There was no other way you could be set free from the chains of homosexuality, the chains of addiction, the chains of mental torment. There was no other way the demonic power could be taken out of your life. And so yes, God the Father did look away, but He looked at me. He looked at you. He saw you in the pit of despair. He saw you in degradation. He saw you with no way out. And so he did. God turned His back on Jesus, His most precious and brightest Jew. Think how heaven—the angels must have cried. God the Father saw me.

A REJECTED SACRIFICE

One day, He is going to look back again and remember all that they did to His Son FOR YOU. You, who have rejected such a sacrifice, will see what that love is going to turn to—you will witness first-hand when love turns to hate! Did you not know when they pierced him in his side, you became a part of His body. The Lord is *expecting you* to take on the same burden for the lost; the same burden that He took on to save your soul. The Lord is expecting you to take it on. We are supposed to be dead with Christ. We should be crucified with him. We should be buried with Him. And Paul said, "Oh, that I may know him in power of his resurrection. In the fellowship of his suffering." Paul declared in one of his letters to Timothy, for am I am now ready. He was going so bodaciously to Nero's chop block. I have finished my mission, Timothy, Paul must have said. And a crowd was standing by. And they watched him, probably whispering under their voice, "Get Him, that Paul, Get Him." But he was jubilant.

Stephen looked up into Heaven and saw Jesus standing at the right hand. And he told Timothy, do not look for me, because I am going to get my reward. Not only for me, but for those who keep their mission in mind. And he told Paul, I am now ready, I have kept the faith. I have fought a good fight. There he went to Nero's chop block with so much joy, because he knew in one instance he would be here, and in the next instance, he would be before the throne. He would see Jesus in living reality. Maybe he had visions and saw angels. For the first time, he could touch the crown of thorns. For the very first time, he would be able to kneel at those feet. He would be able to affix the voice that called him on the road to Damascus. **Saul, Saul, why persecutest thou me** (Acts 9:4)? He said Lord, what should I do? And he is there today, worshipping him. Holy, Holy is the Lamb that taketh away the sins of the world. You are the Christ. And Jesus loved Paul so much. He said, I will show him. I will make him a vessel. I will show him what he must pay for my great name. In Romans, 8th Chapter, What shall separate me from the love of God that is in Christ Jesus. Persecutions, nakedness, he said my God, I have been betrayed by my own brethren. I have been in the dark. I have been naked. But ye, in all these things, I am more than a conqueror. He is saying that this morning. Can you hear him? Can you hear him? Can you hear him? I am more than a conqueror. And there he is talking to Jesus, because he yielded to that love; the gifts of God, the power of God flowing through him in such a way. When love turns to hate. Don't you feel the yearning in your heart? The stirring in your heart? Everybody needs love. The Lord was lied on by audacious men. They hired people to lie, to be a witness against Him, so that you can be here. And you think momma loves you? No. You think your companion loves you? No. It is nothing like the love of God. The love of God covers all of your sins. And the Lord, once you truly repent, will not remember them anymore. But when you will not serve him, then they are ever before Him.

Think about Pilate; how he wished he could change his mind. Pilate, the Lord never lost the vision of why He was made. He had bad days like I have bad days. People left Him, just like they are going to leave me and leave you. In the end, there He is, back with the Father, interceding for me and you, praying for us, caring for us like little children. He is praying for me. And the Holy Spirit is praying for me. You should never feel unloved. Read that story over and over again. They whipped Him. He was brutally murdered. They tore the ligaments out of His back. They beat Jesus to death. They pierced Him in His side. They put a nail into his feet and in both of his hands. And when they put that cross up, it tore His skin. It tore the flesh of the Lord. How could you say you are not loved? In the garden of Gethsemane He said, "I am He." Jesus had to repress His divinity, because He would have killed them. He told one disciple, do you not know I can call twelve legions of angels if I choose? But He loved me more. He loved you more. You have to finish your mission. You must. You must be what God called you to be in this final hour.

Now, I want everyone to say the sinner's prayer. Say: ***Oh God! Oh God! Please forgive me, for sinning against you. But I have come home to never leave you again. Oh Lord, like the prodigal son, I have come to myself and I said, "Oh, lord, I know what I will do." In my Father's house, there are many mansions. I will be your servant today. Just take me back. Just take me back. Take me back when I first believed. Take me back when I first met you. Wash me in the Blood. Wash me in the Blood. Wash me in the Blood. Wash me in the Blood. Set my soul free. Set my soul free. Set my soul free. Set my soul free. Today? Only believe, only believe.*** It is the power of God. It is the power of God.

CHAPTER 11
WHEN LOVE TURNS TO HATE
TAKE ANOTHER LOOK AT GOD

Take Another Look at God. God gave us Christ. Christ gave His life's blood. God the Father and God the Son gave us the precious Holy Ghost. So, we are without excuse. Sometimes, through one reason or another, maybe you were not taught the right way. I hope that through these series of messages you will be able to see what the blood of Jesus can and will do for you, if you let it.

When the love of God turns to hate, when He has no more tears for this old world, when you are suffering, when you are going through something, and then God is not there to help you; that is what we are going to be talking about in this final chapter of *When Love Turns To Hate*. For the last three chapters we have been talking about Christ, and how He gave His life for us. In this chapter, I want to zoom in on the magnitude of that love being turned to hate. Just think about suffering and crying out to a God who will no longer hear you. You say that God cannot be like this. Proverbs 1:24-31 says, **Because I have called, and ye refused; I have stretched out my hand, and no man regarded; But ye have set at nought all my counsel, and would none of my reproof: I also will laugh at your calamity: I will mock when your fear cometh; When your fear cometh as desolation, and your destruction cometh as a whirlwind; when distress and anguish cometh upon you. Then shall they call upon me, but I will not answer; they shall seek me early, but they shall not find me: For that they hated knowledge, and did not choose the fear of the Lord: They would none of my counsel: they despised all of my reproof. Therefore shall they eat of the fruit of their own way, and be**

filled with their own devices. What the Lord was saying through proverbs was, *you did not want My love instruction. You didn't want My love discipline. You didn't want My love, now I DON'T WANT YOU! When you have your problems, and your trials, and sickness, and afflictions not only come on you, but your seed: I am going to laugh at you. Because I extended a courtesy to you, I gave you all I had. So, now you need Me. I am going to treat you the same way you treated Me, all those times I begged you and pressed upon you to turn unto Me. You didn't want Me. I tried to warn you, but you didn't want to listen. I tried to get you to be around My people, but no, you had other things to do. I tried to get you to linger and stay in My presence, but something else took My place. So, you can see how I feel.* Think about the God that made you, saying these very words to your face, in your inner most being where you cannot escape His words or feeling of hatred toward you.

THE TERRIBLE GOD

How many of you know that God has a form. He has a form. He has eyes, He has a right hand. He has a left hand. Read the book. He has feet. And He has feelings. It will be a laughing judge on the *great white throne*. It will be a mocking judge; a judge without sympathy; a judge without love; a judge without compassion. Heaven's judge will be without one tear for those who rejected the shed blood of His precious, precious Son, Jesus. He will not even think about what you are going through. Proverbs 1:27-28 again says, **When your fear cometh as desolation, and your destruction cometh as a whirlwind; when distress and anguish cometh upon you. Then shall they call upon me, but I will not answer; they shall seek me early, but they shall not find me.** Unlike the three previous chapters on this subject, When Love Turns To Hate, I have been giving illustrations of how when you call upon God, He will answer. I have given illustrations of how Adam and Eve. All they had to do was call. I have given illustrations of how Jesus has made Himself so available. Also, in the last chapter, I talked about how they killed Him, and Jesus allowed Himself to be brutally murdered. The Lord allowed Himself to go from judgment hall to judgment hall. Why? Because of love. But, when all that love is turned around, God lets us know He can hate, as much as He can love. Oh My God! And with all the love, John 3:16-17 says, **For God so loved the world, that he gave his only begotten Son**. He loved us so much, that He gave us all. So, it is going to be all of Him that is going to hate. Can you fathom that today? So much love, only this time it is hate, hate, hate. Have you ever thought of God as being a laughing, mocking God when you are afraid or disobedient? You need to learn all about God. This world needs to take another look at God. You need to take another look at God today. Think about it. In Genesis 19th Chapter, God cried when He brought Lot and his family out of the cities of Sodom and Gomorrah. He cried over the men married to the daughters of Lot, because they did not care. They did not believe in God's word. Then judgment fell, and God's tears ceased. The love that He once had for them was gone! No more tears! They, no doubt, blasphemed against the Holy Ghost, and God will never think of them again. The reason why the Lord sent those two angels down in Genesis 19th was to see if anybody would change their mind. Was the degradation as it was being heard in heaven? Abraham in the previous chapter, pleaded with the two angels, "If there be so many righteous, would you save the city?" If there be so many righteous would you save the city?" And the Lord said, of course. But when the messengers of God got down there, there was none righteous except for Lot and his immediate family. The Lord said, let us go down and see for ourselves if the destruction, if the sin, if the defilement against God's word is as great as what we hear in heaven. And the Lord sent the two angels down with love. He sent them down with love, but then that love turned into hate. That love turned to hate. The Lord is sending a strong warning today throughout this old world. The Bible says in the book of Isaiah 24:20 **The earth shall reel to and fro like a drunkard, and shall be removed like a cottage; and the transgression thereof shall be heavy upon it; and it shall fall, and not rise again.**

In the wicked cities of Sodom and Gomorrah judgment fell, and God's love ceased. He did not have any more love. Think about when Lot's wife was turned into a pillar of salt. No more love for her. No more love for her. She met judgment when she disobeyed God's word and turned back to the world. The love of the world was still engrafted in her spirit; she loved it; craved it, and ultimately died for it. She's in hell right now, as you are reading about her life. The Lord sent the two angels down, if you study Genesis the 19th chapter. The Bible let us know that Lot and his wife were physically removed; they were out of harm's way. The angels grabbed hold of them and took them out of the city. And even Lot, he tarried to try to get as many souls as he could. And the angels said, you must go because we cannot destroy the city while you are still here. That was love. That was love.

What the love of God will not do for one soul, He will do for a group of people, for a multitude of people, for a whole nation, for the whole world. But when that love, that massive love, is turned to hate; to have God's back turned on you; when you are on your death bed, when your body is ravaged with AIDS, or when your body or your mother's body, or another dear loved one—and God will not list—oh my God, what will you do now? What will you do when you realize that you are now in the Tribulation Period? What will you do the day that it is announced, "Take the Mark here"? His word will torment you. The words of life will haunt you. You will be reminded of all the months, all the years He was calling you, begging you The Lord was warning you, because He knew you wouldn't make it in the Tribulation Period. Now you're wide awake, but it's simply too late. You were too busy. You better take another look at God; that is His cry to you. Just think about what it will be like, those of you who are playing church. What do you think it will be like? Those of you who are living in sin; those of you who are lukewarm; those of you with your disobediences, sometimes you come to church, sometimes you do not. Sometimes you are on time, sometimes you are not. Sometimes you pay your tithes. What heaven is there for you if you are a thief? The Bible says you are a thief and a robber when you don't pay the tenth. Malachi 3:8-10 says it plainly, **Will a man rob God? Yet ye** have robbed me. But ye say, Wherein have we robbed thee? In tithes and offerings. Ye are cursed with a curse: for ye have robbed me, even this whole nation. Bring ye all the tithes into the storehouse, that there may be meat in mine house, and prove me now herewith, saith the Lord of hosts, if I will not open you the windows of heaven, and pour you out a blessing, that there shall not be room enough to receive it.

THE DEVIL HAS DECEIVED YOU

What will it be like to fall into the hands of an angry God? Oh, the devil has deceived you. You are on dangerous ground, those of you who are failing God. You think you can find the Lord anytime you want? You are deceived neighbor. The Bible clearly states that **No man can come to me, except the Father which hath sent me draw him** (St. John 6:44). You think you can do whatever you want to do? Soon His love will run out. One day that love will not be there. How long do you have left? The Lord has tracked event step that you have made. How close are you to the one sin that there is no forgiveness for? **Where I say unto you, All manner of sin and blasphemy shall be forgiven unto men: but the blasphemy against the Holy Ghost shall not be forgiven unto men. And whosoever speaketh a word against the Son of man, it shall be forgiven him: but whosoever speaketh against the Holy Ghost, it shall not be forgiven him, neither in this world, neither in the world to come** (Matthew 12:31-32). You will be doomed for all time and eternity. You will have no hope. All hope with heaven will be gone. The only escape from damnation for you is in the love of God. See, so you cannot get away from the love of God. You cannot get away from the love of God. There is no other way. There is no other way. Acts 4:12 **Neither is there salvation in any other: for there is none other name under heaven given among men, whereby we must be saved.** And you can only find the Lord through love. Just think, one day heaven will no longer be drawing you. The Holy Spirit will not be drawing on you. The Lord will stop pulling on you. He will not be pleading with you. Jesus will no longer cry over you. When God cries no more for lost humanity, then it will be judgment, judgment, and judgment. Some of that judgment has already begun. **But thou, O God, shalt bring them down into the pit of destruction: bloody and deceitful men shall not live out half their days** (Psalms 55:23). **Destruction cometh; and they shall seek peace, and there shall be none** (Ezekiel 7:25).

The Holy Spirit will not be hovering over you. He will not be waking you up at night and robbing you of your appetite. You should take another look at God. Jesus, in the Bible, is described as two personalities. Right now, we see him as the Lamb, but there is the Lion personality. We see Jesus now, as we read His word; He is that little meek lamb, coming and offering us everything. The Lord appears as a little lamb that had no spot, had no blemish, which they brutally murdered. But soon, He is going to be the Lamb; full of hate, full of anguish, full of fury. Jesus will have no pity for you. There will be no compassion for you. When love turns to hate: take another look at God. Think about when love, God's love, turns to hate. What will you do? What will you do now, as you are reading this chapter? Will you turn to God? Will you repent now and get things right? Will you go on into deeper deceit? Maybe you have never thought about it. Maybe you thought you would always have God's love. It is like some of your children. *Oh, I know how I can get to momma. The only thing I have to do is shed a few tears. I can do my homework for a whole week, and I can be back in.* It will not be like that with God. Today is the day of redemption. Some of you don't respect God, because you grew up in deceit. How horrible. You weren't given discipline, and now you're arrogant and stubborn. Today is the day of salvation. But when God's love, when God's love, not momma's love, turns to hate. In the Tribulation Period, for everyone that will take the mark of the beast, it will be a horrible time. Have you ever thought about that? God so loved the world that He gave us Jesus. But there are those who have spit in His eyes and rejected salvation purchased by His sinless blood. If you have not accepted Him as your personal Saviour, if you are not living free from all sin today, you are spitting in the eye of God, being a hypocrite, coming out doing one thing while saying another. You are spitting in the eye of Jesus.

ONE PLAGUE MORE

Think about the Tribulation Period, the judgments of God will be so severe. It will be so severe. Compare the judgments in Pharaoh's day to the judgments that will take place in the Tribulation Period. Remember when the first born was killed? Exodus 11:1 **And the Lord said unto Moses, Yet will I bring one plague more upon Pharaoh, and upon Egypt; afterwards he will let you go hence: when he shall let you go, he shall surely thrust you out hence altogether.** The Lord said this is it. He will let you go. **And Moses said, Thus saith the Lord, About midnight will I go out into the midst of Egypt: And all the firstborn in the land of Egypt shall die, from the firstborn of Pharaoh that setteth upon his throne, even unto the firstborn of the maidservant that is behind the mill; and all the firstborn of beats. And there shall be a great cry as there was none like it, nor shall be like it any more** (Exodus 11:4-6). All the horrible plagues that will come upon the earth, they are going to be massive, to a greater degree, to a greater extent in the Tribulation Period.

All Adam and Eve had to do was obey. All of humanity, the whole civilization, all authority was placed upon Adam. But he yielded to the voice of his wife, and that's the reason why there's sin, sickness and death today. Take another Look at God. Genesis 2:17 says, **But of the tree of the knowledge of good and evil, thou shalt not eat of it.** God warned them just as He is warning us through these messages. Did you know these four messages are messages of warning? It says first warning, then destruction. Is not that what God's word teaches us? He does not suddenly come upon you. Some of you have been deceived, particularly in Christianity, because we have our grace covenant, which is called Jesus Christ. People believe that God will continue to let people do what they want. God will judge.

Remember this. So many people listen to false teachers and false prophets who misinterpret the word. *They say* nobody can live free from sin, and all you have to do is repent, even when you know beforehand that you are going to sin against God. There are cursing Christians, whoring Christians, adulterous Christians, fornicating Christians, gambling Christians, smoking Christians, and all kind of Christians. Are these kinds of Christians getting into God's heaven? Not so! **Blessed are the pure in heart: for they shall see God** (Matthew 5:8). **Follow peace with all men, and holiness, without which no man shall see the Lord** (Hebrews 12:14). There's no Bible for it! When you know you are going to do wrong before you do it, the Bible says it is sin. When you know to do good, then you do not, it is sin. The Bible teaches us, as I have been teaching you over the last three chapters, everybody's accountable for his or her soul. You are ultimately responsible for your soul. **And the times of this ignorance God winked at; but now commandeth all men everywhere to repent** (Acts 17:30). **Work out your own salvation with fear and trembling** (Philippians 2:12). And as we study in depth in Genesis about Adam, they played the blame game. Adam blamed Eve, Eve blamed the serpent. Some of you, we talked about how we have that same characteristic in our hearts and minds. We talked about companions and when they have disagreements. Instead of confessing and looking at yourself, you want to turn around and say, "But, what did you do.?" It is the blame game. But the gospel said His word was going to go around the whole world, and then the end would come, especially here in America. Not one of us could say, "We were not warned to flee the wrath to come." We will not be able to say, "We did not know about the Rapture of the Tribulation Period," or that "We were not told about the Blood." Not in this church, but when love turns to hate.

THE TREE OF DEATH

I challenge you today to take another look at God. Adam and Eve, in Genesis 2:17 were warned not to partake in that tree, but they disobeyed

God. Many are going to "the tree of death" in this final hour; the tree that's dressed as some of these internet, social media sites. The Lord wanted Adam and Eve to choose Him. He would have, eventually, taken the tree out. You are not a robot. You are a free moral agent. The Lord allowed the tree to be in the Garden of Eden, because He wanted them to choose Him over evil. The Bible tells us to yield not to temptation, for yielding is a sin. We use that every day. Our young people say, "I can't help it. "That's where self-control comes in. How many of you today are living lives of regret because you just would not wait. The book of James tells us, **But every man is tempted, when he is drawn away of his own lust, and enticed** (James1:14). What does that sin turn into? What does that temptation turn into? Destruction. Sin always feels good, but the devil never tells you the end result. The Lord is warning you today. You have no right to partake of anything God tells you not to, no matter what it is. You have to go to the word of God for yourself. He said, **Search the scriptures: for in them ye think you have eternal life** (John 5:39). You take no man's word for your soul. You write the scriptures down. Everybody should be encouraged to bring a notebook. Bring a pen. Read the scriptures for yourself. It is God's responsibility to make sure you are receiving the truth. I've taught you this down through these many years. Do you have a heart to receive truth?

When love turns to hate, do you have a heart to receive truth? I can preach the truth all day long, but I cannot make you accept it. Momma warned me all day long, "Beverly, don't do that," "Beverly, don't do that," "Beverly, would you stop that," "Beverly, would you stop doing that?" It seemed like the more she said to me "don't," to me, it was like "do it, do it, do it, do it." I paid many a price, because I did not listen to what Momma said. My Momma loved me and all her kids. She was a good Mom to all of us, all the way to her great departure to heaven. It was a glorious send-off. But think of a God not loving you anymore; not wanting to be bothered with you anymore. I do not care what people preach in false doctrine. False doctrine teaches people that God does not hate; that God would not send anybody to hell; that there is not really a hell. I beg to differ. God does not send you to hell. Your sins and disobedience sends you to hell. The Bible tells us everything that we are able to do and the things we are not able to do. We have to choose. You are not a robot. Why would you want somebody to tell you what to do every day, every minute of your life? That is not right. That is control. And who's controlling you? That is not love. But God came with love. He said choose you this day that you are going to serve. You are not going to love God and your flesh. You are not going to love God and all things you want to do. You are going to love one and hate the other. This is God's great warning today. This is God's great warning to us today. We have the living Christ to dwell on the inside of us through the power of the Holy Ghost. **And I will pray the Father, and he shall give you another Comforter, that he may abide with you for ever; Even the Spirit of truth; whom the world cannot receive, because it seeth him not, neither knoweth him: but ye know him; for dwelleth with you, and shall be in you** (John 14:16-17). We can have the gift of the Holy Ghost to tabernacle within and be our teacher, to be our instructor, to guide us into all truth. He is the spirit of truth. God will not take the blame for the fall of man. He will take the honour and glory for bringing redemption through His son, Jesus, to fallen men and making them upright. God has provided a heaven where the devil will never be. Not one speck of sin will go into heaven. God will have what He planned in the beginning. Oh, how He has waited and yearned for this hour.

When love turns to hate. You have to think about how God must have felt when His Son, Jesus, left heaven to come down here to suffer, to be afflicted, to be smoted upon, and to be rejected. People kicked him and slapped him in his face. People wanted to be with him one minute, and next time they would leave him. But all of that love restrained Him. All of that love kept Him on the cross for you and me. The Lord looked ahead in time and saw all of us healthy and spiritually cleaned, and He knew He could take the abuse, for our sakes. There was no other way for us. But eventually, He is going to remember all of that love, and it is going to turn to hate on a society, on a world, on a boy, on a girl, on a man, on a woman, on a nation that has rejected all He died to give lost humanity.

THEY SAY

When love turns to hate. False doctrine declares that you cannot help but to sin. *They say*, "Everybody sins. We were born in sin, and we were shaped in iniquity from our mother's womb." Yes, that is true. But then, Christ came. If you want to live free from sin, you can. If you want to be holy as Jesus when He walked among man, you can be, but you have got to make that choice. Choose now while you still have a chance.

One sin destroyed man's life in the Garden of Eden. One sin destroyed man's life, and Jesus had to come with the plan of salvation, with the plan of redemption. One sin destroyed everything that was good. One sin. Just one sin destroyed everything. One sin separated man and woman from their God, drawing them into the hands of the devil. One unrepented sin will take you to hell. Just one sin will take you to hell today. You need to wake up and take another look at God, because of all the love He has given us. He's given us life. He's given us the possibility of having eternal life. Do you think the Lord is just going to sit by and let you do anything you want to do every day and all day, while you turn your nose up at Him? Turn your nose up at His perfect plan of redemption, which cost Him not having His Son sit next to Him on the throne all those years? No! No! A thousand times "No!" The plan of redemption was perfect. It was perfect.

Look at the children of Israel and all the plagues that He brought upon the Egyptians, yet the children of Israel were spared. What did they do? What did they do when they got free? Mumbled, grumbled and complained. That's all they did. The Lord, with so much love, in Exodus told Moses He was going to send him. He had heard their groaning. He had heard their cries. He had heard their afflictions, and He said I am going to send you [Moses] down to deliver my people. Every time you looked up, they were rebelling against him. Every time you looked up, they were rising up against Moses and Aaron.

FAMOUS IN THE CONGREGATION

One magnificent story is the story of Korah. It's an account that we should ever keep before us. Take another look at God. Here, at *A Passion for Christ Ministries*, we have the Word of God. We have the Blood of Jesus. We have the ultimate anointings. We have the Holy Ghost Baptism. We have the Rapture as a way to escape this wicked world. We have fasting. What will we be able to tell God with all of the jewels He has given us, and all of these treasures that have been laid at our feet? What will we be able to tell God is the reason for failing Him? Loved-one, we will be without excuse. I want to admonish you today to take another look at God. Some of you are just playing games.

Number 16:1 says, **Now Korah, the son of Izhar, the son of Kohath, the son of Levi, and Dathan and Abiram, the sons of Eliab, and On, the son of Peleth, sons of Reuben, took men**. Now, I want you to pay close attention to this. This was after they had cried and travailed about how they were being treated under Pharaoh's leadership. Oh, they wanted to be free. They made God all kinds of promises that they did not keep. Have you made God promises that you haven't kept? They had been in bondage for so many hundreds of years. Oh my God, it was after they witnessed with their own eyes the plagues that the Lord brought upon the land. They witnessed the Lord maturing Moses and using Aaron. They witnessed, by the Lord's mighty hand, the Red Sea parting and so many millions of them walking over on dry ground. They witnessed the Red Sea going up right before their eyes. They could see all kind of fishes on each side. But it was like a wall, and they went over on dry ground. They witnessed manna coming down from heaven. They witnessed water from a rock, but they forgot. It's the greatest sin ever, the sin of forgetting God. **The wicked shall be turned into hell, and all the nations that forget God** (Psalm 9:17). They forgot Jehovah God who had parted the Red Sea, gave them manna, gave them angels' food, and gave them quail. They forgot the hand that provided water from a rock to quench their thirst. Have you thought about that? They had to take another look at God. Numbers 16:2, **And they rose up before Moses, with certain of the children of Israel, two hundred and fifty princes of the assembly, famous in the congregation, men of renown.** Now, notice that they were *famous in the congregation*. They were men of renown. They had influence over the people. Now, I want you to pay attention to this, when love turns to hate. When you study God's word, it has always only taken a few people to get the whole crowd stirred up, just a few people; a few *bad apples*. Maybe in your own life, mom or dad, sister or brother, co-worker has distracted you. The Lord has taught us not to cast your pearls before swine. Do not give that which is holy unto dogs. To get these messages, they are the riches of heaven. His presence is with us. The Bible declares it to unlock the mysteries of the Gospel. Some of you have never heard about living free from sin. Some of you have never felt the love of God as you do when you come into these services. Some of you have never heard about the Tribulation Period before you came here. You've never heard about the fact that you could even make the Rapture. You've never heard about the Blood. But soon, you go out like a leaky vessel. Take another look at God.

Numbers 16:3, says **And they gathered themselves together against Moses and against Aaron, and said unto them, Ye take too much upon you.** Where were "the men of renown" when Pharaoh's army was going after them? This is just the way people are today. You are coming to church. He is teaching you how to fast. The Holy Spirit is opening up your mind. He is healing your body. Everything is going good. But where are all these folks at when your rent is due? Where are these people in the mid-night hour when you are crying and nobody is there to help you? Do not be so gullible. When love turns to hate, take another look at God. **Ye**

take too much upon you, seeing all the congregation are holy, every one of them, and the Lord is among them (Numbers 16:3); God is with us. But God did not select any of them. Where were they when people were coming up against Moses? Do you know how much Moses' life was at risk from the time the Lord chose him until the time they crossed the Red Sea? It was God's people; the people that God was delivering time after time, that would *always* rise up against leadership. They forgot about the love of God, so He had to challenge them to take another look at just how strong His love was. **Wherefore then lift ye up yourselves above the congregation of the Lord** (Numbers 16:3)? Who are you? Who are you? Korah decided that they could reach God for them; him and two hundred and fifty princes, famous men overcome with arrogance. They rebelled against God's servant. It was the same as rebelling against God. Notice that. We see the miracles of God in our own lives. God is making a way out of no way. All of us have witnessed the manifestation of God's love in our own lives. Every single one of us today, we have witnessed the manifestations of God's compassion. We have witnessed and seen with our own eyes and ears the mercies of God, each one. Will we let somebody of renown, famous in the congregation come and blind us to the love of God, to the discipline of God, to the order of God? God is God, no matter what people say. Korah rebels against God. And when the people rebelled against the servants, it was like rebelling against God. Upon hearing what was going on, Moses and Aaron fell on their faces.

Numbers 16:28, **And Moses said, Hereby ye shall know that the Lord hath sent me to do all these works; for I have not done them of mine own mind.** Moses did not bring those plagues. He could not separate the Red Sea for millions of people to go over. He was a humble servant that the Lord could use His power through to manifest His greatness. It's not the person; it's GOD working through the person. Always remember that. The devil will seduce you into thinking you are something great if you are not careful and living close to God. In deceit, He uses your weaknesses and personality to try to deceive you at the same time that God is encouraging you. He is elevating you. Finally, you are in a place where He can open up your mind to understand His word. He is healing you. He is given you favor in the market. The Lord is giving you favor on the job. But there is the devil whispering *wicked little nothings;* the same serpent that was in the Garden of Eden.

IF THESE MEN DIE

Take another look at God people. Do not be deceived. It is always the one's you least expect. What got Adam? He never expected deceit out of his wife; precious Eve that was made out of one of his ribs, yet it was Eve. **And Moses said, Hereby ye shall know that the Lord hath sent me to do all these works; for I have not done them of mine own mind. If these men die the common death of all men, or if they be visited after the visitation of all men; then the Lord hath not sent me** (Numbers 16:28-29). So, Moses was saying, if God is not with me, then they are going to die just like everybody else dies. **But, if the Lord make a new thing, and the earth open her mouth, and swallow them up, with all that appertain unto them, and they go down quick into the pit; then ye shall understand that these men have provoked the Lord** (Numbers 16:30). This is not a fable. This happened. This is not a parable. **And it came to pass, as he had made an end of speaking all these words, that the ground clave asunder that was under them: And the earth opened her mouth, and swallowed them up, and their houses, and all the men that appertained unto Korah, and all their goods** (Numbers 16:31-32). **They, and all that appertained to them, went down alive into the pit.** They did not even die. They went straight to hell alive. **And the earth closed upon them; and they perished from among the congregation** (Numbers 16:33).

The love of God; when love turns to hate. Take another look at God. They forgot that the same God that swallowed up Pharaoh's army was the same God that was with Moses and Aaron. I am bringing this to you today to remind you that, even though the Lord has not brought you across *this* Red Sea, he has parted many Red Seas in your life. He did not bring the locust. He did not make it dark. The Lord has performed many miracles in your life. He has pushed people out of your way. He has destroyed people for your sake. So, God is challenging you to take another look at Him today.

Some of us, we know beyond a shadow of a doubt that God rescued us from a *burning literal hell*. We know it today that He saved our children; kept them from harm and danger. But when you go on your way, you lack humility. When you do not have thanksgiving in your heart, there is no humility. When you are always mumbling, grumbling and talking about what you do not have, you forget about the love of God; the blessings of God. You forget about how Christ came down through fourteen generations for you; to rescue you. You forget about how Joseph had to sneak Mary out. You forget about all the little babies that died and God took to Heaven. I challenge you today to take another look at God. So much has been paid for you and for me to be here today. So much has been given for you and to fulfil our mission to help get this gospel to the whole world, then the end will come. We all need to be like Christ. His goal was to make a way for us, and then He was gone. One of these days, our work will be done, and we'll be gone. We'll be gone. We'll be gone. Hallelujah!

The love of God, He is going to ask you at the end of your day, "What have you done with this love?" Have you shown it to anybody today? Have you been long-suffering? Have you been kind? Have you been gentle? Have you forgiven? When love turns to hate. This should serve to us to not hinder what God is doing. We should not judge. We should let God have His way. It has to be God's way. No matter what God does for some, they will never know the hour they are living in. Some of you have become so numb to the tragedies; the devil has desensitized you to violence and abuse. There was this massive train wreck that happened on the day before Thanksgiving in a suburb of Chicago. I think they said the train hit around seventeen cars, and to my amazement, not one soul perished. I think there were only two people in the hospital. But from the pictures they showed, people should not have survived. It was the love of God. God gives life. The devil is the author of death, sickness and all sin. **He that committeth sin is of the devil; for the devil sinneth from the beginning. For this purpose the Son of God was manifested, that he might destroy the works of the devil. Whosoever is born of God doth not commit sin; for his remaineth in him: and he cannot sin, because he is born of God** (I John 3:8-9) **Why do ye not understand my speech? Even because ye cannot hear my word. Ye are of your father the devil, and the lusts of your father ye will do. He was a murderer for the beginning, and abode not in the truth, because there is not truth in him. When he speaketh a lie, he speaketh of his own: for he is a liar, and the father of it. And because I tell you the truth, ye believe not** (John 8:43-45). Even in our own lives, we have all experienced the hand of God upon us. We have all experienced His love. We have all experienced the long suffering of the Lord, or else we would all be dead. We have experienced His love towards us, His patience, His kindness, His gentleness. We have all experience it. The Lord has been mindful of you. He has been so patient with you. He has looked on you with an eye of pity, but He will cut you off without remedy. He will cut you off.

Are you any better than Korah today? Pointing the finger and judging others. We do not know what people are going through. When did we take the place of God? That is what Korah and his boys did, saying, "God is with all of us." And here they were, conscious so seared, the ground opened up right in front of them. How much longer will the Lord call to you? How long before He turns His back on you and not hear your cries? Oh My God!

BUT TOMORROW

Numbers 16:41 says, **But on the morrow, (that means the next day, the very next day), all of the congregation of the children of Israel murmured against Moses and against Aaron, saying, Ye have killed the**

197

people of the Lord. They just saw hundreds of people go down. They saw the ground open and all of these people fell in it. Then, the ground sealed up like it never had opened before. These people were clearly seduced and deceived. The devil can really screw you around and make you think, "I made myself rich." "Thank God I came up with that idea." It's the same deception. "She was going to come back home to me anyway." Think about it today, in your own heart, in your own mind. It is God who moved for you. It is God who moved on the heart of your loved ones. Moses could not have opened up the Earth and swallowed all of those people, their goods, and their houses. *More in the congregation were deceived.* They were taken over by the devil. It is dangerous to fight against the work and the power of God. It is not a matter of what you know; it is a matter of what God knows, and what God puts His stamp of approval upon. The Lord is challenging us today with this great message of warning to be careful how we live our lives. So much love has been given to us; we have no excuse not to do everything God is asking us to do. He is not going to ask you to do one thing you cannot do. You, teenager, if He tells you to be holy and keep your virginity (boys and girls) until your wedding night that is what He means. The hour is so late. He might catch you and kill you right in your sin. He will turn His back on you, and then He will never hear our cries. He won't even care about you anymore. The God of the universe will laugh and mock because He won't love you anymore. And in hell you will be craving sex. Did you know that? The person that dies an alcoholic, in hell for eternity they are craving a drink. The murderer who dies, in hell they will lift up their eyes and always have a desire to murder; they will want to murder somebody. Today is the day to take notes of what God is saying to you. You need to carefully study this message. You need to take another look at God. So many of our leaders preach about the baby in the manger. They preach about the Jesus who changed the water into wine, but He also has another personality. He has a lion personality also. Do you all hear me? You cannot stand against His wrath, against His fierceness. Then, when His daddy remembers all that His died for, you won't be able to pay.

The love of God has kept you alive. His love has kept you out of eternity without hope. His love has kept you from destruction.

Numbers 16:42-45, says, **And it came to pass, when the congregation was gathered against Moses and against Aaron, that they looked toward the tabernacle of the congregation: and, behold, the cloud covered it, and the glory of the Lord appeared. And Moses and Aaron came before the tabernacle of the congregation. And the Lord spake unto Moses, saying, Get you up from among this congregation, that I may consume them as in a moment. And they fell upon their faces.** Pay real close attention to these verses. I want you to see how soon they forget about the blessings of God. Now, the Lord could have consumed all the people yesterday, but He wanted to have witnesses. He has made you a witness of His greatness, His love. For example, the police siren going on around in the back of your head and in the back of your car; you knew you were guilty. Miraculously, they went on around you. But you were the one they should have gotten. You are a witness. You are a living testimony of the love of God. You know you should have been dead and gone. And you let people come by so hardened. You let people come by that are ungrateful, unholy, and unthankful and harden your heart. You know God has been good to you. You know He has watched over you. You know He has kept you. The Lord is not going to always be calling you; chasing after you, but He's calling you now. Will you answer? Will you?

The love of God: take another look at God today. The Son of God is more than just a baby in the manger. God is more than the God that made Adam. He put him out. He is that same God. He came down and scrambled up all the languages. He's that same God. He's the same God. With all that He has given you, you have to pay up. His love is free. It just cost your life. Look at your own life from the time that you were a child. His hand has been moving for you. Take another look at God. You cannot afford to be confused in this hour. If you are lacking in your spiritual walk, it will show up.

I HATE THEM

The people were coming up against the servants of God again. They did not get enough. Moses and Aaron knew God would take action. They had the mind of God. Numbers 16:45 says, **Get you up from among this congregation, that I may consume them as in a moment. And they fell upon their faces.** What I want you to see here is that love turns to hate, all of the love that the Lord used to bring them out among Pharaoh, all of the miracles He performed before them. Love had them when He was delivering them and making a way for them, but it turned to all out hate. He is telling Moses and Aaron, I want to destroy them all. I want to forget about my love. I want to forget about my compassion. I want to forget about my long suffering. I am angry. I am tired of these people rejecting my love. He is a God of judgment, just as His word describes. He will bring judgment. So many, like Korah, have their back to Him. **And Moses said unto Aaron, Take a censer, and put fire therein from off the altar, and put on incense, and go quickly unto the congregation, and make an atonement for them; for there is wrath gone out from the Lord; the *plague is begun*** (Numbers 16:46). Moses had the mind of God. He knew destruction had to come, because the price was so great. He had given all; all of the babies, oh my God, who had died; all of the people that had been destroyed; he parting of the Red Sea, which provided a watery grave for Pharaoh's great army; and all the years before Moses was even born. Now, in his fury, these things have returned, and He is angry. **Awake, awake, stand up, O Jerusalem, which hast drunk at the hand of the Lord the cup of his fury** (Isaiah51:17).

Moses and Aaron, there they are lying on the ground having this conversation. Think about this for a minute. Moses is still thinking about saving lives, because he has the mind of God. Moses is saying within himself, "They don't know what they are doing. They don't have an idea. They don't know God like I know God." Moses, in his mind (think about it for a minute), is thinking about when the Lord first called him. He was so full of excuses. Moses was always whining and crying about what he could not do. Even though the Lord had called Moses, He was going to kill him, because on the eighth day, he had not yet circumcised his son. He is God. One did not have anything to do with the other. If it was not for Zipporah going in quickly and circumcising the baby, who knows what the outcome would've been. Exodus 4:24-26) says, **And it came to pass by the way in the inn, that the Lord met him, and sought to kill him. Then Zipporah took a sharp stone, and cut off the foreskin of her son, and cast it at his feet, and said, Surely a blood husband art thou to me. So he let him go: then she said, A bloody husband thou art, because of the circumcision.** The word said that the Lord waited for Moses by the inn because He was going to kill him because Moses had not circumcised his son. But, yet he was the servant of God. God is God! He's still God! You better take another look at Him. And the plague went out. Punishment had to come. All that the Lord had went through to bring these people out, to bring them deliverance; now they would spit in His face. They would spit in His face so plainly? So boldly? So arrogantly? So full of rebellion? No! His love had to be vindicated. Just like in our day. Just like in my life. Just like in your life. His love is going to be acknowledged by every person. The word says, **That at the name of Jesus every knee should bow, of things in heaven, and things in earth, and things under the earth; And that every tongue should confess that Jesus Christ is Lord, to the glory of God the Father** (Philippians 2:10-11). The Lord has brought forth this very strong, very sobering message, not to condemn you, but to awaken you. Awaken thou that sleepeth. I do not care what they are showing on the television set; that you can whore a little bit and that you can curse. Listen to what the Spirit is telling you today. God is still God. God is still God. He is the same God that your granny told you about. He is the same God that your great-granny told you about: to honour God and don't talk about people. Do not talk about church people especially. Do not pick on people or be a bully. It is the same granny that told you not to steal. "Child, don't you know what you do is going to come back on you?" It is the same God I am preaching about this morning. And God is still God. Oh, you might call him Jehovah, but he is still God.

THE PLAGUE WAS STAYED

Notice the urgency of Aaron. Numbers 16:47-48 says, **And Aaron took as Moses commanded, and ran into the midst of the congregation; and, behold, the plague was begun among the people: and he put on incense, and made atonement for the people.** *And he stood between the dead and the living;* **and the plague was stayed**. That is what we are supposed to be doing as leaders. We are supposed to be standing in between the dead and the living; standing the gap, making up the hedge. What do we have? We do not have the censer, but we have the word of God. We have our holy bodies. We have our holy tongues that are supposed to be seasoned with love. We have our lives that are supposed to be open epistles. We are supposed to be an example for people. We cannot save people. We do not have a heaven to put them in. We do not have a hell to put them in. Through our lives, they need to see the Jehovah. He is still God. If that's what He said He is going to do, He is going to do it. If He said the soul that sinneth; it shall die. That is what He means, precious ones. That is what He means. Do not let anybody trick you out of heaven. Nobody.

Numbers 16:49 says, **Now they that died in the plague were fourteen thousand and seven hundred, beside them that died about the matter of Korah**. That is 14,700 people that died in that moment. **And Aaron returned unto Moses unto the door of the tabernacle of the congregation: and the plague was stayed** (vs. 50)**.** Look at Korah and his group; just a few folks. Korah and his group had been killed, but 14,700 more people were killed for accusing Moses and Aaron of killing the people of God. All of the stuff that is going on is not an accident. All of this is not an act of Mother Nature. But God is getting tired on his throne. He is tired of America. We have Bibles. We have cassettes. We have tapes. We have got braille. You can see it anyway you want to see it, and still we turn our noses up at God. We are so pious. We are so unthankful. We are so unconcerned about the lost, and He is sick of it. We have forgotten about the love of God that was demonstrated to us. We have forgotten in our finances, in our giving. Some of you are worse than Scrooge, but your day is coming. He says in Genesis 6, my spirit shall not always strife with man. Job says work is going to be tried fire. But, I shall come forth as pure gold. Every one of us, what we say we are, how we are saying we are living for God, what is in us, are going to be tested in this hour. All of us will go into the garden of Gethsemane, whether you want to go or not. All of us, we are going to be on trial by the world. We are going to be on trial by the world's church. Some of them are in your family, but there you are without a God on your side. You think you have all day. Don't be so naïve. Don't be so gullible. Take a look at Korah. This was a real man. These people are in hell right now today, as we study about them. Hell is a real place. It is not a figment of my imagination. Korah's rebellion is a vivid picture of people who do not accept the love of God. That same kind of rebellion is happening all over again today, as people are swept into the nets of the devil and dragged away. If the devil can separate you from God's truth and his true people, you are on your way to that same love being turned to hate. You need all the help. You need all the faith of God's people that you can get. Just being in the congregation of God's people gives you strength. And it gives you help from the Lord. I want you to think about Korah today. I do not want you to ever let that leave your mind. Korah, Korah, and his rebellion rising up. The Lord has provided a way of escape for you. In all that He has done, do you think that He will forget it at the end of your day? At the end of your day, do you think He will not bring forth all that He has laid out for you to be a perfect vessel?

TARRY ALL NIGHT

When love turns to hate: take another look at God. Genesis 19:1 says, **And there came two angels to Sodom at even; and Lot sat in the gate of Sodom: and Lot seeing them rose up to meet them; and he bowed himself with his face toward the ground.** Lot put himself in a position to see what was going on. Lot knew they were not from Sodom and

Gomorrah. He had enough knowledge in him to know that they had some form of God in them. The Word says that he bowed himself with his face to the ground. So, he knew that. People are not as nascent or ignorant as they pretend. Lot put himself in a position to see what was coming upon him. In our day, that is called the "spirit of truth." That is the Holy Ghost baptism. That is called John 15:16, who said, you didn't choose me but I chose you. He chose us. No man can come to God, unless the spirit draws him. Lot put himself in a position. He kept himself in a position that he could be abreast; that he could be awake; that he could be alert; that he could be intuitive to see what was going on. If you are spending all day in front of the TV, how can you see what is going on? And you let your kid's watch all kind of stuff on the computers. They are on the phone. You are wrapped-up in your own little world. How can you see what is coming upon you?

Wake up today. Wake up today. Wake up today. Wake up today. Some people visit certain churches, and all they can remember is the fashion display. All they can remember is the choir. None of that is going to take you to heaven, but the Word of God will. And if the word of God is not being preached in truth, if it is not being preached in purity, you are still not going to be saved. It says in Genesis 19:2, **And he said, Behold now, my lords, turn in, I pray you, into your servant's house, and tarry all night, and wash your feet, and ye shall rise up early, and go on your ways. And they said, Nay; but we will abide in the street all night.** So, the angels knew they had come there to see, to spot out. But Lot also knew that night time was when the devil really starts acting a fool. And while he may not have had his eyes open to these two angels, Lot wanted to protect them. He did not want them to be infested. He did not want them to be contaminated, because he knew his city. He knew his city. He knew the folks that he dwelled among. He did not want these people to be contaminated. He wanted to protect them. He wanted to shelter them, because he knew, especially at night, stuff was going to be jumping off. He knew it. This is the way we must be about what God has given us, our miracles, our healings, the fact that we can come here and open up his Bible. We can understand what he says and the truth. We have to be the same way about the truth; to not let anybody speak strange doctrines to us and say the wrong things. He says search the scriptures, for in them you have eternal life. Don't take my word, but take my word to the Word. What is God saying to you? He's talking right to you today? He is making you accountable today for the love He has shown you all your life. He's watched over you. He has treated you just like you were a little baby. He has been so long suffering. Some of you have spit in his face over and over, over and over, over and over again. You have lied to him. You made vow after vow. He has healed you of cancer. He has taken the lump out of your breast. He has cleared your mind. He has healed your marriage. He has put food on your table. But he has come to the end of His long suffering, and He's going to make some of you an example of what His love will do when it is neglected, when it is not held high. Some of you still do not have family altars in your home. You still let these children do whatever they want to do. You are going to be held accountable. You are still not showing love. You are still saying all damnable things out of your mouth. And then, you want to take those same lips and put them on your companion. But God's watching you. You are still indulging in pornography. You are still giving into lust. You are still giving in to lasciviousness. He said "Go away, sin no more, unless a worse thing comes upon you." Now, maybe some of you have said by your own admission that you almost died. Surely you will. He went through so much to save you. He wants you to remember. When we take account of ourselves, the Bible says, "Let a man examine himself." He said to judge yourself. Stop and think about how He saved you. That was love. He has been watching over you and protecting your family. He has been keeping you week after week, day after day. Remember, when you just could not sleep, but now you sleep so soundly they have to come and shake you. He's saying to remember His love, His long suffering. He's done for you what no other God could do. You made idol gods, but they could not redeem you. They could not save you.

Take another look at God today. Genesis 19:3 says, **And he pressed upon them greatly; and they turned in unto him, and entered into his house; and he made them a feast, and did bake unleavened bread, and they did eat.** As you go on and read the rest of the story about Lot, he pressed upon them. Lot offered the wicked men who wanted to perform homosexual acts upon the two angels his two virgin daughters. Notice the characteristic of Lot as you go on to read this profound chapter. Lot was willing to risk his life. Would he let them in? We let anybody come into our Eden. We let anybody come in. You come to the services. God has blessed you. By the time the night comes, you are so discontented because you have not stepped out. You allowed them to come in and pollute you; to come in and contaminate you, some disgruntled member of the church; somebody who left the church. Shut that rascal up. What has he done for you today? He picked you up from the muck and the mire. You have got a story to tell. You have got a testimony. Don't let anybody rob you. Don't let anybody deceive you. Remember when you were staying in a shelter? Come on. Remember when your body was racked with pain? Don't let the devil deceive you. His love comes with a price. Whether you want to or not, you are going to have to pay up. You are going to pay up. You are going to have to pay. And He's coming with such a strong message. Sometimes you don't know what you have, and He's trying to warn you. He's giving you a way of escape called the Rapture. That is when Jesus will come back for His bride. The bride of Christ will be those who are living holy, full of the good Holy Ghost. Hebrews 9:27-28, **And as it is appointed unto men once to die, but after this the judgment: So Christ was once offered to bear the sins of many; and unto them that look for him shall he appear the second time without sin unto salvation.** Those who are looking for Jesus to come, they will be clean. They will be ready. He has made a way of escape for you, just like Lot when he was in those wicked cities of Sodom and Gomorrah, yet his righteous soul remained faithful. He was not intermingling and intertwining with them. The word says he sat at the gate. He sat at the place where he could get a view of everything that was coming in and going out. You might be saying, "Reverend Thomas, where is that gate?" It is at His feet. That is the gate. It is the key to the city. It is at the feet of Jesus. It is in your prayer time. When you push your plate back, afflicting your soul, that is when your vision becomes crystal clear. When you push your plate back; when you start crying out, your mind becomes enlightened. Oh my God! A member of our congregation sings a song. She says "it's when I'm on my knees." She says, "When I close my eyes there is no darkness there, because He meets me there." He meets me in my prayer time. He illuminates me. He strengthens me. He lifts me up while the storm maybe going on inside outside of me. In my prayer time, it is me and my Saviour. He's telling me all about how I am going to make it over. He's strengthening me. He's pushing me on, telling me, "You can make it. You can make it."

The great gospel Historians, they are there to remind us. The Lord will bring back to your memory such soldiers as Shadrach, Meshach and Abednego. He's saying, "See, I will be with you all the way until the end." There was a king in the day of the three Hebrew boys. He had no knowledge of Christ, but in the furnace he said, "I see four men, one looks like the Son of God." Who taught him? It was the spirit of God. It was the spirit of truth. He told them He would be with them all the way until the end of the world. Then, there was Daniel. He was in the lion's den. But love, love, love shut up the lion's mouth. Love, love shut the lion's mouth. Esther, there she was, yielding to love. Mordecai came and said, "Don't think you are going to hide away in this palace." But who knows? You were brought to the kingdom for such an hour as this. Don't you see your responsibility? You were born, shaped, and molded for this hour. You were born right on-time. I do not care what they say about how you were premature. I don't care what they say about how your mother had to stay on bed rest. I don't care what they say about how you were a month late. You were right on-time to hear the gospel of Jesus Christ. When love turns to hate: Take another look at God.

YOUR WAY OUT—TAKE IT!

This is your way out. He made a way out for you. 1 Corinthians 15:51, **Behold, I shew you a mystery.** He is saying, I am showing you a way out. Don't you feel like leaving this world sometimes? You just want to pack your bags. But here I have a destination in mind for you. **Behold, I shew you a mystery; We shall not all sleep, but we shall all be changed. In a moment, in the twinkling of an eye, at the last trump: for the trumpet shall sound, and the dead shall be raised incorruptible, and we shall be changed**

(1 Corinthians 15:51-52). We shall be changed, We shall be changed, We shall be changed. Hallelujah! We shall be changed. Oh, that excites me. We shall be changed. There is no demon in hell Lucifer can't stop me. We shall be changed. Oh my God! Job is saying, "Though he slays me, yet shall I trust him." He said, even though, I may be dead but in my flesh I am going to see the Saviour of the whole world. I am going to see him for myself. I am going to kneel down at His feet for myself. We shall, we shall, we shall be changed. No matter what this old world says, we shall be changed. **For this corruptible must put on incorruption, and this mortal must put on immortality. So when this corruptible shall put on incorruption, and this mortal shall have put on immortality, then shall be brought to pass the saying that is written, Death is swallowed up in victory. O death, where is thy sting? O grave, where is thy victory? The sting of death is sin; and the strength of sin is the law. But thanks be to God, which giveth us the victory through our Lord Jesus Christ** (1 Corinthians 15:53-57). See, it is only through him; not their way. You can't make any way to heaven. Ask the guys in the tower of Babel. **Therefore, my beloved brethren, be ye stedfast, unmoveable, always abounding in the work of the Lord, forasmuch as you know that your labour is not in vain in the Lord** (1 Corinthians 15:58).

ARMAGEDDON

When love turns to hate, take another look at God. The nations are lining up today for the battle of Armageddon. Look around; this is such a late hour. This is such a later hour. In the battle of Armageddon, if you don't know it today, is how the Tribulation Period will end. And the Tribulation Period, in case you do not know it today, is the answer. The devil himself will be destroyed at the very end of the Tribulation Period. The Tribulation Period has been made for everyone who is not full of the good Holy Ghost. You may be saved, but you may not, if you have not obeyed him. Luke 24:49, **And behold, I send the promise of my Father upon you: but tarry ye in the city of Jerusalem, until ye be ensued with power from on high.** Receiving the Holy Ghost is a command to all of us. Remember, in the first few chapters of Revelations, He said you are lukewarm. Because you are not cold, you are not hot. I am going to spew you into the Tribulation Period. Who was so close within his mouth that he could spew him out? Christians, Christianity. He loved you so much that He held you in His mouth, close to his heart. But you would not go on, so he will have to spit you out in this hour. And you will be ready for the Tribulation Period. Look around, look around, look around, in this late hour, at what God will destroy in the Tribulation Period. Many stand against God. They blaspheme his name, no matter what He does. They want no part of Him, seeking instead their fornication, their thefts, their devil worship, their witchcraft, and their sins. No value is placed on a soul. On and on they go in their sins. They die without calling out to God for forgiveness. Men's hearts are going harder and harder. Things will not get better. The spirit of the antichrist is changing the behavior of people more and more. It is influencing the actions of the government. How many people are really living holy and free from all sin? How many are looking for Jesus to come? The world mocks people like that. Scoffers, they make fun of the ones who really believe in the coming of the Lord. They are mocking. Some of us give into the mocking; we are worried about what people say. We better be worried about what Jesus is saying. And the nations today, they are preparing for the battle of Armageddon. The stage is being set. Nations are crying for peace. But when they cry for peace and safety, sudden destructions will come upon them. As travail upon a woman with child, and they shall not escape. America. Yes, the United States of America, she will be caught lacking. As a whole, America has forgotten God. When the Bible and prayer in schools were taken away, we were set on a path that we will never recover from. Many ministers no longer preach about the blood of Jesus, a born again experience, or that sin belongs to the devil. Think about that. You think about that. People, they are ready right now for the battle of Armageddon. Just think, the shadows of Armageddon, they are falling upon the Earth. The nations are right on-time. The nations are right on-time. My God, you say what kind of message is this? This message is that when love turns to hate, you better take another look at God. Think about nations. The shadows of Armageddon are falling upon the Earth. Did you know the nations are right on-time? They are lining up right now. When you read the newspaper, you see more and more nations trying to join the EU nations (or the common market, as it is being called today). Study Ezekiel Chapters 36-39. Ezekiel prophesied that Israel would become a nation. The Israelites started going back to their home in 1921. In May 1948 they became a nation. That is what the Bible talks about in Matthew 24, the fig tree. He is talking about the holy land. He is talking about the promise land. Whether you know it or not today, we are right on-time. The nations are lining up. They are lining up for the battle of Armageddon. Where would you be in the wicked and perverse hour without the love of God on your side? Will He turn His back on you? Was He talking to you about mocking and calamity coming? You, young people, will you be caught in your sin? Will you be caught today? Will you be caught without a Saviour on your side? The shadows of Armageddon, the nations, they are lined up. They are lined up for the greatest battle ever. The Jews paid and continue to pay for crucifying the Messiah. The antichrist is alive and on Earth today. When he makes his appearance, the Jews will follow him. Their eyes have been blinded by deceit. But when he sets himself up as God, they will realize. They will realize that they tried to destroy love, which was Christ. They will realize that their true Messiah had already come. They will realize, oh my God, when the antichrist goes up and says I am god, they will realize. They will realize that the little lamb, Oh my God, that it was true what the wise man was saying; that they came from afar. They said where is His star? They say they have seen it; they have come to worship Him. They will realize. Oh my God! They will realize that the crown was masked into His head. They will realize what had been done when they pierced him in his side, when they scourged him with vinegar, and beat him. They will realize that was our true King. They will realize that was really our Saviour. Yet they cried, "Let his blood be on us. "And it is. Think about it. Think about the footsteps of Jesus. His footsteps will be visible to every child of God. But there is still hope today. You can make it with God today. You can make it with God today. Through consecration, through dedication, through prayers and fastings, and living in the Word, you will be able to step right into His steps. You will do His works. Your hands will be His hands. Your eyes will be His eyes. Your mouth, your vocal organs, will be His. Your feet will be His. Your body will be His. You will be totally possessed by Him, and you will be used by Him, if you dare to walk in His steps. What about you today? Do you dare to walk in the steps of Jesus?

A RAGING SEA

When love turns to hate, take another look at God. Have you thought about being possessed by Jesus? Have you thought about the man that walked the Sea of Galilee? It says that the people came looking for Jesus, and He had to get in the ship. He had to get out of the water, and He taught them from the ship. But there was a storm, and the sea was raging. Peter looked at Him, and he was trying to see. He said who is master that you bid me come? And the Lord is telling you today come, come, come? It is a stormy sea. The storm is raging. Oh my God! He is saying come to Jesus. Come to Jesus. Don't you hear Him talking to you today? He is saying come to Jesus. Oh my God! The shadows of Armageddon, the nations, they are lining up. Maybe you do not understand this message today. Some of you do not understand. But why get an understanding? Just obey God. Come to Jesus. Think about how long He has been waiting on you. The Lord God Himself has yearned for this hour. He has yearned for vengeance. Have you thought about it? He has yearned for vengeance of His son, Jesus. He's yearned, He's yearned, and He's yearned. He has been yearning for His son, Jesus. And all in heaven, our loved ones that are in heaven today, they are youthful. But then you will look upon Jesus and see where the crown of thorns was placed upon His head. You will see where they tore the ligaments out of His back. And you will see where they whipped Him. If you look at His hands, you will see the holes. They will still be there where they pierced Him and went through the bone of His arm. And you will, if you look down at His feet, see where the nails went through them. He will challenge you to thrust your hand in His side, like He did Thomas. What about you? Have you thought about being possessed by Jesus Christ? When love turns to hate, take another look at God.

Oh God! Oh God! Please forgive me for sinning against you. I have come home, never to leave you again. Oh Lord, I want to love you with my whole heart! I want to love you with all of my might and with all of my mind! And by faith in the blood, give me that love. Save my soul! Save my soul! Save my soul! Come on in Jesus! If you mean that, then you will have that love tonight.

Part 4

When A Sinner Dies

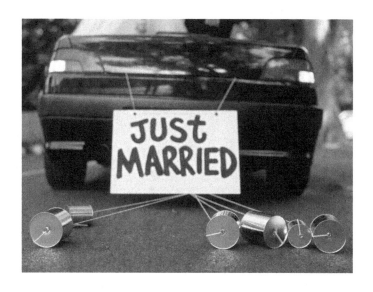

CHAPTER 12

WHAT, YOU DON'T LOVE
ME ANYMORE?

What, you don't love me anymore? 2 Timothy 4:10 says, **For Demas hath forsaken me, having loved this present world.** You know, it's really something to think about how the Lord drew each and every one of us through great love. Not only did He draw us in with His love, but John 3:16 says, **For God so loved the world, that he gave his only begotten Son, that whosoever believeth in him should not perish, but have everlasting life.** God is our Father, and Jesus is our Saviour. God is our Father, and Jesus is our Saviour. The Holy Spirit is our teacher, comforter and guide. The Holy Spirit is the one that convicts us. The Holy Spirit is the one that is used to make us aware something is wrong in our lives, so that we can cry out to God through Jesus Christ. So, let's make sure we keep that straight. God is our Father. Jesus is our Saviour. The Holy Spirit is our comfort, our guide and our teacher. Yet the mystery is that they are all God. There are some religions that only teach to baptize in the name of Jesus. That's false doctrine, for the Bible teaches us that we need to be baptized in water in the name of the what? The father, the Son, and the Holy Spirit. Isaiah 29:13-14 says, **Wherefore the Lord said, Forasmuch as this people draw near to me with their mouth, and with their lips do honour me, but have removed their heart far from me, and their fear toward me is taught by the precepts of men.** The Lord is saying, yeah, they come near Me, but they don't give Me all of themselves. They only give Me mental assent, the Lord is saying. That's something we can see in our daily lives. People say the words, "I love you" so loosely. Some people use "I love you" when they mean "I lust you". Some use "I love you" when they want to justify getting married after they've been shacking up and living like dogs. Others use "I love you," oh my God, when they get married, because they want to have sex instead of waiting on the right one. What, you don't love me anymore? Listen to it. The Lord says, yet they draw to Me, but only with their mouth. Their lips issue forth honor, the Lord is saying. The Lord desires to be honoured and praised in the heart, but most people won't give Him their whole hearts. People will talk about what they're going to do, and how they're going to do this, but if that desire does not come from the heart, nothing will take place beyond thinking about it or saying it. People can say all day long "Reverend! Reverend! I'll be there for you Reverend! I'm going to stand by you and for you. Reverend, I'm going to support this ministry with my finances." But if you look in their heart, they never intend to do any of the things they have said. **Therefore, behold, I will proceed to do a marvellous work among this people, even a marvellous work and a wonder: for the wisdom of their wise men shall perish, and the understanding of their prudent men shall be he hid** (Isaiah 29:14). So, Isaiah was saying here, especially at the end of verse 13, there are people that don't even love the Lord, but he was trying to teach his people how to love Him. Listen to that! He said at the end of verse 13, **and their fear toward me is taught by the precepts of men.** No doubt, men who don't even know God, men who haven't studied the Word of the Lord are attempting to teach others about a God they don't know. **For when for the time ye ought to be teachers, ye have need that one teach you again which be the first principles of the oracles of God; and are become such as have need of milk, and not of strong meat. For every one that useth milk is unskillful in the word of righteousness: for he is a babe. But strong meat belongeth to them that are of full age, even those who by reason of use have their senses exercised to discern both good and evil** (Hebrews 5:12-14). I Corinthians, Chapter 13, that's the love chapter that teaches us all about the quality we should have in our lives. Our love for the Lord should equal up to Matthew the 5th chapter, that's the beatitudes, and John the 17th chapter, which is the high priestly prayer, the Sermon on the Mount. Does your life add up to all of those chapters in the Bible? 1 Corinthians 13:4-5 says, **Charity** [or love] **suffereth long, and is kind; charity envieth not; charity vaunteth not itself, is not puffed up, Doth not behave itself unseemly, seeketh not her own, is not easily provoked, thinketh no evil.** So many people marry under false pretences. Others help people under false pretences. For it says, love *suffers long*. Don't be sick more than a few days; don't be broke more than a month. What, you don't love me anymore? The Bible says, what you do to the least of these, you have also done this to Me. The world is starving for love. The world is starving for love. So many marriages are destroyed because of a lack of divine love; human love is not enough. Many homes are just a bombshell of corruption; a bombshell of disappointment, because there is no love.

YOU NEED LOVE

You can grow up without many things such as wealth, fame, brand-named clothes, ***but you need love*** to thrive. You need love. You need love to grow into a valuable adult. So many people, so many children are growing up in this world and don't even have a chance, because love hasn't even been demonstrated to them. What, you don't love me anymore? That's what the Lord is talking to us about today. You love Him when it is convenient for you. You love the Lord when it makes you feel good, and you love doing stuff for the Lord when it's going to shine a light on you; make you appear as a true winner. But that's not really love. It says, love suffereth long and is kind. Charity envieth not does not have any jealousy. You have that jealous spirit? Are you envious of other people? It says, charity vaunteth not itself. *Look at me! Look at me! Look at what I've done! Look at how well I did! Look! Look! Look!* He said, that's not real love. Verse 5, **do not behave itself unseemly**—act a fool. I just summed that one up. **Seeketh not her own.** *Look at me!* **Is not easily provoked.** Some of you all get mad so quickly. You can't have the love of God. **Thinketh no evil; Rejoiceth not in iniquity, but rejoiceth in the truth**, love's the truth. What, you don't love me anymore because I told you the truth about yourself?

217

When you go to God's Word, some always want to read about them walking on the water. They want to read about only the good, using the power of the Lord. Yeah, well, the Lord's love also chastens, corrects and knocks down, so it can be rebuilt. That's God's love too! God's love is judgment to shake you; shake your little boat so you can wake up and see that you don't have that much time left; get your act together. That's still God's love. God's love is to warn you to get yourself together! Some of you are so deceived about love. You've got such a controlling spirit. You want people to do what you want them to do when you want them to do it. You think that's love. No, you act like that because you are incomplete. And if you go on and check people in your family, they get mad just like that. They want to be controlling too. The Bible says you need to get that destroyed! You need to get it destroyed from the root. In my family, my mom had cancer, but it stopped with me. A whole lot of different things have happened in my family, like have happened in your family. But when you get a real born again experience, such as the love of God, it has to stop, because light and darkness can't dwell in the same place. So, if you're still doing some of the same things you did when you were lost, maybe you didn't get the love of God, because that's part of salvation. When you receive a real born again experience, you get love, faith, joy, peace; all of these things. And if you are still doing the same bad things, I'm telling you, you need to check your salvation. Everybody's saved today. Everybody's saved. Everybody's an evangelist. Everybody can prophecy. Everybody *has a word*. The Lord does not use lay people with His gifts. As a matter of fact, I don't believe there are too many people in this final hour with His gifts. There is a great price to be paid so that the power of God can flow through a person on a continuous basis; not many can have His gifts. The separation and praying, how much you have to be in God's presence, separated from people; that is the price you pay. That's something to think about. How humble you must be, how you have to be so possessed by God, knowing His word, having that word hid in your heart, standing for the truth in opposition of whoever it is. The Lord said **because strait is the gate, and narrow is the way, which leadeth unto life,** in Matthew 7:13-14, **few** be there that find it. Find, seek, search, hunt for it. **Charity suffereth long, and is kind; charity envieth not; charity vaunteth not itself, is not puffed up, Doth not behave itself unseemly, seeketh not her own, is not easily provoked, thinketh no evil; Rejoiceth not in iniquity, but rejoiceth in the truth; Beareth all things, believeth all things, hopeth all things endureth all things** (I Corinthians 13:4-7). As soon as you get mad, you want to run and separate yourself from everyone; you want to leave the church when the truth finds you out; *no, that is not the church for me.* But you still are taking *you* with *you* wherever *you* go. *You* are the problem. What, you don't love me no more?

We love it when our refrigerators are full. We love it when the Lord is blessing us, and people are saying good things about us. But it's the same God that wants to whip your butt. It's the same God that knocks you down; causes you to trip over yourself. The Lord said in His Word, But if you're a son or a daughter of mine I'm going to chasten you. I'm going to correct you, because I want you to do well. Hebrews 12:5-10 says, **My son, despise not thou the chastening of the Lord, nor faint when thou art rebuked of him: For whom the Lord loveth he chasteneth, and scourgeth every son whom he receiveth. If ye endure chastening, God dealth with you as with sons; for what son is he whom the father chasteneth not? But if ye be without chastisement, whereof all are partakers, then are ye bastards, and not sons. Furthermore we have had fathers of our flesh which corrected us, and we gave them reverence: shall we not much rather be in subjection unto the Father of spirits, and live? For they verily for a few days chastened us after their own pleasure; but he for our profit, that we might be partakers of his holiness.**

THE TRUE VINE

John the 15:1-2 says, **I am the true vine, and my Father is the husbandman. Every branch in me that beareth fruit, he purgeth it,**

that it may bring forth more fruit. Verse 6 and 7 says, **If a man abide not in me, he is cast forth as a branch, and is withered; and men gather them, and cast them into the fire, and they are burned. If ye abide in me, and my words abide in you, ye shall ask what ye will, and it shall be done unto you.**

What people define as "love" nowadays, you can't even find in the Bible. As long as you got money, "I love you." As long as you can do what I want you to do, "I love you." You'll be surprised how many marriages in the churches are buying love. "Come on. Go with me to this dinner. I'll get you a suit. No, you're supposed to want to be with me. Come on go to this affair." You can't even enjoy the service, because you're wondering if your husband is looking at somebody else. That is not love. That's not love. That's not love. Many people have been so deceived about what love really is. Love is enduring, it lasts; it holds on. Love builds up. What is that? Virtuous woman, that's a woman that's full of God's love. The Bible says she gets up early and gets her house ready. She gets up before the rest of the family and makes sure they have food and clothing. She knows who's coming in and out of her house. A virtuous woman knows how to please her husband.

I Corinthians 13:8-10 say, **but whether there be prophecies, they shall fail; whether there be tongues, they shall cease; whether there be knowledge, it shall vanish away. For we know in part, and we prophecy in part. But when that which is perfect is come, then that which is part shall be done away with.** But prophecy's, they have not stopped. Tongues have not stopped. And some people, when they read this scripture, want to justify why they don't allow tongues in their church. The Bible tells us that a person does not have the baptism in the Holy Ghost until the Lord has the tongue. Speaking in tongues whenever you get ready, well, that can't be the Holy Ghost, can it? **And they were all filled with the Holy Ghost, and began to speak with other tongues, as the Spirit gave them utterance** (Acts 2:4). Some people speak in tongues and use that same tongue to blaspheme God's name [curse]. Curse words blaspheme the name of the Lord. You've got to think about this; you're not going to be any holier in heaven than you are on the day you receive the baptism in the Holy Ghost. He's not coming to an unclean temple. Most of the people you know that speak in tongues do not have the real bible Holy Ghost. They have a form, but they have denied the power of God. The Lord said if you love me you're going to keep my commandments. He said in Acts the 5th chapter He gives the Holy Ghost to those who obey Him. There's no way you're going to have the Holy Ghost with the evidence of speaking in tongues while you're shacked up with somebody, while you're with somebody that's not your husband, not your wife. There is no way you have the baptism in the Holy Ghost, and you're smoking. Your body is supposed to be the temple of the Holy Ghost. There is no way you're going to have the baptism in the Holy Ghost by not speaking to your neighbor. It's not going to happen. There is no Bible for it! What, you don't love me anymore? There's no way.

BELIEVE ME

Jesus saw Peter and asked him a profound question in John the 14:11-12. It says, **Believe me that I am in the Father, and the Father in me: or else believe me for the very works' sake. Verily, verily, I say unto you, He that believeth on me, the works that I do shall he do also; and greater works than these shall he do; because I go unto my Father.** Now, people always want to say this; that he that believeth on me is going to do the works of Jesus. But what the Lord is talking about is if you believe in Him, you're going to believe the part about being holy. If you believe in Him, you're going to believe that part about being separated from the world. If you believe in Him, you're going to believe the part about the soul that sinneth it shall die. That's what the Lord was talking about. So, this applies to you. People always want to quote Romans. Oh, and we know that all things work together for the good of those who love the Lord. Don't forget the rest of it; and *are the called according to his purpose.* People take the scriptures and try to justify themselves for staying in sin. *No weapon formed against me shall prosper.* No! You're getting evicted because you didn't pay your rent! That is not a weapon formed against you, rascal! Your lights are out because you bought shoes instead of getting on a payment plan. Now stop lying on God! Oh, no weapon formed against me. I don't care what they're doing on these jobs. You've been gossiping and tearing other people down. Now it's your turn to receive some of what you put out. All of a sudden, **no weapon formed against you shall prosper.** Cut it out! Cut it out! "Oh, my husband, he's not talking to me." You have talked down to him and treated him like he was such a dog. Now, all of a sudden, he's starting to wake-up, and you're quoting **no weapon formed against me shall prosper.** No, you should have said that scripture when you wanted to say something back, yet you should have shut your mouth. You should have just said, "No weapon formed against me shall prosper, tongue. No weapon formed against me shall prosper. I know what self I know; what I'm about to do to you." You're about to go on a fast. "You are not about to tear my house up." Instead, you just lash out. *You just have to get the last word,* and it has cost you over and over again, hasn't it? People just have to know you're in charge. You want everybody to obey you. When I read the gospel, it said that the man was the head of the household. He said to follow your husband as he follows Christ. If he is not following Christ, don't you follow him. He might lead you into a ditch. That husband—that wife will lead your soul right to the pit of hell.

Some are not paying tithes. You fool! That ten percent belongs to the Lord. You don't let anybody talk you out of missing church; paying the tenth that you owe. The tenth is holy, child! Not paying will cause God's hands to be tied for you, and you will go lacking. That's the reason some of you haven't achieved more in your life; robbing God. When I start talking about sex, money, and these nappy head companions, and these wayward children, people just start scratching and blinking. They start nodding. They go into a deep coma. But I talk them right back up out of that coma. You hear me neighbor? What, you don't love me anymore? People always want to talk about "Oh my God, the woman with the alabaster box of oil, did you know she was a prostitute? She was out in the streets." But how are you treating the Lord? In Jeremiah, the Lord said you go away and lay up with other gods. You go up and lay up with the basketball games. Oh my God, March madness. And you know, huh? You go watch the championship instead of being in Sunday school. Those people in that game don't even know you're around. But you need strength for your mind; missing the services and missing your prayer time to be out in the street. You know you got service on Sunday, just wearing yourself out completely; then, always nodding in the church and then wonder why, "I don't know why my prayers aren't being answered." What, you don't love me anymore?

A GOOD INVESTMENT

When you first came into the knowledge of the truth; when the Lord first looked at you and accepted you and put that blood on your soul; you wanted to spend as much time with him as you could. You had reckless faith; nothing could stop you. Now, nothing can get you going. Your relationship with the Lord is only as strong as how much you invest in it. It's the same way with your marriage. Your marriage shouldn't be over with when you get married. When you get married, you know you have to work at it every single day. You've got to work at it every day, and it requires work, and it requires communication. In the Song of Solomon, it's such a wonderful love song, such a wonderful love story. It talks about a lady who went out looking for her love. She didn't find him at first. When you are in a relationship with the Lord, He has feelings. Did you know that? Go back to "in the natural," when you first met your companion. You couldn't even sleep. Boy, your heart started beating fast. And now some days you wish your heart would just stop. That'll show them, if I just died right in the service. But you better not bank on that. They might start clapping. You better not bank on that. And some of you, you talk the love right out of your marriage. You are not perfect. You are not all of that. Wouldn't anybody else want to marry you? Do what's right in the eyes of God. You have to serve your companion as unto God. Some of you, when you got married, were not saved, but now you are. God will help you. It's very hard to have a companion that doesn't know God, but you do. Maybe one of you in the marriage lost your job. All of a sudden, you're impatient. That's not love. The man, his hair is receding, "Oh, you're not fine like you used to be." "But I'm still me." Gain a little weight, lose a little weight; I'm still me! *You have to marry for love*. You have to marry for love, no other reason. This is where many couples miss it. Nothing else is going to keep you together. When you first came to the Lord, nothing stopped you. You didn't miss services, and you spent time with the Lord. Everything you're ever going to be is through your intimate relationship with the Lord. When does that take place Reverend? In your prayer time. What the Lord reveals to you, what He's expecting of you, all the sweet you know, the Bible is little love letters that He gives you. When you spend time with Him, when you study His word, and you study the history along with it, the Lord is letting you know what great price His Son paid for you to be in this moment. Resent it, or be thankful for it. You are in such an hour as this right now. Regret it, or be excited. You are in one of the greatest hours ever, and you ought to rejoice! You are in an hour when the prophets of old wished they could have been in our day. You're not excited about the Lord, because you haven't studied Him. Jeremiah 29:11-14(a) says, **For I know the thoughts that I think toward you, saith the Lord, thoughts of peace, and not of evil, to give you an expected end. Then shall ye call upon me, and ye shall go and pray unto me, and I will hearken unto you. And ye shall seek me, and find me, when ye shall search for me with all of your heart. And I will be found of you, saith the Lord.** We know that the joy of the Lord is my strength. You're not happy today? You don't have peace? You need to go back to the Word. The Lord promised to keep you in perfect peace whose mind is stayed on Him. Jesus said when He was here, that said if you *continue* in His word; dwell then you'll be His disciple. The Lord in the book of John said that the sheep of the Lord know His voice, and the voice of a stranger they're not going to entertain.

But how can you love the Lord if you don't even know anything about Him, His ways, and His promises? People blame God for sin, sickness, and death. He's not the author of any of it. When my son, Daniel, got killed, people were talking about, "Well, I guess God had another plan for him." God didn't have anything to do with Daniel's death! The truth is, if it had not been for God, Daniel could have died a more horrific death. He could have died much earlier. But because of the grace of God, He got me ready, which I will never cease to honor and give Him thanks for looking out for me. Certainly, I would have fallen apart, but His grace kept me. The Lord held me, and I held on.

LIVING IN A WORLD OF SIN

I am in this world, but I'm no longer of the world; no longer a sinner! Yet I had cancer. Who did sin? My mother or me? Neither one of us. I'm in a world where sin has control. The bible says that healing is the children's bread. Yes! Yes! Yes! I live in a world where you can live in so much fear, because so many things are happening. But I'm going to have peace, because that was what the Lord died for. When He died, He left me peace. When He died, He left me joy. When he died, He left me healing. When He died, He said I could have a sober mind. When He died, he said I could stay in my youth. I didn't have to get bent over and be all crippled up over, even though there are good people, holy people who have afflictions. But this is what He promised me, as Him being my lover; the lover of my soul. He says He belongs to me, and that I belong to Him. And when you have an intimate relationship, you don't let days and weeks go on without communion, without talking to them. You don't go to bed without saying, "Goodnight." You don't go to bed without talking to the Lord and revisiting your day to see how you can do better the next. What is it? Did I treat every person right? Did I speak what You wanted me to speak to every person? If not, then you need to repent, then, you can go to bed knowing that all is well. When you wake up in the morning, the first thing you do is talk to that love, that great love. "Good morning sweetie." You are thanking Him for the blood that kept you all night. Some of you are stumbling in your life, because your faith is wavering. But an unexercised faith is not going to work for you. He says but grow in grace in the knowledge of our Lord and saviour Jesus Christ. You're having major things happen to you in your life, but you are unprepared. Think about when you first meet somebody. Now, in the world, I read that they are having sex on the first date. There was a time when you got to know one another. You didn't just meet somebody the first day and bring them over to your house. They might be a serial killer. They might be a paedophile, talking about, "I'll watch the kid." People's minds are bad, degraded. So, when you first meet somebody you kind of get to see what you have in common. Don't try and make something fit that is not fitting. You're engaged. You're thinking about getting married. You got any questions? Don't do it! You have any concerns, other than being a little nervous? Don't do it! Don't do it! I wouldn't. Don't do it! Because everything calms down. At first, when you're married, you're all under each other. You're just all over the place. Yeah, but wait. After a while, you start living life. You want to marry somebody that's compatible to you. Many people marry for the wrong reasons. Even though a person might be called by God to be your companion, you still have to grow together. For when you marry a person, that's the Lord's will for you. You have less friction.

WO-MAN

People are getting married for the wrong reasons today. I'm bringing up marriage because it's a close similarity to our relationship with the Lord. When the Lord made woman in the book of Genesis, He didn't go way across the world to get a part that she would become. No, He put man asleep, and Eve came out of his rib. That's how close the Lord desires to be with you. He wants you to know his thoughts. He wants you to know that when you see different things going on, He wants you to be able to discern it, not through the gift of discernment, but if you have the Holy Spirit, and you're walking with the Lord, the Lord said before things spring forth, I'm going to tell you of it. You might not know exactly what's going on, but because you're living with the Lord, the Lord can make some connection in your heart about certain things. There are certain things the Lord's not going to tell us about that, we must experience them. There are so many things you can save yourselves so much trouble from, if you just had an intimate relationship with the Lord. I mean, really knowing Him; learning Jesus. You have to learn Jesus in this final hour. There are so many Jesus' in the world today. There are people who literally call themselves the saviour of the world, but they're just cults. That's all it is, just a bunch of false doctrine. If you don't know your Lord, you're going to be swindled. You're going to be deceived. You're going to be talked out of attending the services. You have to know what your Lord will do and what your Lord will not do. Mathew 17:21 says, **Howbeit this kind goeth not out but by prayer and fasting**, and I'm adding *living in the word*. He says in 2nd Timothy to study, to show you're self-approved unto God, a workman that need not be ashamed rightly dividing the word of truth. You have to know that God is not a God who does not compromise with sin.

It's just so amazing to me when you have friends, and they go "Oh Reverend, you're such a great leader!" They come here and see this place. They come here, and we have published some books, and we're on T.V. They're so amazed! But when I start talking to them about the truth, which is the love of God, all of a sudden I'm not so great. All of a sudden, I'm not really a good preacher. No, they don't love the truth. But I am a lover of the truth! I love what the truth says! I love the word of God! I love thus saith the Lord! I love the Psalms! I love Genesis through Revelation! Oh, I love that Word. It's like manna in my bones! I love the Word! Oh, I love what it says! I love the hope that I have in it! I love how it encourages me. I love how the Lord knows everything that's going on in your life, even on this day that this message is touching each and every one of you reading it. What, you don't love me anymore? Think about all that God has done for you down in your life; every time He has brought you out. He didn't leave you to wallow in the mud! He didn't leave you to drown you in your own blood! The Lord gave you His blood so that you could live! He gave you His divine blood so that you could stand up! Jesus gave you His blood so that you could rise up! He gave you divinity! Yes! What, you don't love me anymore? You think about the price that He paid for you, and you think about God the Father, God the Son, and God the Holy Ghost. We didn't evolve from a monkey. But the Lord—the trinity—took His time. He thought about us having two eyes, and that we could live with one. He thought so much. The body is so complex; it's such a magnificent thing. The mind is so magnificent, no wonder it needs to be on the control of the Holy Spirit No wonder it needs to be under the control, the mass control of the Holy Spirit. Our minds can move a million miles a minute. How many countries have you been in since you've been in this ministry? How many thoughts have you been perplexed with, instead of yielding over to the power of the almighty God? How much is your mind, how much of your mind is leached today? How much is your mind leeched today with control? How much is your mind just so taken over? The Lord has delivered you over and over again, but you just keep on going back to the past; back to hurt feelings, causing you to be re-leached. And now, you're in a worse state than before you even knew God.

How often this week have you thought about committing adultery or engaging in pornography? It's going to be your death! What, you don't love me anymore? You love the praises; you love for people to pat you on the back. But many people don't want to be corrected. What, you don't love me anymore? When you're soaking in sin, degraded people just love a message that makes them feel comfortable. Everybody knows a sore that's covered up won't heal. The air has to get to it. It's not going to heal. In Jeremiah it says my people love this mess. They love deceit. You would be surprised how many churches open today are teaching nothing but deceit. They are teaching that damnable doctrine that no man can live free from sin. Can you please tell me why did they beat Jesus to death and He shed His blood? What, you don't love me anymore? Our world was dying. You were dying in your life, but then Jesus came along and rescued you. You have an opportunity in this ministry; you have an opportunity in T.V. land to be a person you never thought you could be, but you have to lay aside the sin and the weight that so easily besets you. You have to choose real love. Jesus said to know me is truth. He said to know me is to be free! Oh, not a freedom like this world talks about. In this world, people talk about being free when you win the lottery. Do the research on people who have won the lottery. Some wished they had never won it.

REAL LOVE

Real love is patient. Real love is longsuffering. Real love is kind. Real love forgives and understands. When you think about intimacy in marriage, it's something that God planned. Just because Adam failed the Lord, it didn't take the power out of intimacy. No! You think about two virgins coming together; they don't have to worry about the past. They will have no worries. There's no shame, because they haven't been touched by anybody else. I'm offering you, and you're offering me yourself. The Bible teaches us in one of Paul's writings that the woman's body does not belong to herself, neither does the husband's; it belongs to the wife. We have it all mixed-up. I had a person come in my office some years ago. I was talking to her because I wanted to know if my couples were getting it on [making love]. I want to know. I want to know if they're getting it on, because it's important. So, this lady came in, and I was talking to her (they no longer attend PFC) about something and said, "Sweetheart, when is the last time you and your husband made love?" "Oh, it's been about four months." I said, "Really? Four months?" I felt like saying Lazarus' been in the grave for four days. By now Lord, he stinketh. I said, "Why haven't you all got together? She said, "Because he didn't do what I said." This is what she told me out of her mouth. I thought to myself, "How horrible!" Love-making is very important. That's important in a marriage. It's a bond, a form of communication that the Lord has developed in marriage. It's an intimate way that a *husband* and a *wife* communicate towards one another. I'm not talking about how the world has degraded it and made it so filthy and so nasty. I'm talking about how the Bible says that when Adam saw Eve he saw they were both naked, and they were unashamed, because they were in God's truth. They were in the love of God, and they responded to the will of God. You have to think about the way we're made.

What, you don't love me anymore? "My husband, he does not really treat me like he used to." Are you the same person now that you were then when you got married? What? You put up all your favorite gowns; they're all you have. Locked them away with a triple lock. That's so unfair. What, you don't love me anymore? Some harbor resentment and bitterness in their hearts against their companion. You forget about what you have done. You know what the greatest thing about love is? Consideration, compassion, forgiveness and tenderness. This is missing from so many marriages today. Many people come into marriage already lame, halt and blind, both of them. They're already scarred. That's why the Lord encourages you to be virgins. Oh, don't be so stuck up today if you got married and you weren't a virgin. Learn, help some other person, teach somebody else. Those scars and deep wounds that are taken into our marriage, you just limp along.

Men have to learn how to be a companion; a helpmate. We are not help wanted. We are a helpmate, but we are not help wanted. We're not soliciting any ads. Men have to learn how to love their wives. You have to do the same thing you did in the beginning. Some men don't even want to help their wives with the children. But when people come over, they're just jumping up, running all around. No wonder the wife is stunned. She's watching. She knows it's all a show. Women and men, they're different. They're different. Women need to be primped. We need to be pre-meditated for, prepared for and sought after, and we need to be, you know. You get it, right? We need flowers and roses. When our hair is all over our head, we still need to be told we're beautiful. Don't just come in talking about, "Let's get it on!" with bad breath, have not washed up, haven't said hello to your wife in three days.

What, you don't love me anymore? That's the reason why the Lord gave us the scenario of Eve coming from Adam, not only to symbolize what He wants you to be in marriage, but how close He wants to be to us. Isn't that a type and shadow of when Jesus died on the cross, when they pierced Him in His side and out came the blood? We were born because that blood brought us redemption. So, I don't understand why people can constantly preach in and out that nobody can live free from sin, when they beat Jesus to death for sin-free living. In the Old Testament days, they used to sacrifice bulls and goats, but that spilled blood could not keep them; that was not the remedy; that was never God's divine plan. He just allowed it. We needed a remedy for sin, which was the spotless lamb, Jesus Christ. In John the 21, Jesus was straight forward when he asked Peter, do you love me. He was traveling with Him, and he had witnessed some great miracles, some great manifestations of the Lord. It's easy for us to love the Lord. It's easy for us to feel good about what's going on in the good times. Anybody can do that! But can you still love your husband when there's a disagreement? Can you agree to disagree without arguing, without cursing, without fighting? I can't see how you can say you're going to heaven while you're fighting with each other and fussing. I can't see it. Can you still love your wife, even though you don't understand her at this time? Can you still love her without taking the love out of your marriage, without going to the in-laws, without going to your family? When you just go to your prayer closet and tell what you say about me, right?

Oftentimes, when an accusation is brought up against a person, it's really that person with the problem. But they have to discover that they're the reason they are having a problem with you, right? So many times we point the finger; you, you, you, you, you, you, you, you, you, you. We have made a song out of it; you, you, you, you, you. But when you really get quiet before the Lord, "It's me Lord, standing in the need of prayer," that's what it's really all about. You may be so unhappy with yourself until you start pointing things out in your companion. What's wrong with you? I know you want stand up, bless your little heart, and say "Wait a minute. I've always been like this." You're uneasy, you're unhappy, you're discontented about who you are and the decisions you have made in your life. So what, you don't love me anymore? Some of you should be glad you have a companion, because nobody else would deal with you. The Lord barely deals with you, and He just keeps on anointing your companion. In the marriage vows that you recited, it says that you promised to obey, you promised to love, you promised to cherish in sickness and in health; through the good times and the bad times. You have good days at work, you have bad days at work, but you're still working. You have good days in your marriage, you have not-so-good days, but you still respect one another. She's still your queen and he's still your king, right? The Lord gets on us, doesn't He? We study His word, He gets on us and corrects us, but He's still our Saviour. It's because He loves us that He points us to the Word for the things going on in our lives. He knows you. He loves you, but He does not like the things that you are doing. Think about how the Bible teaches us that when the Rapture happens, the Lord is coming back for a church without spot, wrinkle, or blemish. Think about it, and look up all those words; spot, wrinkle, blemish. He's coming back for that. One's going to be in the field; two are going to be in the field; one is going to be taken, and one is going to be left. Two are going to be in the bed; one is going to be taken, and one is going to be left. Wouldn't it be nice if both of you were taken right? Show love. Make love. Showing love is for everybody. Making love is for the people that are married; a man and a woman.

NO BIBLE FOR IT

The scriptures don't endorse same-sex unions. There's no Bible for it. The scriptures do not endorse same-sex unions, and since I'm a believer of the scriptures and responsible for the whole Bible, I (this church) do not endorse it either. There's no Bible for it. There's no Bible for it. The bride is for a husband to love his wife, as Christ loved the church and gave His life for it. Some of you men don't even cook for your wives. You just think they're always supposed to be laying around waiting for you to get home. You want to go out and play all day; golf, basketball, but we can't even go to the beauty shop and get our nails done ("What are you going over there for?"). No, take care of yourself for yourself. Reverend Thomas looks beautiful. I look beautiful for myself. I look beautiful for myself. Do something for yourself; your hair, your nails. Get a pedicure every now and again. Keep yourself up for yourself. Look beautiful for yourself. You young girls keep yourselves dressed modestly, neatly and clean. Don't let these young guys put their hands all of over you, and don't you be all over them either. We have too many chemicals, products and processes that can help you look like a beautiful young lady and smell like one too. You go and hang out with your friends, and they think you've been in a salon. You come to church, and you look like you've been out there beating some trees or something. What are we going to do? And your hands, you want them to see your hands; you got your nails done. You know it's freezing out, but you got some shoes with your feet out, because you want them to see that your feet match the color of your nails. When it comes down to the church, your hair looks like a bird is nesting at the top of it. Your teeth are not brushed; your clothes, iron your clothes, then go to sleep in them, pop up and run down to the services. Lord, I honor you. You're so tired when you get here.

One of my kids, she's very talented. She can play by ear, she can write songs, she can mime, and she sings very well. She's grown and on her own now, but many years ago I was asking her to do some stuff in the church. It was like pulling teeth. Come on, sing! Write a song! Come on, play. You know, she played the keyboard. Oh ok. So, one time I went to her school. Everybody was like, "Yeah! Yeah!" I was like, "Who is that?" "Yeah! Yeah! Yeah!" "Who is that?" One day I went there, they had some kind of program at her school, and she was miming. I was like, "That's the one that lives with me?" People were standing up and yeah! They were standing on their feet. Yeah! Yeah! Yeah! I'm like, "Is that our child?" Another time, I went and she was singing, she was blowing up the song! She was singing off the chain! She was singing! I was like, "Our kid?" But that's where she wanted to be, so she put her heart into it. You're only going to get out of your relationship with the Lord what you put in it. The Lord has forgiven you, so now you have to learn how to forgive others, or else He won't hear you when you pray. Some of you would be more successful if you would just shut your big mouth. You always have an opinion. You can't raise a grown man! Cut that mess out! You can't raise a grown woman. Give her the money to get her nails and her hair done. And you're going to try and withhold your body so that you can teach him something. Ahh, but you better think about that one. You better think about that one. You can't make anybody sin, but you better make sure you're not a part of it. You can't make anybody lust or look after another woman or another man, but you better make sure that you don't have anything to do with it. You can't complain about something if you're not doing your best.

When is the last time you all have been out to dinner? When is the last time you all walked down the street holding hands? I'm not talking about fists, I'm saying holding hands. When is the last time you touched when you were riding in the car? "Don't touch me! Get your feet off of me! You're scratching me with those long corns!" Some of you, your mates could be gone for weeks. You haven't seen them; don't know where they are. You want to wear anything out of the house. Miss-match, match colors; you don't want them to. The first time some woman looks at your man; or maybe if you looked at him, you know what look I'm talking about. Some of you men, I'm telling you, you complain about your companion, but I know that song they used to say. I'm not going to sing it. When is the last time you all have been out to dinner? When is the last time you all did some stuff without the kids around? When is the last time you said, "I love you," to your companion? When is the last time you told him how beautiful he was to you? When is the last time you thanked him for doing something for you, instead of going, "You oops . . . ," "You should have had it done."? When is the last time you just said thank you? When is the last time you brought lunch up to her job? When is the last time you were up out of bed when they got home? I'm talking about you. You know you're still in the bed from the morning. When is the last time you gave them breakfast, either one? When is the last time, you know those outfits, where are they? Where are they? Are they taking up the draft in the window? Where are those outfits—you know, the one you wore in the beginning of your marriage? Are they closing up in the attic or the basement? Come on now. When is the last time you read the Word together? Stay together, stay in love.

CHAPTER 13
A CALL FROM THE BURNING BUSH

God is calling every single one of us. What He has called me to do may be different than what He has called you to do. When God calls you and you respond, you will be a success. If you respond, and if you do everything He is asking you to do, there is no way for you to fail. Why? Because there is no failure in God. This is what you have to get in your mind. Matthew 22:14 says, **For many are called, but few are chosen.** In order for you to rise up, you will have to overcome some obstacles in your life, maybe from childhood, such as jealousy, maybe it's low self-esteem, or not having a high school diploma, whatever it might be; any past failures.

You are the only one that can hinder yourself from what God has called you to do. In Exodus 2:11, we see that the Lord was calling Moses, but the first thing that he called him to was separation. Moses got ahead of God. He felt that in his heart, in his spirit, there was a need to defend his brethren. But he did not have it all figured out. The Lord doesn't give you all the "*pieces*" at one time. You must wait upon God. Waiting is key. God is calling you. God wants to use yourself in this final hour, but you have got to become a person that God can use. Exodus 2:11 says, **And it came to pass in those days, when Moses was grown.** So, we know he was a grown man. So, just because you are grown does not mean that you have it all figured out; that you have all the answers. It's precept upon precept. Amen. You still need direction. All sheep need a shepherd. I have a shepherd (Reverend Angley). I am a part of his sheep. Everybody needs a leader. Everybody needs direction. **The steps of a good man are ordered by the Lord: and he delighteth in his way** (Psalm 37:23).

BOOK SMART

You don't have it all figured out in your own life. You can have an inclination. You can study to be a nurse. My sister is a nurse. And my other sister has a certificate in pharmacy. But when you are in the classroom, all that stuff is good. Until you get out into the real word and put all that knowledge to use, you do not have anything. All you have are book smarts. But you have to have application. You might have it in your heart that God wants to use you. Now, you have to be made ready for that position. It is sort of like prayer. You can pray "Lord help me, God I want you to move for me." God works on both sides of the spectrum. He is working on that part of your life in what you are petitioning from the Lord. How many of you know that when you are living in the divine will of the Lord, He puts it in your heart what to pray for. The Holy Spirit will put it in your heart, in your spirit what to pray for. Those things that you need to pray for. And way on the other end, God is working, touching people's hearts and maybe dropping you to part-time so that you can go to Bible College. Maybe He is moving upon you to take some of the classes on the website from our home church. Maybe He is moving upon you to separate more. "Lord, I want to do your will." It is not easy. Don't ask for God's will in your life if you are not going to do it! You do not even know what that all means as we study our lesson today: A Call from the Burning Bush. Moses was there. He felt an inclination in his heart that he needed to defend his brethren. Yes, that was God's calling upon Moses' life, but not the way he thought.

WHAT THAT *SOMETHNG* IS

Many times we know, we believe, we feel, we sense, in our heart, "it is something God wants me to do," but that is not the time to run off and do it. You have to find out what that *something* is, and you have to be sure. You have to know what that something is, and you have got to be sure. As we read this chapter, you will find out that Moses ran out and killed one of his brethren. He slew one of the Egyptians, which were his brethren. He thought nobody saw him, but somebody did see him, which led him on a chase. So, Moses thought he would go and hide out. You have to be comfortable with what God has asked you to do. When you first start out, you might be in some classes. You might come in the church and get counselling. You have to come into the reality that *my calling is my calling and my calling alone.* You know it is good for all of us to sit in here and believe in our hearts that the Lord is calling us. I cannot go with you, and you cannot answer for me. There is no way that I can still be the person that God is calling me to be after 16 years. There is no way the ministry could still be in existence, if I owed allegiance to anybody and everybody. People want to tell you what to do. You have to find your place in God. You have to find your life in God, or put your life in God's hands. A time is going to come in your life when the real you, and where you stand with God, is going to be paramount. Oh, yes it is! You are not going to be in this ministry and riding the bus, so-to-speak, or riding in the car with somebody else. No! You are going to have one of those Harriet Tubman moments in your life. You are going to have an opportunity to go back; it just might cost you your life, to bring somebody out who might be pinned to the gates of hell; snatching them as if it were, brands from the fire. Are you going to do it? You are going to have a Rosa Parks experience where you decide, "Today, I am not bowing down. I am not compromising." And they might shackle you and chain you up. You have to know where you stand in this whole scheme of your calling with God.

THERE'S NO WAY

Some of you are so complacent and "everything is okay." That is why you have not received the Baptism of the Holy Ghost. It may be that you are not saved. There's no way you can have a real born-again experience and are seeking earnestly the Baptism of the Holy Ghost. The Bible let us know in Acts 5:32, that the Lord gives the Holy Ghost to those who obey Him. The Bible asks us in the Gospels, how is it that a natural man, if his son is hungry, will not give him bread. Why would that father give his hungry son a serpent or something deadly to eat? So, how much more so will your Father give you the Holy Ghost to those who ask Him? He said it is expedient for you in John 15:7 says, **It is expedient for you that I go away: for if I go not away, the Comforter will not come unto you; but, if I depart, I will send him unto you.** He will bring all things back to your memory, whatever He told you. He won't leave you comfortless, but He will come to you. Acts 1:8 says that you are going to be an effective witness. But you have got to find your place. He's calling you from the burning bush even as you read this. Clear your mind; focus on these thoughts that are before you. Take the pot off the stove, sort of speak. Dwell on this chapter; make it your own. Think, dwell and meditate on what's here. It is for you. You cannot lump yourself up with anybody else.

THAT GOOD ICE CREAM

You know it is something to go into a store, for example, and you might get some Neapolitan ice cream. It might be an ice cream that is sponsored by the store. It might have a lot of preservatives in it. The ice cream might have a lot of other things in it, might not hurt your stomach. But then, you might go to an ice cream place where they have pure ice cream. It runs right through you, because your system is not used to having pure ice cream. So it is with the Word of God. So it is with the call of God upon your life. You have been sitting around at the banquet table. You have been eating and feasting. You have been fellowshipping with your friends. But the banquet is over. It's biblical right there in Exodus 3:1 says, *Now Moses kept the flock of Jethro his father in law, the priest of Midian: and he led the flock to the backside of the desert, and came to the mountain of God.* All of us will have this experience in our lives where God is going to call us. If you have not had this experience, you will. Moses was willing, and God was too. We do not know how long that bush burnt, but in the time that Moses was ready. God was ready. God was ready, because Moses was ready. God is always ready. We are so comfortable in our own environment. Some people cannot do anything, unless somebody goes with them. Maybe that is not the plan of God for you. You do not want your family or friends to reject you. That is not the plan of God for your life. You have got to come out of the shadows of other people. Some of you do not have your own opinions about who you are. You only know who you are based upon who people say you are. No! Who are you? Will you die for the gospel? Will you die for the sake of Christ? Will you leave all for the sake of Christ?

FROM AFAR

If we study the book of Acts, we can let that book be a pattern for us. They did not have anything. The Bible says people saw the disciples and admired them *from afar* off. I think it was on Solomon's porch. The bible says people admired them, but they dare not join them. They knew the price that they were paying was great. Nobody was in the lion's den but Daniel and those lions. Nobody else was there. The three Hebrew boys; nobody else was there but them. And then the fourth man came. The fourth man only came when they were in the furnace. Jesus only locked the lion's mouth after Daniel was in there. Daniel did not go into the lion's den, and the lion's mouth was locked. No! That was after he was in there. He did not take the sting out of the fire or the stench out of the flame on their way to getting in. No! They had to be in the fire.

Exodus 3:2-5 says, **And the angel of the Lord appeared unto him (Moses) in a flame of fire out of the midst of a bush: and he looked, and, behold, the bush burned with fire, and the bush was not consumed. And Moses said, I will now turn aside, and see this great sight.** Now, you have to think about what it took for him to say all of that. He was not like the children of Israel just saying and talking about the Lord, yet their hearts were far from him. No! His lips and his heart meant the same thing. It is not like some people today who are hypocrites. They say they love God, but they want everything else. People say they love this ministry, but they won't support it with their finances [tithes and offering]. They do not love this ministry. Love is an action word. If you love something, you are going to sponsor it with your finances; you are going to volunteer. You are going to sponsor it with your time. You are not going to leave something you love to the care of somebody else.

When my children were little, I loved them. I did not leave them all around. And my mother did not leave me or my brothers and sisters. I did not leave them all over on somebody else's house. That was my responsibility. I had them with me. When my mother was sick, I had every opportunity to just go on with *my* life; maybe I could have gone and visited instead of moving there to help my father. But that was my mother. She was sick. I did not know how long I had with her. I wanted to be there with my mother. I wanted to talk to her. I wanted to see her face every time I had a chance. Love is an action word. It motivates you. It provokes you. It invokes you to do something. The Bible challenges us. It says how in the world could you love God, whom you have never seen? But you have got the homeless. You have people that do not know God, and you can do something about it.

SEE THIS GREAT SIGHT

Moses said, I will now turn aside and see this great sight (Exodus 3:3). Notice that nobody can say that for him. Nobody can make up your mind about your walk with God but you. Nobody, nobody can. You have to be the one to make the decision about whether or not you are going to really live this life that God has laid out for you. It is not a happy path. People are going to hate you on this path. I am preaching a Gospel that is in opposition to ninety-nine percent of the churches now. I am preaching a

Gospel that has stirred up a hornet's nest. I believe there are many pastors and evangelists that watch our program. I believe there are many who are replicating the things that they see and hear on our program. That is fine. If they are replicating righteousness, so be it. If they will duplicate holiness, then duplicate it. It is not my holiness. If they take a sermon and preach the Word, preach the Word. It is not my Word. *Let the Word do the work.* That is what I say. Yes! I mean, at some point you have got to make your mind up about this. Honestly, you have got to make a conscious decision about your walk with God. Either He is your daddy, or He is not. Either you love Him or you don't. If you notice in this passage of scripture, it says "and Moses said", that is a conscious decision he had to make himself about himself, about going up into the mountain. He did not know. He had heard stories. And if you watch, his wife or somebody told him that no man has ever been up there and lived. Something drew him. Something compelled him. He was willing to take that risk. What are you will to give? What are you willing to do so the promises of God can be fulfilled in your life? Not only for you, but for others.

TURN AND SEE

Think about living your whole life for the sake of other people to find God. That is a harsh reality. Amen. **And Moses said, I will now turn and see this great sight, why the bush is not burnt. And when the Lord saw** (Exodus 3:3-4). Now, the Lord was all ready to move, but what provoked action in the Lord was the fact that Moses was now being obedient as much as he knew how to be; that is what provoked God to move on his behalf. God is always ready to move. He is always ready to move on your behalf, but you have got to do your part. And it said, **when the Lord saw** (Exodus 3:4). I told you to underline that, and I am going to give you a reference scripture. The thoughts that the Lord has towards you are good as are stated in Jeremiah 29:11-14a. These are the things you have to really reflect on. John 15:16-17 says, **Y have not chosen me, but I have chosen you, and**

ordained you, that ye should go and bring forth fruit, and that your fruit should remain: that whatsoever ye shall ask of the Father in my name, he may give it you. These things I command you, that ye love one another. When you have done all you can, He is going to come see about you. But you have got to do all that you know you are supposed to be doing. Some of you have turned cold up in here. Oh my God! When you first start coming to church, we could say a word, and you would just start crying, your hearts were so tender. Now, you barely come; let alone your heart getting tender. When you come in now, we have to come in with the chisel to knock away at some of that debris of anger, strife, fear and doubt. Maybe you might warm up by the time we say, "Alright everybody, see you later." Proverbs 3:5-6 says, **Trust in the Lord with all thine heart; and lean not unto thine own understand. In all thy ways acknowledge him, and he shall direct thy paths.** These are things that have to become a product of your life. Moses is at the burning bush. And so it says there, and **when the Lord saw that he turned aside to see.** (Exodus 3:4). That is so magnificent. You have got to ponder that in your life. Ezekiel the sixteenth chapter talks about the children of Israel, how they were drowning in their own blood, and nobody pitied them. The Lord said, "Hold up; I stopped and said it is a time of love". You do what you do for God because you love Him, because He is your God. The things that the Lord has asked us to do, or that is on our plate, may not be easy. So, stop looking for an easy way out. People are not going to like you. Stop looking for that. You have got to be tough. Stop crying and whining over them. Cut it out and grow up. Paul said when he was young he spoke as a child. He played those mind games, those pity games. He played those anger games. But when he became a man, he put all of that mess away and moved on to do what he knew God was calling him to do. He was trying to redeem the time, because the days are evil, and he had wasted so much of it. When you really come into the knowledge of God about what he is asking you to do, you will be like, "Man, I have wasted so much time. I was chasing women. I was chasing skirts. And then when I got it, I realized. Hmm. I could have passed this up." Some of you have been after people. You have been after stuff. And you have been after things. Then, when you finally got it, you hated it. You want the thing that is in God's will for you. The blessing of the Lord maketh rich and added no sorrow. There is nothing like begging the Lord for something then, when you get it, you spend all of your time crying about it. That is a hard thing. You say, "Lord, I want to be married." Do you know what it is, sure enough, like to deal with somebody else? Think about cavemen; they had their wives (on the Flintstones) and used to drag them by the hair and have this big stick. It is not about you anymore. You have to learn how to perform. You know who the problem is with; yourself. It took a married man to tell you that.

WHEN A MAN LOVES A WOMAN

When you decide that you want to be with somebody for the rest of your life, marriage is about giving all the time. When a man marries a woman, she is his responsibility. He has got to make sure she has what she needs. I do not know what you think marriage is about, but that woman is his responsibility. When she has her monthly, you have got to rub her head and her feet or whatever. If you want the storm to pass over, you men have to take some clues. Sometimes, you have got to talk to them from across the room. "Is today a good day?" "No!" "I will be back. Love you." When you get married, that woman is your responsibility; to take care of her, to love her to protect her. She is your "little ewe lamb". If you are not getting along, do not marry that person. Just the way they are now is the way they are going to be when you marry them. You are a fool if you think you can train a grown person. When you are alone by yourself, you are free. You can go to the store and get you a salad. If you want chicken in it, that is good. You might want you a parker house polish today. You might want you some light yogurt. You might want you some ham today, and not turkey. When you are married, you better not come into that house without two hotdogs. Oh! Did you want one? Oh! Do you want some? Did not Reverend Thomas tell you that if you want some honey, you have to be sweet? Say it, sweet.

You are not really crying about how you forgot that hotdog. You are crying about something else. But you will have the whole night to think about it.

HERE AM I

And when the Lord saw that he turned aside to see, God called unto him out of the midst of the bush, and said Moses, Moses. And he said, Here am I. And he said, Draw not nigh hither: put off thy shoes from thy feet, for the place whereon though standest is holy ground (Exodus 3:4-5). When he got in contact with the Lord, when Moses recognized that it was God, when he was in the presence of God, the Lord told him to take his shoes off. And what the Lord was doing here, you can symbolize it in some many different ways, but He was telling Moses to leave the world behind. All the paths, that you have been on before, forget about them, it is just Me and you. That is the way it is in your life with your calling. It is just you and God when it all boils down to it. If you have a companion, if you have children in your home who will pray with you, man what a blessing! If you have someone you can search the scriptures with and have a little bit of light, a little bit of insight into your calling and how God helps to use you, man, you are blessed beyond measure. But it rarely and seldom happens. The Lord was telling Moses to take those shoes off because He wanted Moses to leave his history, his past failures, and everything he have done. The Lord did not want anything to come in between Him and Moses. "Take those shoes off." Abiding in your calling and answering the call that the Lord has for you, it will grow you up pretty fast, if you are going to please God. In John the 6th chapter, a large number of people were following Him. Jesus already knew why they were following Him. He thought He would put them on the spot to bring them into the reality of "self"; why do you do the things that you do? What motivates you? Sometimes people do stuff and say stuff, without the knowledge of their heart. In John 6th chapter, the Bible says Jesus got in the boat, and was going to go over across the shore. He simply had to turn around and ask the people, "Why are you following me? What is all this noise about? Why are you following me? He brought that to their attention to get them to examine themselves. He said you are not following because of the miracles and the greatness that my Father has bestowed upon me to show you. You are following me because of what you think you can get out of me. Why are you following the Lord tonight? He has asked for your life, every single one of us, for the rest of our lives. Moses might have thought it was so great to be in the presence of God. Just think about that, as a human being, to be in the presence of the Lord. Think about how the Lord had to anoint him to even be in His presence in a bush.

IN HIS PRESENCE

Sometimes the Holy Spirit takes me over, and I can hardly get my breath. I cannot imagine a divine visitation, like the one Daniel had in Daniel 10th chapter. He was calling out to God for his people. He had been on a fast for twenty-one days. Daniel was crying out to God, crying out about what was happening in the people's lives. And the angel of the Lord told him, "Daniel you are greatly loved." He told him that from the time you set your heart right, I have been on my way to see about you. But the enemy, the adversary held up the answer to Daniel's prayer. Thank God for the blood that our prayers can go right on through to heaven. Nothing can hold them up. Nothing can hold-up our prayers. Nothing can stop the connections.

Nothing can block God from moving for us. It says, **Daniel, you are greatly loved.** He said, *I heard your prayers from the minute you called upon me. I have been on my way to see about you.* We must know that the Lord will take time with us. He will give us His undivided attention; He will take the time to be with us in all of His fullness. The Lord seeks to draw us closer and closer to His bosom, to gather us into His love, into His faith and into His vision for each one of us. He loves you. He loves you with an unending love and in His presence in where the great, great plan for our lives will be uncovered. Remember, you can always reach God, when all else fails, with Bible fasting. In Bible fasting, your complete focus will be upon Him and His will for your life; you will become a part of Him, a person in a different world.

The Bible says that in order for Daniel to even be in the presence of the Lord, the angel had to touch him to give him strength to understand what was being said. Think about what the Lord had to do and what was the atmosphere that He had to create just for a man to be in His presence. Initially, just like our call, just like walking with the Lord, when you first start off, you are exuberant; you are encouraged and you sing all the songs. You want everybody to be saved. But after the honeymoon has elapsed, and you really get down to business, you will realize Jesus must not bear the cross alone. No! There is a cross for everyone. And yes, there is a cross for you. The crucifixion becomes reality; lost humanity is your main focus now; no more playing games. The Pharisees and the Sadducees, you recognize their spirit. The Judas' and the Barrabas', you can sense them now. The false witnesses [some hired], you know about that now, because now, you are walking in the shoes of Jesus; a call from the burning bush. Yes God! So, Moses is in the very presence of God and the Lord is telling him to take his shoes off. Then, God begins to introduce Himself to a human being. Can you imagine what that must have been like? **Moreover he said, I am the God** (Exodus 3:6). If you ever listen to our home pastor's cds, he will tell you in a minute, "Yeah, the Lord came to me this week." You are like, "The Lord came to you this week?" He will say, "No, God told me Himself." You are like, "God told you Himself?" You know it is real. I know he is God's holy prophet!

GOD TOLD ME TO TELL YOU

Unlike some of the other people on and off TV who are talking about, "The Word of the Lord came to me," or "The Spirit of the Lord told me." You are like, "Shut your mouth, talking about God told you to tell me something." Their lives do not match. God is holy, and He only deals in holiness.

I AM THE GOD OF YOUR FATHERS

I am the God, of thy father, the God of Abraham, the God of Isaac, and the God of Jacob. And Moses hid his face; for he was afraid to look upon God (Exodus 3:6). To think, that the God of the universe has a need [has chosen to need us] of man (mortal men, mortal women, mortal boys, and mortal girls). What a privilege it is, for God to have need of us! Just think about how wise and awesome God is. He knew what was in the heart of Moses. The Bible says He knows what we have need of, even before we speak. So, the Lord in His awesomeness, His Greatness, His Majestic-ness, He already knew that Moses was saying if you are God why are you allowing all this suffering? If you are really God, the God of my Father; who has told us from generation to generation that a deliverer would come; if you are that God, why? In Exodus 3:7 says, **And the Lord said, I have surely seen the affliction of my people which are in Egypt, and have heard their cry by reason of their taskmasters; for I know their sorrows.** Notice, before Moses even had a chance, God already knew what was in his heart. He already knew what was burdening him down. He already knew how he felt. The Lord spoke so emphatically to Moses. He wanted him to know even before he thought about it, the Lord already knew what was on his mind. Moses had to be, "Oh my Lord, the God that speaks the thoughts that is in my heart. A God that answers, before I can even calculate my thoughts. He knows what I need and He answers me." Yes! Yes! Why? Because He is God! Because He is God! He is the God of all flesh. God of all living things, He is the God of it. The Lord told Moses, "I know their sorrows." Think about the God of this world coming down to deal with you. He said, **I have come down to the mountain.** Think about it. He had to come down to the height that Moses could come up to. Think about it in your life. God comes down to you, so you can come up.

He says, Exodus 3:8, **I have come down to deliver them out of the hand of the Egyptians.** Think about this, Moses had to be excited that finally after all of these years; *Yes! You are that God. Yes! You are that Saviour.* But the Lord did not give Moses the whole picture at once. He was happy. He was excited. Deliverance was on the way. Exodus 3:8 says, **And to bring them up out of that land unto a good land and a large, unto a land flowing with milk and honey.** Oh! How Moses must have felt. The dying of my people, the dying of my ancestors, it is not all in vain. **Unto the place of the Canaanites, and the Hittites, and the Amorites, and the Perizzites, and the Hivites, and the Jebusites, Now therefore, behold, the cry of the children of Israel is come unto me; and I have also seen the oppression wherewith the Egyptians oppress them. Come now therefore, and I will send thee unto Pharaoh, that thou mayest bring forth my people the children of Israel out of Egypt** (Exodus 3:8-10). Hold up. This was good at first. Now, the Lord has changed the scenario. It goes from being a *great method* to being a *great burden.* It goes from *great possibilities; every single one of us.* You are the hands I am going to use. You are the instrument. You are the tool. Think about how that must have affected Moses.

I ORDAINED THEE

To give you a better synopsis, go to the first chapter of Jeremiah. It reminds me so much of our ministry. I have read this so many times, but not like this. As you know, the Lord is calling Jeremiah now, like He is calling you. It says here in Jeremiah 1:4, **Then the word of the Lord, came unto me, saying, Before I formed thee in the belly I knew thee; and before thou camest forth out of the womb I sanctified thee, and I ordained thee a prophet unto the nations.** As I was studying this, the Holy Spirit really challenged me to dwell on the conversation that Jeremiah and the Lord were having. I spent a couple days on the first chapters. The Lord pointed out different things about the conversation and the order of things. It says here, **Then the word of the Lord, came unto me, saying Before I formed thee in the belly I knew thee; and before thou camest forth out of the womb, I sanctified thee** (Jeremiah 1:5). I already set you apart to be my prophet. And the Lord was letting Jeremiah know at this time, in his young life, that he is going to be an instrument. Jeremiah was not sent to people he did not know, but people he knew. The Lord told him upfront. Jeremiah 1:6 says, **Then said I, Ah Lord God, behold, I cannot speak for I am a child.** He was already talking about his weaknesses. He says, **but, the Lord said unto me, Say not that I am a child; for thou shalt go** (Notice that this—the Lord is empathic—no questions. "You are going to do this."). I do not know where you are in your life. I do not know where you are in the call of God in your life, but you better listen to me. He says, for ye shall go. Verse 7 says, **to all that I shall send thee, and whatever I tell thee, that what you are going to say.** How about that one? You thought when your mama told you to shut up while she was whipping you that was bad. I told you about my momma, when she use to whip us [we needed it too]. She would constantly bring that belt down on my backside, but she was telling me to shut up. Now, I am thinking in my mind. "How can I do this?" She is just whipping me, and whipping me. I am thinking under my breath, "If you give me a break, I might be able to be quiet." My mom, she had a bionic arm. I do not care what nobody says. The Lord says you are going to go where I want you to go. And you are going to say what I tell you to say. That is it. He says, (now, this is what really got me. I told you that I have been studying this for a couple of days, just a couple of verses) **Be not afraid of their faces: for I am with thee to deliver thee, saith the Lord. Then the Lord put forth his hand, and touched my mouth. And the Lord said unto me, Behold, I have put my words in thy mouth. See, I have this day set thee over the nations and over the kingdoms, to root out, and to pull down, and to destroy, and to throw down, to build, and to plant** (Jeremiah 1:8-10). That is our mission. **Moreover, the word of the Lord came unto me, saying, Jeremiah, what seest thou? And I said, I see a rod of an almond tree. Then said the Lord unto me, thou hast well seen: for I will hasten my word to perform it** (Jeremiah 1:11-12).

So, what the Lord was letting Jeremiah know was, *Listen, I called you. This is what I called you to do. These are the people, and these are the circumstances by which I have called you.* And it says that he is telling Jeremiah *Whatever I told you to do, I am going to confirm what I say.* Oh yes! He says, **And the word of the Lord came unto me the second time, saying, What seest thou? And I said, I see a seething pot; and the face thereof is toward the north. Then the Lord said unto me, Out of the north an evil shall break forth upon all inhabitants of the land. For, lo, I will call all the families of the kingdoms of the north, saith the Lord; and they shall come, and they shall set every one of his throne at the entering of the gates of Jerusalem, and against all the walls thereof round about, and against all the cities of Judah. And I will utter my judgments against them touching all their wickedness, who have forsaken me, and have burned incense unto other gods, and worshipped the works of their own hands. Thou therefore gird up thy loins, and arise, and speak unto them all that I command thee: be not dismayed at their faces, lest I confound thee before them** (Jeremiah 1:13-17). Let me summarize verse 17 for you. *You better go and say what I tell you, and you better act like you are confident about what I am saying, or I will make you look like a fool in front of the very people I sent you to speak My word.* I am sending you on a mission, the Lord was telling Jeremiah. You better do it with confidence. You better stay in my presence.

Howbeit this kind goeth not out but by prayer and fasting (Matthew 17:21). **Thy word have I hid in mine heart, that I might not sin against thee** (Psalm 119:11). You are not walking with the ungodly. You are sitting in the seat of the scornful (Psalm 1:1). And you are going to proclaim my word and act like you know what I am talking about when I speak, that's what the Lord is saying to each one that He has called to speak His word. How about that? And are you going to do it? As you go on to read, Jeremiah and the Lord just kept on going back and forth. Jeremiah was talking about how he was young, and how he did not understand. He told the Lord about how he was just tired of proclaiming His word. People would try to kill him. But then, when I try to shut up, Jeremiah told the Lord, I can't shut up, because it seems like if I do not get it out, I am going to burst. I have to proclaim your Word, Lord. And we better proclaim the Lord, because He is God. Yes! The Lord is calling each and every one of us.

THOSE SAME PEOPLE

Moses went up to that burning bush. He was so excited at first, to think that God had chosen him. The Lord prepared Moses with the rod, throwing it down, and showed him how to pick it up. Moses got in trouble when he asked for the company of Miriam and Aaron but those same people that he thought he needed caused Moses the most trouble. The Lord is calling each and every one of us into His great plan for our life; to do a great work for Him. The Lord has let us know that, if He calls us, we have to get to a place in our lives when we have to study along with the Lord. The Bible tells us to study, to **shew ourselves approved unto God, a workman that needeth not to be ashamed, rightly dividing the word of truth** (2 Timothy 2:15). You have got to know how to handle the truth. You have to be able and have the right words for the people at the right time. But we have to go forth and be the witness of the Lord that he has called us to be in this final hour. The Lord has given us so much. He has given us wealth. He has given us miracles. He has given us food. He has given us peace. He has given us jobs. He has given us joy. And now it is pay up time for a debt. It is pay day. Should we look for another? No! He called you. He called you.

I CAN DO ALL THINGS

We want a life that is easy. We want everything to go well. When He was here, Christ was our example in all things. He fasted as long as forty days. He spent so much time in prayer. But He also handled the power of His Father. The Lord told us about His gifts. He told us about His power. Jesus told us about His greatness. And it says that we can have the mind of Christ. **Let this mind be in you that is also in Christ Jesus** (Philippians 2:5). **I can do all things through Christ which strengtheneth me** (Philippians 4:13). **We are more than conquerors** (Romans 8:37). **For I am persuaded, that neither death, nor life, nor angels, nor principalities, nor powers, nor things present nor things to come, Nor height, nor depth, nor any other creature, shall be able to separate us from the love of God, which is in Christ Jesus our Lord** (Romans 8:38-39). What's separating you from what God has called you to do? You have to weigh that out. Matthew 22:14 says, **For many are called, but few are chosen.** John 15:16 says, **Ye have not chosen me, but I have chosen you.** The book of Hebrews talks about how the children of Israel rejected the Lord God. And we realize that because they rejected Jesus that caused us to be grafted in. But our time is winding up. People are going to come against us. People are going to say stuff. But with God on our side, we do not need anybody else. Come out of the shadows! Come out of the shadows! Stop being a follower, rise up and take your place. When they talked about Gideon and why they were so successful, He said because every man was in his place. They didn't need as many people as they thought they needed. About how many people did they start with? God's perfect number. And that was all he needed. In the eyes of the enemy it looked like, "Man, what are they going to do?" But they had the power of God. When they walked around the walls of Jericho, my God, how could anything great come out of these people just marching around? What was their success? They obeyed God. God tumbled the walls, not the people. So, all we have to do is obey God. We have to obey God. It takes fasting and praying and living in the Word. You are not going to be victorious without it. This is not a ministry that you can come into halfway. No! No! We cannot look around to somebody else to do the work that we have been called to do. Do it, we must! Do it, we will! Do it, we must and do it, we will! It's your call from God. That's your call from God. That's your call from God. That's your call from God.

CHAPTER 14
WHEN A SINNER DIES

There is so much false doctrine being preached today. It's alarming. Preachers are telling their congregations that when they die, it is all over. They say that anybody and everybody can make it to Heaven; people from all religions will be accepted. All they have to do is repent. People are being taught from pulpits across America that it does not matter what you do, you will make into heaven. But that is not according to the Word of God. There's no Bible for it! There's no Bible for it! We talk about how glorious it is when a child of God dies, but in reality, to those of us left behind, it breaks our heart. When a momma is gone, or a daddy is gone because the Lord saw fit to take them to Heaven, instead of letting them suffer over and over again, we don't always understand—at that moment but we do know that God is just in all of His ways. There is another spectrum to that story; it's when a sinner dies.

RECOGNIZE FALSE DOCTRINE

During funerals today, yesterday and even tomorrow there will be an alcoholic who died, and some poor preacher will tell his or her grieving family that the Lord took them. That is false doctrine neighbor. There will no doubt be people who will die as a result of AIDS, because they were addicted to drugs. People will stand in the pulpit and say that God took that soul. But let hell be uncovered today. God is not the author of sin. He is not the author of sin, sickness or death. I want to take on you a journey today to witness just what happens when a sinner dies. How long do you have to live? How long, how long, how long is your life span? How long do you have to live? Those of you living in adultery, fornication, same-sex union, and those who are robbing, cursing, those who blaspheme the name of the Almighty God, those who embezzle, and those who sit in the seat of the scornful, have you thought about it? How long do you have to live? When will the clock stop ticking for you and you end up in hell? I cannot imagine living one moment without God. I cannot make it without God. I cannot live; I cannot breath; I cannot think without His power to help me. There is no way I can live without Him. My mind and body are so feeble without His power to keep me going. I need the presence of the Almighty God with me and inside of me all the time. I wouldn't be able to collect my thoughts. I would not be able to reason. What purpose would there be for me without God in my life?

A BLOOD-LESS GOSPEL

In many churches today, there are so many messages being preached, but no blood messages. The messages, so many, are bloodless. It was the religious world that gave Jesus trouble. It is the religious world that is giving the true children of God trouble today. The Gospel has been watered down to fit the accommodations of sinning individuals. Many preach a gospel that makes Jesus appear as if He is not the Son of God. So many preachers, teachers and religious leaders have taken the place of God, and they say "nobody can live free from sin." The Bible tells each and every one of us, that **Behold, all souls are mine; as the soul of the father, so also the soul of the son is mine: the soul that sinneth, it shall die** (Ezekiel 18:4). When a sinner dies!

SOUL MAINTENANCE

Neighbor, when is the last time you gave thought to your mortality? When is the last time you really gave a thought to your life? People spend so much time building mansions. Neighbor, they are looking to their investments.

They are looking in their 401k, and they are making so many plans for the future. You may get your nails done. You may get your weaves done or even get your braids redone. You may even go to the chiropractor. You get a brace on one leg when it is broken. You may go to the therapist when something is wrong with your back. We go and check when we get a new prescription in our glasses. But you are not preparing for an eternity. As a whole, you are not ready. You need to give some thought to this. You have a destination with death, except you make the Rapture—the one flight out. So many people have given in to the spirit of this age. What is the spirit of this age? It is an age of mocking God. It is an age of rebelling against the things of God; fighting against true holiness and righteousness. This is the most rebellious generation on planet Earth right now. This is the most ungodly, unholy, unthankful, lacking mercy generation ever.

When a sinner dies! When a person comes to the end of their life and dies without God. Now, they have to face an angry God. There is so much false doctrine that talks about purgatory and soul sleep. There is no truth to it, neighbor. There's no Bible for it. If you cannot find it in the Word of God, throw it out—it's garbage. Roman 6:23 says, **For the wages of sin is death; but the gift of God is eternal life through Jesus Christ our Lord.** Everybody is going to get paid; everyone will be awarded their wages. What will you get? I like to watch the Discovery channel. I like to watch those investigative programs. I love mysteries. I like the way the Lord has blessed our nation with doctors, modern technology, and how that crime committed forty or fifty years ago, the perpetrator may think they got away, but now through the modernization of DNA, they can find you out. It is just really something to think about. Nobody is going to get away with anything. I do not know what you are being taught in your church, but when a sinner dies, that is a person that dies without the true and the living God. And from the time that the breath leaves the body, your soul goes to the place that **you** have prepared for. **When you die, that is not it; that's only the beginning**. That is false doctrine.

THE REAL YOU

Our world and the spirit of this age—the spirit of the antichrist, teach you to do whatever it is you want to do. It is your life, do anything you want to do. You are grown, nobody can tell you what to do. Oh, but there is one. The Lord says I am Alpha and Omega. I am the beginning and the end. That is the real part of you that is part of you that will never die; your soul. I do not care what people are teaching and preaching, the Bible is right. When you die, that is not it. Your eternal life just begins, either with the Lord in heaven or without God in hell. The Bible states in Romans 9:27 **And as it is appointed unto men once to die, but after this the judgment.** It is an appointment. Every one of us, we have an appointment, except you make the Rapture.

LET HELL BE UNCOVERED

The devil has covered up hell all these years. He has covered up hell all of these years, and he is primarily working in the pulpits across America today to cover up hell. There is no way the devil could have accomplished what he has been able to do without the leadership of those in false doctrine across America. The devil has seduced people into thinking that there is not a literal burning hell. But according to the Word of God, it is! Churches, they are covering up blaspheming against the Name of the Lord. But it is going on today. Ministers, Pentecostals, full gospel churches, they are blaspheming against the Holy Ghost and area guides to the blind. The Bible clearly states this in Matthew 15:14, **Let them alone: they be blind leaders of the blind. And if the blind lead the blind, both shall fall into the ditch**. But, Oh Neighbor! When a sinner dies, when a person dies without God, I told you a minute ago, Ezekiel 18:4 says **the soul that sinneth, it shall die.**

Some of you are doing so much wickedness. You are so perverse. Something is wrong with you. You do not fear God now, but you will. You have no fear of God at all. You are just stealing, and you are profane. Maybe even some of you might be preachers, you might be leaders. You might be an evangelist. It does not matter what title you name yourself. The Bible says that if you sin, the devil is your daddy. If a person tells you, no matter who they are—pastor or leader, that you can't live free from sin, they are sinning and trying to make a side door to Heaven, but I promise you they won't get in, and neither will you if you endorse such as that. It does not matter who that person is, if they tell you a person cannot live free from sin, you can check their lives. They are sinning somewhere. But, oh neighbor, when a sinner dies! Heaven is going to forget about you, and hell is going to hate the fact that you are coming there. Hell will hate you before you even get there. God is going to hate you. He will never remember you again; the Lord has power to remember as well as forget. He is God! There are people walking on the Earth today, God has turned them over to a reprobate mind. He will never hear their prayers again. Some of you reading this book are on the borderline of blaspheming against the Holy Ghost. God has called you out according to His Word in the first chapter of Proverbs. You do not want to be bothered with that. You do not want the **"Thou Shalt Nots."** You do not want to live pure, clean and holy. Well then, the Lord will not want you. Think a moment, the God who gave all for your life, the God who purchased your salvation with the precious blood of His Son, Jesus—to forsake you—to hate you—to regret allowing you to be born—whew! There are dead men; there are dead women in the pulpits across America. There are dead men; there are dead women walking around here now. God has completely turned them off. He will never hear them again. The God of Heaven will never hear their prayers again. He does not care about them. His frown is on them, and He hates them. Then, they die and go to hell. But are they dead?

When you die, are you dead? Is that it? Or is it the beginning of a different life? When a sinner dies! It is appointed unto to man, once to die, and after this the judgment of God.

JUDGMENT MUST BEGIN

The book of Peter is a really good book to study. 1 Peter 4:17-19 says, **For the time is come that judgment must begin at the house of God: and if it first begin at us, what shall the end of them that obey not the gospel of God? And if the righteous scarcely be saved, where shall the ungodly and sinner appear? Wherefore let them that suffer according to the will of God commit the keeping of their souls to him in well doing, as unto a faithful Creator.** Now, this word speaks so opposite to the way America is today. This word speaks so opposite to so many churches today. God has been disappointed and forsaken by so many churches in this hour. He is depending on them to rise up and do right. The Lord is depending on them to not compromise. He is depending on parents not to compromise with their children, but be parents according to His word. Christ is depending on parents who are bringing children into this world, to live Godly and to teach them to fear Him. But people are failing God all over the world now. People are failing God, and that makes me feel so sorry for God. It is not a big thing now to have a wife and a whore. It's no big thing to have a husband and a whore. I am talking about from the pulpits of God. It can be a man or a woman. It does not matter; married and have whores out in the congregation. But neighbor, I am telling you today, when a sinner dies, there is a hell to shun, and an angry God you are not going to want to face.

PLEASURE AND LUST

So many people today are caught up into the spirit of this world. This is such a pleasure-seeking, lustful age; completely worse than the time of

Sodom and Gomorrah. What is the spirit of this world? People rejecting God and blaspheming against His name and the Holy Ghost. When you blaspheme against the Holy Ghost, you will never, ever have another chance with God. He will cut you off. That is the one sin that there is no forgiveness for, neither in this life, nor in the life to come. Don't talk to me about God, some have screamed. I am tired of hearing about God. I don't want to hear about God. Don't tell me about the Bible. I don't want to go to church. I want to wash my car on Sunday's. I want to spend all day watching the game. I don't have any time for God. But Oh! You will wish you did. You will wish you did. This is your message from God. When a sinner dies.

When a sinner dies. Proverbs 10:8, **The wise in heart will receive commandments: but a prating fool shall fall. He that walketh uprightly walketh surely: but he that perverteth his ways shall be known.** Proverbs 10:8-9). The Lord says the years of the wicked shall be shortened. Proverbs 11: 1-3 says, **A false balance is abomination to the Lord: but a just weight is his delight. When pride cometh, then cometh shame; but with the lowly is wisdom. The integrity of the upright shall guide them: but the perverseness of transgressors shall destroy them.** This is something for you to think about; how the Lord is talking about the wicked. He is also talking about the just. Proverbs 11:7-8 states, **When a wicked man dieth, his expectation shall perish: and the hope of unjust men perisheth. The righteous is delivered out of trouble, and the wicked cometh in his stead.** What is the Lord saying about the wicked? Then, think about what He is saying about the righteous. It's amazing how some people think what they are doing is right, and nothing is going to happen to them. But it is wrong thinking and wrong believing. Wrong thinking leads to wrong believing. When is the last time you thought about the end of your life? When is the last time you thought about meeting your maker? When is the last time you thought about when your life is over? Some of you reading this don't even realize how close to death you are. You are just playing games. God has watched over you. He has protected you.

The Lord has taken you out of one jam and out of another problem. He has been there for you. The Lord has shown you nothing but compassion and watched over you, especially if you were a little one. No more! He is sick of you. God is getting sick and tired of you. You are crying out to Him and prostituting him. And when you get in trouble, you call on Him. But you won't live for Him. God has spared your life more than once and more than twice. He is telling you, go on to hell sinner. Go on to hell sinner! There, you will wake up. There, you will wake up. Did you know everybody in hell is a believer? Everybody in hell is praying. And the gospels let us know that fire is so much torment in hell. The Bible let us know that they are screaming out. They are screaming. They are screaming out. In one breath they are praying, and with the next breath, those sinners who died without God, are asking for grace. One breath, they are asking for compassion. And in the next breath, they are blaspheming God's name, because they know they will never get out. *Everybody in hell is a believer. Everybody in hell, they have all of the answers about life. Everybody in hell is loyal; walking hand-in-hand. There is no division. They are no atheists in hell.* No, all the people in hell today, they are true believers, but it is too late. There is nothing they can do with their belief in hell. Oh my God! In hell, everybody believes that God is God. Everybody that is in hell knows Jesus is the son of God. Everybody that is in hell knows Jesus came, and He was the spotless lamb. Everybody that is in hell now knows that **the soul that sinneth it shall die** (Ezekiel 18:4). They know it. They know it. When a sinner dies! When a sinner dies! No doubt, the Lord is talking to some of you. Please respond. Please respond.

WARN THEM FROM ME

I hear the call of God upon Ezekiel's life. The Lord told Ezekiel, I am making you a watchman upon the children of God. You have to tell them the truth; you have got to let them know. So many churches, they don't even talk about hell. They won't even read or teach from the book of

Revelation. But let hell be uncovered today. Sometimes love doesn't draw people to God. Sometimes God has to use judgment. Some of you come to church and hear the messages of God. You hear calamity happening. You hear this happening. And for a minute, it moves you. *Only for a moment.* You are so deceived. Your mind is covered with many leeches. Oh my God! You are so seduced. You think you can just go on doing your own thing, right in the face of God. But when a sinner dies.

Every one of you, you have an appointment with death. From the time they spanked you on your bottom, you had an appointment with death. You have got to think about this. You can only live one day at a time, and then your final hour comes. Even today, how much has God gotten out of your day? From the time that you woke up this morning, how much profanity have you spilled out? How much hatred? How much unbelief? How much unforgiveness have you spewed out today? Yet you call yourself a child of God. You only can live one day at a time. Tomorrow you might be dead. But you have a chance now. You might be a sinner today, but you can change that. You can change your life today. You might be leaving God. You can change your condition today. I feel like Lot, sitting at the gate, viewing the wicked cities of Sodom and Gomorrah. In Genesis, 19th Chapter, Lot ran all around those cities. He did everything he could to reach, not only his family, but everyone. But no one wanted God; not even his wife. Those two cities—Sodom and Gomorrah—are just like America, just like Chicago. You can get shot down taking your garbage out or walking to your car. It is just like Illinois. It is just like these churches. Everything in the world is going on, and they are saying it is in the name of God. The only thing Lot could do was sit at the gate. But the angels came down to see if it was as bad as they were hearing in Heaven. I am convinced that the angels have been down in this world. They have concluded, "Yes, it is worse." It is worse. How can you say that Reverend? Because in the Bible, in the gospels it says that it is going to be worse than the days of Sodom and Gomorrah. It also says just like in the days of Sodom and Gomorrah, when Jesus came back, people would not give any thought to it. They are going to be partying. They are going to be marrying and giving into marriage, thinking nothing about being married. The Lord is not into same-sex union. He is not into shacking up. The Lord has no part of it. There's no Bible for it. He has nothing to do with sin, sickness or death.

RECKLESS FAITH

We have to be bodacious. We have to stand up. We must display *"reckless faith."* We have to have our pride. We have to have pride about who we are, which is being a true born-again Christian. You have to say, "True born-again," because everyone, no matter what you do, is a Christian. You have got to think about this. So many people have their own pattern of living. They are seeking to please themselves and to please others, but not to please God. It is dangerous when people put God off. "Oh, I will do that tomorrow. I am not going to pay my tithes this week. I will double up next time." It is so dangerous. Don't play around with God's money. It's dangerous. Some people get mad at the pastor, and they won't even pay their ten percent. The Lord clearly states that tithing is His financial plan for the church. He gave people the health to get the wealth. They have to bring tithes into the storehouse. When you don't pay tithes, you rob God of souls. **Bring ye all the tithes into the storehouse, that there may be meat in mine house, and prove me now herewith, saith the Lord of hosts, if I will not open you the windows of heaven, and pour you out a blessing, that there shall not be room enough to receive it** (Malachi 3:10) You are responsible. But, oh, when a sinner dies! When a sinner dies!

VENGEANCE

People get joy out of being evil. They get joy out of being mean. They get joy out of treating other people bad. But oh, when a sinner dies, God is omnipotent! He is everywhere all at the same time. The Lord told us that vengeance belongs to Him, and He will take care of our enemies; He will take care of our battles, etc . . . When is the last time you thought about God? Some of you should have been dead. Some of us should be dressed in our grave clothes, but God is merciful and compassionate. The Lord feels so sorry for you, because He knows that you just don't know what is ahead for you. He knows that you are punk. You are so weak. He knows that you definitely are going to catch it in hell. He knows it. I just want to ask a prophetic question today. What in hell do you want? When you are drawn to sin, you are drawn to hell. The Bible says it so plainly in James. He says God does not tempt people. He says a man is tempted when **he is drawn away with his own lust and enticed.** When sin is done with you, you are going to die. When is the last time you thought about your life? Revelations 10:5-6 says, **And the angel which I saw stand upon the sea and upon the earth lifted up his hand to heaven, And sware by him that liveth for ever and ever, who created heaven, and the things that therein are, and the earth, and the things that therein are, and the sea, and the things which are therein, that there should be time no longer.**

GUILTY!

I want to tell you about your future. People want to run to astrology. They want to read about the zodiac sign. They want to find out what kind of star they are under. Well, I got it all for you right here. When a sinner dies, that is a person who dies that does not belong to God. That is a person who dies that has not lived for God. So many young people, they are busting hell wide open. They come across like they are tough gangsters. They are just unstoppable. And then they land in hell. They land in hell. Oh my! What a surprise! You just think about that. Where will you be when the angel declares that time will be no more? Some of you will be in glory and others not. Time no more. My God! How awful for those who have made no provision for their souls; haven't made themselves ready; haven't got their lives straightened out with the Lord. It doesn't really matter what people say. You have to work things out between you and your God. You got to work things out between you and your God. You got to work things out between you and your God. You got to get things right with Him in your life. Some of you are just going on. You are not even giving a thought to God, but you will. Some of you, you know He is dealing with you. You know the presence of the Lord is hovering around you like a person following you. He is trying to chip away at that wicked heart; free you of those leeches, so that you can think clearly. This is your chance to be free. But there's those seducing devils swarming all around you, making you think you are invincible. Some of you are guilty of murder and rape, aren't you? Those murdering devils possess you and won't let you rest until you kill, and kill and kill again. You are beyond feelings. But you will feel. You will feel. Anytime you can steal from your own momma; that is degraded. That is wicked. Anytime you can go into your father's wallet, the father that works so hard so that you can have your needs met; he goes without so you can have. That is wickedness. Then, you come and lay down in their bed that they paid for, lie on their sheets, eat their food. The shoes that you put on, they bought them with their money. It is wickedness. No doubt, many devils bound you. Let hell be uncovered this day. Yes! Yes! When a sinner dies!

AND THEN YOU DIE

There is unforgiveness and anger in your heart, being disobedient. And then, you die. You sneak out at night. And then, you die. You leave out to go to work in the morning, just cursing and fussing. And then, you die. You sneak out to be with some girl or some boy. And then, you die. You smoke your blunt, drink your wine, do your reefer, snort your cocaine, but then, you die. When a sinner dies, how tough are you, really? I heard the word say, I am God, and besides me there is nobody else. If it is, I want you to show me. Job was feeling so pitiful for himself. He began to question God. And God said, stand on your feet like a man and answer me. Can you form a world and shape the stars? What can you do? You are nothing. And that is what we better know today. We are nothing. But when a sinner dies, people are indulging in divers sin, and they don't even have time for God. But they have time for pleasure. We live in such a pleasure-seeking age; an age of looking out for *self.* There's no time for God. People make time for more and more sin. Each day, they degrade themselves before the God that made them, and it displeases Him.

DEATH, JUST THE BEGINNING?

When you die, that is only the beginning. This life is a short journey in comparison to eternity. We are all on a small journey; on a journey that will decide our eternal future. But when you die, eternity is yours. When you get to hell, you cannot get out. When a sinner dies, when a person dies without the blood of Jesus on their soul, what do you think happens to them next? Are you really dead? Can you think? Can you feel? Can you see? Do you have senses? Can you smell? Yes, to all. While your body may go back to the earth, that soul, the real you will never-ever die. It will never die. It will never die. That real you, it will never die. And you cannot defy God. Think about this. Mark 9:43-44 says, **It is better for thee to enter into life maimed, than having two hands to go into hell, into the fire that never shall be quenched: Where their worm** [your soul] **dieth not, and fire** [fire of hell] **is not quenched.** Belshazzar, from the book of Daniel, spent his last day revelling in a wild party, just partying. How many people dropped into hell last night on their way from a wild party or had an accident due to being drunk? And now they are in hell. Not only are they dead, but they took some people with them, no doubt. But they have all the answers now. Some poor mother, some poor father, their hearts are broken. Going to the morgue, the body is right there on that window, identifying. Is this your child? "Yes." When a sinner dies they [the real person; the soul] is not dead, but their body has been returned to the earth. That real you, the inner man, lives on forever, and ever, and ever, and ever. When a sinner dies, God will hate you. He will hate the fact that He spared your life all these years. He hates the fact you were even born. Not only will the Lord hate you, but He will forget all about you. The Bible declares that when you are in hell, the Lord won't even remember you no more. You will be shut away from His mind; shut away from His thoughts. And I say again, there are some people on Earth that are hell bound. God is no longer dealing with them, because they refused for the last time, and He let them go. Whew!

THE HOUR OF BLASPHEMY

Today, there are pastors and leaders that have blasphemed against the Holy Ghost. They are the walking dead, the Bible declares. God will never hear another prayer from them. He does not care. The Lord hates them, and they are still alive; physically, at least. But oh, when a sinner dies. Again, Belshazzar spent his last day having a wild party. Devils had taken him over to the extent that he thought he could do whatever he wanted to do. Wow! That spirit is in the world today. "You can't tell me what to do." "I can do whatever I want to do. I work every day." "I can party. I can stay out. I can have a social drink." "If I am tired of my wife, I can get me another one." Oh! But when a sinner dies! "I can have men in and out of my house." "My kids, they are just children." But dear one, they are precious souls; oh, they are sponges. Devils had taken Belshazzar over to the extent; he thought he could do anything he wanted. Belshazzar forgot about his father's experience with God. He forgot about Nebuchadnezzar and how he had gloried himself, despite a warning through a dream that Daniel had interpreted for him. Daniel 4:24-27 says **This is the interpretation, O king, and this is the decree of the most High, which is come upon my lord the king: That they shall drive thee from men, and thy dwelling shall be with the beasts of the field, and they shall make thee to eat grass as oxen, and they shall wet thee with the dew of heaven, and seven times (seven years) shall pass over thee, till thou know that the** most High ruleth in the kingdom of men, and giveth it to whomsoever he will. And whereas they commanded to leave the stump of the tree roots; thy kingdom shall be sure unto thee, after that thou shalt have known that heavens do rule. Wherefore, O king, let my counsel be acceptable unto thee, and break off thy sins by righteousness, and thine iniquities by shewing mercy to the poor; if it may be a lengthening of thy tranquillity. "Listen to me; I am trying to give you a warning. Listen to what I am saying to you." That's what the prophet Daniel was trying to tell Nebuchadnezzar, but he did not listen. Belshazzar did not learn from Nebuchadnezzar's mistakes. He [Belshazzar] gave no regard to the Lord. It is like some people who are incarcerated. They get caught. They are not sorry, but they are sorry they got caught. They have not changed in their hearts. They are just waiting for another opportunity. What they do when they are released proves that.

SORRY . . . SORRY I GOT CAUGHT

The Bible says Godly sorrow worketh repentance. When you are sorry, you don't do that again. If you keep on falling, rising and in and out with God, and treating people wrong, you are not sorry. You hypocrite! You are not sorry. You are just mad you got caught. When you are sorry, you change. When you are sorry you change. When you are sorry, you change. When you are sorry, you don't go onto deeper deceit. You do not go on and look for another way to con people. You don't go looking for another woman. You do not knowingly pass HIV because you have it, you change. HIV, AIDS and STD's, they are right here in South Shore [the Reverend's neighborhood]. Some people, they have AIDS, and they will never tell you. They will sleep with you unprotected and never tell you. In turn, you end up sleeping with every person they've slept with, and it just goes on and on. Sexually transmitted diseases, they are right here in South Shore. A man or woman will have the audacity to say, "I do not want you using a condom," but he or she will give you something you cannot get rid of.

Oh! But when a sinner dies. Some of these women have got so much low self-esteem. They take anything that comes along with two legs, wearing pants. God makes a man. Simply, because you wear pants does not make you a man. The Bible says in the book of Genesis that God the Father, God the Son and God the Holy Ghost got down in the dirt and made us. And God said, Let us make man in our image, after our likeness (Genesis 1:26). And He stepped back and looked at us, and He said that he thought it was good. Why? Because there was no sin in the man and woman God had made; they was pure and the Lord meant for them to stay in that holy condition. Flowing in his veins was divine blood; no iniquity. But then Adam was deceived by Eve and they were both kicked out of the garden forever. How many days did they go back to the Garden of Eden trying to plead with God to see if they could get back in? The Lord put that very fact in His word to show us that when you go so far, you will be cut off forever.

HE UNDERSTANDS

I do not care what these churches are preaching about. "Oh, God, he understands." Take your life to His word. What does the Bible says about it? That is what we will all be judged by. God understands alright. He understands you are a sinner. No, He understands His Son died. No, He understands audacious men beat His boy to death. No, He understands they put a crown of thorns upon our Lord's head. No, the Lord understands that they beat Jesus all night, taking Him from hall to hall. Remember, that was HIS son! No, God understands that they mocked the Lamb of God; took off his clothes, and put on Him a purple robe and some other kind of garment. No, the Creator knows that His Son died so that you could live free. So, He doesn't want to hear what you talking about! When a sinner dies. When a sinner dies. It said before Jesus came, God winked at ignorance. But every time He thinks about Calvary, everybody has to pay. For the wages of sin is death (Romans 6:23).

SOME PEOPLE NEVER LEARN

In Daniel 4:28 it says that all this came upon the king Nebuchadnezzar. At the end of twelve months, he walked in the palace of the kingdom of Babylon. Some people never learn. It says the prophet came to him, spoke to Nebuchadnezzar. Nebuchadnezzar had a whole year. He had a year before his judgment came upon him. The Lord pronounced judgment upon him a year before. You think he would have gotten down in the dirt. You think he would have had his head bowed down. You think he would have been fasting and praying. You think he would have tried to change his ways. No, it says twelve months later, he was the same way. The king did not change. He did not want to be free. Some people they are only alright, but only for a moment, because they are scared. But they have not changed. They have not changed.

The Bible says that God calls all men to repentance. When a person is really sorry, and they have really repented, it shows up. They are changed. People who are in and out with God were probably never saved. In and out, up and down, cursing and doing all kinds of stuff, one minute they are prophetic. The Bible says you have to make the garment good or bad, you can't make it both. **No man putteth a piece of new cloth unto an old garment, for that which is put in to fill it up taketh from the garment, and the rent is made worse. Neither do men put new wine into old bottles: else the bottles break, and the wine runneth out, and the bottles perish: but they put new wine into new bottles, and both are preserved** (Matthew 9:16-17).

A CURSING PROPHET

How can you be a prophet one moment, and cursing and smoking the next? You are not saved, let alone be a prophet. *How can it be*? There's no Bible for it. It don't line up with the Word of God. It cannot line up. And if it doesn't line up, throw it out, because it's just worthless—just garbage. You can't curse, drink, smoke and do all this stuff and then, talking about how the Lord told you to tell me something. Those are lying devils talking to you. God is not speaking to you. He uses a Holy tongue and a pure heart. Oh, but when a sinner dies.

WHILE THE WORD WAS IN HIS MOUTH!

Daniel 4:29-34 says, **At the end of twelve months, he walked in the palace of the kingdom of Babylon. The king spake, and said, Is not this great Babylon, that I have built for the house of the kingdom by the might of my power, and for the honour of my majesty?** Notice this! How quickly judgment can fall. (vs. 31) **While the word was in the king's mouth, there fell a voice from heaven saying, O king Nebuchadnezzar, to thee it is spoken; the kingdom is departed from thee. And they shall drive thee from men, and thy dwelling shall be with the beasts of the field: they shall make thee to eat grass as oxen, and seven times (seven years) shall pass over thee, until thou know that the most High ruleth in the kingdom of men, and giveth it to whomsoever he will. And in that** same hour, the same prophesy was fulfilled upon Nebuchadnezzar: and he was driven from men, and did eat grass as oxen, and his body was wet with the dew of heaven, till his hairs were grown like eagles' feathers, and his nails like birds' claws. And at the end of the days I Nebuchadnezzar lift up mine eyes unto heaven, and mine understanding returned unto me, and I blessed the most High, and praised and honoured him that liveth for ever. The king got seven years. The Lord took out a normal heart and gave him the heart of a beast. But God is not doing that in this hour! He is not doing that in this hour. This was before Christ. This was before the Blood. This was before the Anointing. This was before the Bible. The Lord is not playing them games with you now; you have to get down to business. You have to get yourself together.

ALL RELIGIONS

All these religions are not going to heaven. That is not right. That is not true. That is not right. That is not true. The Beatitudes said, only the pure in heart shall see God. That's it. The Lord said, without holiness, no man shall see His face (Hebrews 12:14). Act 4:12 says, **Neither is there salvation in any other: for there is none other name under heaven given among men, whereby we must be saved**. So, if you are saved by any other name besides Jesus Christ, you are not saved. Romans 10:9-10 says, **That if thou shalt confess with thy mouth the Lord Jesus, and shalt believe in thine heart that God hath raised him from the dead, thou shalt be saved. For with the heart man believeth unto righteousness; and with the mouth confession is made unto salvation.** You must be very, very careful who you listen to nowadays. Everybody is saved; everyone has a gift; everyone can heal the sick. You better watch it. The bank robber is saved. The prostitute is saved. The whoring deacon is saved. Oh my God! The same-sex bishop is saved. Saved from what? What are they saved from? Saved? What kind of Heaven would it be if all these kind of people were able to get in? But thank God! Thank God! The Lord is not against the thief, liar, homosexual or murderer; He hates the acts of sin that they commit. No sinner is greater than the other; except for blasphemy against the Holy Ghost. Matthew 12:31-32 says, **Where I say unto you, All manner of sin and blasphemy shall be forgiven unto men: but the blasphemy against the Holy Ghost shall not be forgiven unto men. And whosoever speaketh a word against the Son of man, it shall be forgiven him: but whosoever speaketh against the Holy Ghost, it shall not be forgiven him, neither in this world, neither in the world to come.**

THE TEMPLE OF GOD

I Corinthians 3:17 says, **If any man defile the temple of God, him shall God destroy; for the temple of God is holy, which temple ye are. I**

Corinthians 6:19 says, **What? Know ye not that your body is the temple of the Holy Ghost which is in you, which ye have of God, and ye are not your own? For ye are bought with a price: therefore glorify God in your body, and in your spirit, which are God's.**

Some people are not going to wake up unto they are in hell. The devil can deceive you for so long. He can work on your mind and work on your mind. You can only play the role of the hypocrite so long, until the Lord turns you over to a reprobate mind. In a reprobate mind, you don't know if you are coming or going, speaking in tongues at will with your cigarette, cursing and smoking. Then you are telling people to speak in tongues so the devil won't know what you are saying. What nonsense! The Holy Spirit speaks through a holy tongue. The Bible teaches that Mary, the mother of Jesus, was up in the upper room with the other people, tarrying for the Baptism of the Holy Ghost. But you can do what you want to do? You can say whatever you want to say? And you can still go to Heaven? That is not true! That is absolutely false. There's no Bible for it.

GOD IS GOD!

And I praised and honoured him that liveth for ever, whose dominion is an everlasting dominion, and his kingdom is from generation to generation: And all the inhabitants of the earth are reputed as nothing: and he doeth according to his will in the army of heaven, and among the inhabitants of the earth: and none can stay his hand, or say unto him, what doest thou? At the same time my reason returned unto me; and for the glory of my kingdom, mine honour and brightness returned unto me; and my counsellors and my lords sought unto me; and I was established in my kingdom, and excellent majesty was added unto me. Now I Nebuchadnezzar praise and extol and honour the King of heaven, all whose works are truth, and his ways judgment: and those that walk in pride he is able to abase (Daniel 4:34-37). This was a lesson that king Nebuchadnezzar **had to learn**. Our world is so polluted with hypocrisy. Our world is so polluted with lukewarmness. When you talk to people about living free from sin, they act as if you are preaching some other gospel. But it is in the word of God. If you start talking to people about really being saved, they say we are judging them. If you talk to people about living free from sin, they want to know what kind of Gospel is this we are preaching. It is the Gospel of Jesus Christ. This mess about once saved, always saved. Oh, when a sinner dies. Now it is on. You thought you were tough. It is on. It is on. Again, in Daniel 4:24-37, Belshazzar gave no thought to the experience of Nebuchadnezzar. He was pleased that his party was going well. Thousands were in attendance, and they were eating and drinking. He never thought about his tomorrow. Belshazzar just thought about today, "Man, I am living. The lust of the eyes. The pride of life. Lust for sex. Lust for money. Lust for drugs; I got the porn going on. I have sex whenever I want to. I smoke all the bud, I smoke all the weed I want. I am toting my pistol. Everybody is bowing down to me." But oh, when a sinner dies. Oh, when a sinner dies. So many churches, they have covered up the reality of hell. But let hell be uncovered. Hell is a real place, it is not relative. It is real. It is not a figment of my imagination or something I have to think on. It is there now. The Bible says, as a matter of fact, not only is it there, but it has enlarged itself. People are going to hell by the thousands every day. They are dropping into hell like pennies in a bank; just dropping into hell, like a swarm of bees. Like a swarm of flies, they are just falling into hell. That is what happened to Korah and those boys, when they rose up against Moses and Aaron. They were talking about, "God is not using you. You are not right." It is dangerous to talk about the people that God is using. It is dangerous to talk about the things of God. It is dangerous to come up against God's true people. It is a dangerous thing. Korah was talking about Aaron and Moses and how they were doing all of this stuff themselves. Moses told them, "Tomorrow the Lord is going to let you see who is on his side. If Korah and his group die a normal death, then God is not with me. But if the Lord does something that has never been done in our day, then you will know." Look at all these judgments that are happening all around the world today. All these storms and tornados are no accident. Some of them are shaking mankind to try to get them to wake up while there is still time. God is shaking this old wicked world. This world is comatose. The world is comatose with sin, laziness. We are comatose in the houses of God; comatose with lukewarmness. They don't even fear the true and living God anymore. The Lord is sending some of these judgments. He is trying to rock these people and wake them up, before it is too late. Oh, before it is too late. There goes Belshazzar. There he is, and he doesn't care. He is having him a party. This is his thing. This is the thing he wants to do. He is having him a party. It says in

PARTY ONE LAST TIME . . .

Daniel 5:1, **Belshazzar the king made a great feast to a thousand of his lords, and drank wine before the thousand.** Just partying, he is getting it on. Belshazzar has no worries about tomorrow. He is not thinking about God. Belshazzar is not thinking about anybody. It is his life. He is going to do what he wants to do with it. That's the same spirit of many people today. It says Belshazzar had a thousand of his lords, and drank wine before the thousand. Belshazzar, while he tasted the wine, said *oh, bring out the gold and silver vessels that my father, Nebuchadnezzar, had in the temple of Jerusalem. I am going to drink out of God's stuff,* comparing himself to be equal with God. *Bring me that, I am worthy. I am worthy.* People in so many of today's churches have adopted that spirit of taking God's glory. *God, do something for somebody.* Well, you know. The Bible says to acknowledge the Lord in all your ways. To acknowledge the Lord, He is the one to give you the strength, to give you the wealth that you have.

A MIGHTY ARMY

Many of our youth today, they are so wayward. They are so rebellious. The antichrist, no doubt, will use them in his might army in the Tribulation Period. But so many of the youth learned from their parents; the disrespect; the lack of reverencing God in the home; a lack of commitment. They learned how to degrade God from their parents. They learned how to be disrespectful of God in the home. Some of these people that have grown up, they grew up in deceit, and now they treat God the same way that they treated their parents. The lying, stealing, they think that God is just another parent, BUT He is not. If your kids talk back to you, and you think they are going to get down and pray to a God that they don't even know, you are sadly mistaken. The Bible says, *how in the world can you serve a God, you have never seen and your brother is right there with you every day and many won't even look after nor have compassion on that one.* They are building these big houses for these leaders and buying them big Cadillacs. No! What about God? What about God? What about holiness? What about righteousness? "Oh, I have to have this. I have to get this for my pastor. You know the pastor said." No! You better read the Word for yourself. The Bible says, *mark the perfect man.* People say, "Ain't nobody perfect." Ain't nobody perfect, everybody sins." Then that is to say that Jesus died for nothing. But I know that is a lie. That is one of the greatest lies the devil has ever told. Many are in hell today because of that one lie, "nobody can live free from sin."

In Psalms 37:37-38 it makes it clear, **Mark the perfect man, and behold the upright: for the end of that man is peace. But the transgressors shall be destroyed together.** Paul says follow me, as I follow Christ. He said the woman should obey her husband as *he is in the Lord.* I am not obeying you in embezzlement. I am not about to drop any drug bags for you. That is not the "obey" the Lord is talking about. He is talking about obey your husband, as your husband is obeying the Lord. If that joker is talking about the church, whether it is a man or woman, turn them off.

Your responsibility is to the true and living God. You first responsibility is to God. **And thou shalt love the Lord thy God with all thine hear, and with all thy soul, and with all thy might** (Deuteronomy 6:5). It is probably because of you that many of your loved ones are still alive. It is probably because of you that they are not a cripple or in worse shape. Belshazzar was drinking and partying and not giving any regard to God. That is spirit of the devil. He wants to make you think that you are invincible. This is so paramount in so many of the youth today. You can do whatever you want to do. You do not have to pay. Pay day is not coming, until you land right in hell. Then, when you wake up in hell, you'll want God. It says that in the Bible, **In the same hour came forth fingers of a man's hand, and wrote over against the candlestick upon the plaister of the wall of the king's palace: and the king saw the part of the hand that wrote. Then the king's countenance was changed, and his thoughts troubled him, so that the joints of his loins were loosed, and his knees smote one against another** (Daniel 5:5-6). Now, the kings want to call for the people to tell him what the sign means. The sign means you have been found, and today you are dying. You are dying today. The kingdom is going to be taken from you. Amen. He came there, and they told the king what was going on. **And thou his son, O Belshazzar, hast not humbled thine heart, though thou knewest all this; But hast lifted up thyself against the Lord of heaven; and they have brought the vessels of his house before thee, and thou, and thy lords, thy wives, and thy concubines, have drunk wine in them; and thou hast praised the gods of silver, and gold, of brass, iron, wood, and stone, which see not, nor hear, nor know: and the God in whose hand thy breath is, and whose are all thy ways, hast thou not glorified** (Daniel 5:22-23). Think about the great God of the Universe bringing such an accusation against you! *The God in whose hands our breath is, you have not glorified.*

BORROWED TIME

You only have today. You are not promised tomorrow. But you have got today, just through the mercy of God. How are you living it? How do you treat God? It is God who brought the sun up for you this morning. If a person dies without God, he or she will have no chance to escape the tormenting flames of hell. You will not get out of hell. What is your life? **Whereas ye know not what shall be on the morrow. For what is your life? It is even a vapour, that appeareth for a little time, and then vanisheth away** (James 4:14). You do not know how long you have. Some of you treat each other like dogs; talk down to each other. Some of your companions, it is like a bull fight. But this is the one you picked out. This is the one you said God gave you. But it was *the god of lust*. You just had to have that one. Now, you have him and your life is a living hell. But you have to deal with it, because there is only one biblical reason for divorce. I don't care what people are saying. You just cannot drop him or her and get another one, not according to the word of God. **It hath been said, Whosoever shall put away his wife, let him give her a writing of divorcement: But I unto you, That whosoever shall put away his wife, saving for the cause of fornication, causeth her to commit adultery: and whosoever shall marry her that is divorced committeth adultery** (Matthew 5:31-32). There is only one bible reason, other than death. If that person goes outside of the marriage and commits adultery on you, *and you keep yourself clean* in the meantime, then you are free to remarry. Not talking about, "They got somebody. Well, I'm going to get me somebody". No! You are not free. And to show you what the Lord thought about divorce, they went down in the Old Testament days trying to talk to Moses about it. **And they said, Moses suffered to write a bill of divorcement, and to put her away. And Jesus answered and said unto them, For the hardness of your heart he wrote you this precept. But from the beginning of the creation God made them male and female** (Mark 10:4-5).

LEFT OVER TROUBLE

In most cases, a divorced person is a lot of trouble. There is some reason why they could not stay together with the one they had. Now, you have got to think about his. There is a reason why they are not with that person. Then, you run over there to marry them with their troubles. They got bad credit, got bad feet. They got bad debt. They got bad breath. They got a bad back. What can they do for you? In most cases, a divorced person is trouble. They are bringing all that garbage from somebody else to you. In our economy, the way our society is going, these kids are having sex at ten years old. They are getting pregnant at eleven years old. And they are having, I do not know how many abortions, by the time they are fifteen. And you are going to marry somebody like that? You better think twice. If you are arguing now and fussing, don't get married. If you are *throwing down* now, that's not the one for you. I want to tell you ladies, you cannot make a man change. "When I marry him, I am going to change, him." Yeah, and now you see who got changed. You are taking a pill to go to bed. You are taking a pill to stay up, while you are up. You got more hell than you bargained for. But your compass was the lust of your eye. It was not your heart. *You must marry for love.* I would be so very careful about bringing children in this world today. I would be so careful. If you all are not getting along now, please do not have any kids. Think of those you know, who already are dead. They had come to their last day and didn't even know it. They had plans for tomorrow. They had plans for their future and never made it. And if they died without God, they are a sinner who died. *And they are alive right now.* They will be alive forever more. Just think maybe some of them were young and healthy. You thought they had a long life ahead of them, but just one wrong move, and they were dead; gone from this earth. Suddenly something happened to them, and they were killed. They died unexpectedly, lost and eternally damned; eternally shut away from the face of God as the eternal ages roll. Think about it again and again.

YOUR LAST DAY

When is your last day? Do you know? **And he spake a parable unto them, saying, The ground of a certain rich man brought forth plentifully: And he thought within himself, saying, What shall I do, because I have no room where to bestow my fruits? And he said, This will I do: I will pull down my barns, and build greater; and there will I bestow all my fruits and my goods. And I will say to my soul, Soul, thou hast much goods laid up for many years; take thine ease, eat, drink, and be merry. But God said unto him, Thou fool, this night thy soul shall be required of thee: then whose shall those things be, which thou hast provided** (Luke 12:16-20)?

There are those of you who are evil and wicked and treat people bad, talking about people and stabbing them in the back. You just curse and curse. You are evil. Your kids don't even want to be around you. Now that is something; to bring kids into the world, and they can't stand you. It is sad for a parent to have gone through a lot with a child and almost hate them. *I don't want to see your face.* You have done so much to them. You have stolen money. You stole their jewelry when you were on drugs. Oh my God! You lied, stole their social security number and messed up their credit. Then, all of a sudden, they want to know why momma did not want to have anything to do with them. When momma doesn't want you no more, that is a deep, deep thing, because the Lord compares a mother's love to the love of Jesus. You have the love of God, and then momma's love is right there. That love is way up there, because a momma will deal with you when nobody else wants to deal with you. But when momma says, "I am sick of you now," that is something to me. When momma says, "Don't come back here, anymore!" That is something. That is something. But momma can't heal you. Momma can't save your soul. Momma can't put you in heaven or hell. You are the only one who can put yourself in hell.

A TYPE OF JESUS

Luke 16th chapter talks about a rich man and a beggar. This scripture talks about how there was a rich man that did well every day. Also, there was a beggar. The beggar was a type of Jesus. The beggar did not have the appearance that the rich man thought he should have. The beggar did not smell like the rich man thought he should have. The beggar did not wear the kind of clothes. He did not have a lot of money. But it was symbolic; that beggar was the symbolic Christ. That beggar was the last hope for that rich man. It was his last hope. Jesus literally came and sat at his door, because Jesus knew his days were numbered.

YOUR DAYS ARE NUMBERED

Some of you, your days are numbered. Your days are numbered. The Lord has been pulling on you. He has been trying to get you to wake up. The spirit of the devil has taken you over. You are so deceived. You are so stubborn. You are so rebellious. You have got that murdering spirit in your heart. You are going to die with that in your soul. You have got that vengeful spirit in your heart. You got that spirit in your heart that you don't care. You have got that jealous spirit in your heart. Oh my God! And you just don't care. But you will care one day. I have not met one person that could outdo God. I have not met him yet. He has not been created.

The Bible says that when iniquity was found in Lucifer, he was cast out along with so many of the angels. There was Jesus, who said, *I saw Lucifer fall as lightening from heaven.* It was because iniquity was found in him. If the Lord did not spare the angels, He is not going to spare your wicked evil self. You better let hell be uncovered today. Some of you are really wicked. You are very evil. You talk down to people. You have got your kids scared of you. You better let hell be uncovered. You better cry out today for the true and living God. You better turn away from this mess. You better turn away before you go to hell. As you go on to read in Luke's gospel, it says that both the rich man and the beggar of them died. Oh! Oh! Isn't that something? They both died. It amazes me how people are when they are near death.

AT DEATH'S DOOR

When I was a chaplain, I did an internship at a major hospital here in Chicago. It is really amazing to me when people think they are going to die. They do not care anything about you being black; they are looking for some help. When people would call for chaplains, I didn't care if they were Jewish, Catholic, or a deep rooted Baptist from the south. It doesn't matter, when people are getting ready to die, they want somebody that can pray for them. They don't care. They don't have time for prejudice. They don't have time for any racism. They are not there trying to count their money, because they are near death. None of that stuff matters. They are trying to get their next breath. Sometimes the doctors use to call me down. They would say, "You need to come on down now to talk to the family, because the organs are there and are now coming out through the tube. It will just be a few moments, and they will be dead." The worst death I have ever witnessed is a person who died with AIDS. That disease is so horrific. It is the worst disease I have ever seen in my life. It is the worst disease that I have ever seen in my life. And when you're dead, it is really on. It is on now.

As we finish this lesson in Luke, one of them went to heaven, and one of them went to hell. This is the thing I have to get you read here and notice about Luke 16 chapter. This is not a parable. A parable does not have proper nouns. This really happened. The Lord put this in the Bible. He does not give us a whole lot of information about Heaven, but that doesn't mean it is not real. This is not a parable. This is factual. This happened. It says here, in verse Luke 16:22, **And it came to pass that the beggar died, and was carried by the angels into Abrahams bosom, the rich man also died.** Notice that the rich man died too. It says he was buried. But

282

in the next verse, it says in hell he lifted up his eyes. Only his body was buried, but his soul went to hell. When a sinner dies. When a sinner dies. When you die, that is just the beginning. Your life is so short. People are so deceived. They will not realize it. Your life is so short. You won't even give over to God. You won't even live for God. You won't even give God glory. Some of you won't even pray over your food. Some of you won't even pay tithes. This life is so short, but you won't even honor God. There you are, spending an eternity separated from your God forever. Forever. Then, you will think about all the times He tried to warn you. Then, it will come to your mind of how deceitful you were. Then, it will come to your mind that the Lord was really trying to help. But there is nothing you will be able to do about it. When you get in hell, there is no getting out. If you got any sin in you, hell is your destination. One lie, hell is your destination. The book at the end of Revelations says, all liars will have their part in the lake of fire. There is no such thing as lying Christians. There is no such thing as smoking Christians. There is no such thing as a cursing Christians. Curse words blaspheme the name of God. You are not saved. The blood of Jesus is not on your soul. You do not belong to Him. You do not belong to Him. I never read about Jesus taking a social drink. That wine that they made was not fermented like it is today. But **in hell he lifted up his eyes** (Luke 16:23). This was instant; the next breath.

DEAD . . . NOT AT ALL

Go back to Luke 16:22 where it says when the rich man died, he *was buried.* So you know, flesh and blood cannot enter Heaven or hell. His body was placed in the ground. Not his soul. His body was buried, not his soul. Your soul will live forever. Your soul came from God. Your soul is going to live forever. Your soul came from the breath of God. That is the real you. You will never die. You will never die. The Bible says in Heaven we will be known as we are known. I am not going to be known by my hair, but by whom I am, my soul. I am going to have a glorified body, but you are going to know me, and I am going to know you. It says, in hell he lifted up his eyes. His body was buried, but his soul was alive. His soul was alive. His soul was alive. His soul was alive. His soul was alive. Get that! His soul was alive. He lifted up his eyes. The Bible said he had eyes, and he was in torment. How was it that he could realize he was in torment? His consciousness. You better wake up and hear this today. Some of you, you are walking on a thin wire. You are so close to eternity. Oh my God! If the Lord could open up your eyes today. If he could pull a shade down and play your life, you would see how close to eternity you are. But your arrogance is stifling. Your disobedience, your rebellion is stifling. Nothing is going to wake you up, but the fires of hell. The Lord has shaken you, trying to shake you awake. He has incarcerated some of you. He has let something happen to some of you, and you still won't give over to God. It is amazing. But it is the spirit of the antichrist. It is the spirit of Lucifer. Some of you have many devils in you. You have many devils in you. That devil is putting in your mind about murdering people. But let hell be uncovered. That is what the Lord told Cain. You live by the sword, you die by the sword. Some of you have no fear of God, and it makes me frightened in my heart. It says he was in torment. He saw Abraham afar off. And Lazarus was in Abraham's bosom. Abraham's bosom is heaven. In this context, Abraham's bosom is heaven. In Luke 16:24 he is supposed to be dead. Again, this is not a parable. A parable doesn't have proper nouns. It says, **and he cried and said**. So, he is crying and talking. Get this! Get this! So when you die, that's it? No! It says in verse 23 he lifted up his eyes. He recognized he was in a tormented flame. Verse 24 says, **he cried and said**. He cried and said. Father Abraham, have mercy on me, and send Lazarus, that he may dip the tips of his fingers in water, and cool my tongue; for I am tormented in this flame. Now, he wants mercy. He could see. He could feel. He had a consciousness. He could cry. He could speak. He was conscious that only that body was in the ground. But the real him was in a place he had prepared, in a living, tormenting hell where the fire is not quenched. It is not going down. The fire is not going out. You will never get out. You will never die. You will never get out. You will never get out. You will never get out.

YOU BETTER CHANGE

Some of you better change. Some of you better change toward God. Some of you better change toward God. Some of you better change toward God. God is not playing. How long do you think this world can last? People are dying by the thousands every weekend, all over the world, all of over the city. There are disasters everywhere. There are hurricanes. Tornadoes are in places that they have never been recorded. Lift up your heads, redemption draweth nigh. Abraham said, *Son, remember when you had it good? You did not want to pray. You did not want to fast. You did not have time to tarry. You did not wait to pay your tithes.* But remember, he suffered. Remember all the stuff he went through. The tables have turned. It is not like what you thought. Most things are not like what you thought. Most people are not what they say to be. Most people are not what they seem. Most people are not what they seem. Most people say that they are your friend. They aren't your friend. Your friend isn't going to tell you to steal from momma. Your friend wants you to do well. They are not going to tell you to shoot up. That is not a friend. That is co-dependency. No, a friend wants what is right for you. That is a friend. A true friend will tell you "Boy, get out of that place before you die. Boy you better serve God." That's a true friend. The Bible says that if you want friends, you have got to show yourself friendly. It says a true friend will stick closer than a brother, Jesus Christ. They don't judge you. They are long suffering. They are gentle. They are kind. They want the best for you.

CAN YOU SEND SOMEBODY?

You have got these rappers, talking about I am going to hell. I am going to hell. I am going to hell with my gun, blaspheming God's name in these songs. They are talking about how they are praying unto God. God does not have any part or lot with them. He told him in Luke 16:25, "Remember you had it good on the earth but you did not have time for me." Now, all of a sudden, he has a missionary spirit. "Well, even if I can't get out, can you send somebody? Anybody? Can you please tell my brothers, because they believe like I believe? They were profane too. Can you send somebody over to my brother's house? They are all shacking up with women. Somebody tell them this is for real. Can you send someone to my brother's house and tell them to come in and start praying, because this is real? Can you send somebody to my brother's house and tell them God is vengeful? Can you send somebody to my brother's house and tell them God see's everything we do? Can you send somebody to my brother's house to tell them when you're an alcoholic, when you are in hell, you crave alcohol? Can you send somebody? Can you send somebody to my middle brother's house? He introduced me to porn. Can you tell him that down here I want porn, but I can't do anything about it? Can you send somebody to my brother? He got high all the time. Can you tell him that down here you get high, but you never sober up? Can you send somebody? Send somebody to my brother. He said he was hearing voices. Can you tell him those are devils? Can you send someone to my brother? He's a pastor, but he's not teaching the truth. Can you tell him, "Whoa! Whoa! To the pastors who scatter my sheep." Can you tell him God is watching? Can you tell him God is watching? He is weighing him on his scales. I am a witness. But Abraham said, No we aren't. They got all the prophets. They got the Bible. They got the Holy Ghost. They got the anointing of God. They got Jesus. They got the word of God. They got angels who minister to those who are heirs of salvation. If they are not going to believe them, certainly sending them somebody back from the dead won't change them. When a sinner dies! I hope you take this message to heart today.

You cannot afford to die without God. You do not have to be all deep in religion to realize there is a God. People might say there is no God. There is no God. I prefer to die believing in Him, then to die not believing in Him. I give my whole self to this Bible. I give my whole self to this Bible. The Bible says that Jesus is coming back, and He is going to the pay for everybody for the deeds they have done. The Bible says Jesus is going to pay everybody for everything that they have done. Everybody who mistreated me, I do not have to do anything about that. I have to forgive them, because I have got to have the right heart to deliver the message to you. Everybody who mistreated me, Oh I forgive them, because I know hell is real. They have to work that out for themselves. I cannot have any unforgiveness in my heart. He said when you are praying, and you don't forgive them, God is not listening to you. With all that unforgiveness in your heart, he is not listening to your prayers. You have got to let go and let God in. You have got to let go of all that past and all that stuff people did to you. I know it is hard, but you have got to let God be God in your life.

TO DIE WITHOUT GOD IS TO DIE WITHOUT HOPE

I hope you were blessed today. When a sinner dies. To die without God in this hour is a dangerous thing. Neighbor, you need God. And I need God. We can live without so many things. We can live without so many people, but oh my God! I just feel like Lot in the days of Sodom and Gomorrah. Lot was trying to tell his family that Jesus was coming. And you know what? They just mocked him. "Oh, you crazy man." "Aww, she doesn't know what she talking about." Can you prove I don't know what I'm talking about? Can you prove it? Has anybody come back and told you? No! I want to tell you today as we close. Hell is a real place. Hell has been prepared for those who will not follow God. You were created to serve the true and living God. Some of you only have a few more days, relatively speaking. Your days are numbered. Some of you in this congregation, your days are numbered. God has been after you and after you, and He's just about to let you go to do your own thing. Everything He does, you rebel. Everything He does, you kicked against Him. Everything He does, you turn your nose up. Everything He does for you. You will run a little while, but as soon as someone says something, you get mad. Neighbor, He is getting sick and tired of you. He says it right there in the book of Proverbs, *you did not want my law.* You did not want thus said the Lord. But when you get right down to that hour, I am going to turn away like I have never seen you, like I don't hear you suffering. Neighbor, God bless your hearts today. I want to pray for you.

LET HELL BE UNCONVERED

I pray that this message will shake you up. I pray that you will allow hell to be uncovered. Neighbor, things are winding up now. Things are not like they use to be. Things are winding up. But just by repeating this simple prayer, you can change your life today. All of us know somebody that is in hell today, but we can't do anything for them. We can do something for ourselves. We can do something for our children. We can do something for our neighbor and our friends, and that is to live right. Neighbor, I want you to lift those hands up. All my boys and girls in the prisons, you can still have Christ. Your life is not over. Your life, it is not over. Your life is not over. Your life, it is not over. Just think about that when a sinner dies. It is something to think about those last moments on Earth. Just think about that person. No doubt, those demons are waiting right there to take that soul. Now, they are laughing, mocking God, saying that they have got another one of God's children. When a sinner dies, it is so profound when I think about it over and over again. That person, even though they go to the grave on Mother's Day, they go to the grave on Father's Day, that person has been in hell for years and years and years. Belshazzar has been in hell. Korah and his boys, they are still in hell this morning. They are there. Saul and his beloved son, Jonathan, they are still in hell. Judas who betrayed Jesus, he is still in hell. Some of my family members, they are in hell today. They died lost. They did without God on their side. And there is nothing I can do for them. There is nothing I can do for them. But today is the day of salvation for some of you. Some of you are in really big trouble. You need to cry out. You need to cry out to the true and the living God. If you ever asked God to help you, you better get down to business. You better ask God to help you. You better pray until you know something has changed in your life. Some of you are so far away from God. Just one more step. Just one more step, and you can end up in eternity. Just one more step. Just one more step, and you will blaspheme against the Holy Ghost. I don't want you to leave this chapter until you are absolutely sure where you stand with God. I want you to make sure. We are living in evil days. And the Lord did say that our life wouldn't get cut down, but He said He would be with us. And you young people, you are living in a devilish hour. Oh My God! You need God. You need God.

I want you to say it with all your heart today. Some of you better not play around today, because you are in deep trouble. You better call on God while He might be found. This might be your last day. This might be your last day. You don't know when your life is up. You don't' know when your life is going to end. Today, God might say, that is enough, I am cutting you off. I am cutting you off. You might be walking around, but He might not even help you. You might lose your mind. I want you to repeat this simple prayer:

"Oh, God! Oh, God! Oh, God! Please forgive me, for sinning against you. But I have come home, never to leave you again. I am so sorry. I am so sorry that I failed you Lord. But I have come home, never to leave you again. I need your help. I don't want to die lost. I don't want to die lost! And by Faith and the Blood, I believe you are the son of God. I believe that you shed your blood for me, so that I could be free. Save my soul! Save my soul! Save my soul! Save my soul! Save my Soul! Save my soul! Save my soul! Save my soul! Save my soul! Save my soul! Save my soul! Save my soul! Save me Lord!

And if you mean that, He has come. He has come, neighbor. Now, do some Bible fasting. If you are within our area, come by and see me sometime at the church. And if I never meet you on this side of the Earth, I will see you in Heaven.

Part 5

This Is My Blood

CHAPTER 15
DRINK YE ALL OF IT

I was thinking about when you go to the doctor, particularly little kids, and they have you give them some kind of antibiotic or other medicine. They tell you, "Make sure they drink all of it." Make sure they drink all of it. The Lord is saying the same thing to each and every one of us. We want the blessings. When you receive salvation, the Lord just moves for you. I'm sure many of you, if not all of you, can attest to that; healing your body, finding you a place to live, getting you good employment. Then, you stop drinking. The Lord is admonishing each and every one of us that, if we're going partake of the Lord, we have to drink, and we have to drink it all. In John the 18th chapter, verse 10-11 says, **Then Simon Peter having a sword drew it, and smote the high priest's servant; and cut off his right ear. The servant's name was Malchus. Then said Jesus unto Peter, Put up thy sword into the sheaf: the cup which my Father hath given me; shall I not drink it?** Every single one of you; that cup became yours when you received salvation. All of the happiness, all of the joy that the Lord experienced, that became ours. But the suffering, persecutions, long-suffering, the compassion we must have on the lost, and forgiving one another, that's all in the cup for us to drink. Some choose what they want to accept and what they don't want to accept. But according to the Word of God, then we can't say we really are partakers of Christ's suffering. Some of you want the blessings, but you don't want to suffer. You don't want people to not like you. Well, they killed Jesus. So, the Lord is telling us we have to drink all of it.

TAKE THE MEDICINE

Sometimes you take medicine, and you start feeling better. So, you figure, "Well, I know more than the doctor, and I'm feeling better. I don't need to take anymore." One of the members in my church shared with us not too long ago about one of his doctor's appointments. His doctor was cautioning him and reminding him about taking care of his new kidney. "I know you seem like you feel well on the outside, but the inside is still healing. And so when you take that medicine you might start feeling good, but maybe the inside is still healing," the doctor cautioned him. So, the Lord admonishes us to drink ye all of it. I think about another person who attends my church. He said that when he first received salvation, he jumped on the bus telling the bus driver, "I'm saved," and the bus driver just kind of pointed to the back like, "Dude, sit down. Dude, I see this all day, just go sit down. Just head on to the back." The reason I'm bringing that up is because many of you started out like that. You all used to get those giant little books. Now, your spirit is saying to me, "Reverend, go on now with that Jesus stuff." It's like you are telling me, "Go on to the back with that, Reverend. Go on to the back". But the Lord is telling you, drink ye all of it.

John 12:23-27 says, **And Jesus answered them, saying, The hour is come, that the Son of man should be glorified. Verily, verily, I say unto you, Except a corn of wheat fall into the ground and die, it abideth alone: but if it die, it bringeth forth much fruit. He that loveth his life shall lose it; and he that hateth his life in this world shall keep it unto life eternal. If any serve me, let him follow me; and where I am, there shall also my servant be: if any man serve me, him will my Father honour. Now is my soul troubled; and what shall I say? Father, save me from this hour: but for this cause came I unto this hour.** If you're not where you think you should be with the Lord, you have to think, did you do everything that was required of you to receive salvation? Have you done everything that's required of you to receive the baptism of the Holy Ghost? Because Acts the 5th chapter lets us know that the Lord gives the Holy Ghost to those who obey Him. So, if you don't have the Holy Ghost, something is wrong on your end. If you're not hungry, you're not honestly seeking the baptism in the Holy Ghost; you're not saved. How could you have the blood of Jesus on your soul and not want to go deeper with Him? That's the purpose of engagement; to learn a little bit more about the person you plan on spending the rest of your life with. Is this person really my soul mate? Is this the person I really want to be with? An engagement is kind of like the idea squirming around in your mind that, "I'm no longer myself, but I have to also think about somebody else." I was talking to one of our recent brides in our church, and she was explaining to me about how it just seems like she does not have any time. I said, "Well, you're married." Well, she used to be able to do stuff for herself. I said, "It's no longer. There isn't an 'I' anymore. See, when you were alone you could have all that prayer time you wanted, but now it's not like that. You can't pray all day." Do you get what I'm saying? Some of you guys, it's the same way. You have turned that car into a statue. Drink ye all of it. You have to learn how to blend those personalities together and gel together. You have to realize, "I'm not married to you, but now we are a team. We have come together to become one." Your child shouldn't be able to go to mommy and rise up against daddy. When that child goes to mama, mama should say, "What did your daddy say?" I know that's the way it used to be when I was coming up. But we knew better. We didn't play that! Always, "What did your mama say?" My daddy was like, "Hand's off baby." But now, it's not like that.

EXCEPT YOU DIE

Again, in John 12:23-27, **Jesus answered them saying the hour is come that the son of man should be glorified. Verily verily I say unto you, except a corn of wheat fall into the ground and die; it abideth** (what?) **Alone.** I encourage you to underline that, if your Bible is a workbook. Except you die, you're going to be alone. It's the same way, naturally. Except you die to self, and what you want. Nobody is going to stay with you and put up with your mess! You don't have a maid. God gave you a helpmate. He isn't your sugar daddy; you're not a cougar! It says, but if the seed dies, it bringeth forth much fruit. He that loveth his life shall lose it. Those of you married couples, those of you who think you want to be married, and those of you who think you shouldn't have married, here it is; right here in this verse. The Lord said, **if you seek to save your life you're going to lose it. Now you can't save your life when you're in marriage. You can't have your own way when you're married. The Lord said, if any man serve me, let him follow me; and where I am, there shall also my servant be: if any man serve me, him will my Father honour. Now is my soul troubled; and what shall I say? Father, save me from this hour: but for this cause came I unto this hour** (John 12:26-27). Jesus was born to die. He knew when He left Heaven that the cup was before Him. He knew when He left Heaven that He was going to suffer. The Lord knew people were going to hate Him, nevertheless, He still left Heaven to save us and to make us free. We thought the Emancipation Proclamation was something great. No! Freedom for the soul, deliverance for the body, and healing for the mind. So, the Lord is admonishing you to drink ye all of it. You can't drink this with selfishness in your heart. Things happen that you have to encounter in your life; just accept it. Stop going back and forth with God. Just accept it; just drink ye all of it! God said no whoredom, no fornication, no shaking up; drink all of it! One prophet said the word of God may not taste good going in, but once it gets all the way down, once you accept all of the Word pertaining to you and your situation, it will be good to and for you.

CASTOR OIL

When I was growing up, I didn't like taking castor oil, but I wanted to go back out and play. My stomach cramped, but in the morning I was singing By and By When the Morning Comes. I was able to go outside, even though I had to sweat a little bit. God forbid if you had asthma, like

I did. Anybody who came into my room was getting a contact high off of the camphor. Your eyes could have had cataracts, but that camphor was knocking those cataracts off! You could have had a lump on your arm, that joker was going to fall off with all that camphor! My mama had me wrapped up. I think I was embalmed about five times when I was little. You know, they rubbed those mummies down so they could stay mummified like that. My mama wrapped me up more than once. I had that little light on me; wasn't a bright light, and I had that wheeze. Anybody coming in was instantly delivered! Instantly delivered! Every pore was open when you came in from my mama putting that camphor on me; you know, old-time mamas are the greatest ones. My mama didn't run to the doctor for everything. We couldn't afford it anyway, having five kids. She parted my hair, put that camphorated oil on me, ran that camphor all over my face, rubbed it all over my whole body, under my feet, then she would wrap me up, and I would sweat all night. But the next day, I was ready to go. The Lord is talking to you tonight. You have to drink ye all of it.

THE PART THAT MAKES YOU FEEL GOOD

Some of you drink it when it's good for you. Some of you drink it when the scriptures talk about walking on the water and feeding five thousand. But you have to drink all of it! You can't just drink the part that makes you feel good. You have to drink the part that corrects you, because the Bible tells us that the Lord deals with us as children. If we were bastards, He wouldn't even try and chasten us; He wouldn't even try and correct us. Don't you want to make the one flight out? Don't you want to be ready when Jesus comes? You have to challenge yourself and ask yourself, "Why am I not all I can be in God?" You and God are the only ones that can get that worked out; nobody else. We can preach to you, we can have all the counseling, but you have to get before God and say, "What is my problem?" You have to stay right there and let Him work on you and work on you. Depending on how deep your scars are and how bad you were mistreated, you have to let Him work on you and work on you. The Word will back you up. The Bible lets us know that Jesus will work on us until the day He comes back. He's going to work on us toward perfection. You have to accept some things in your life; that something is wrong with you. If you're mean and low-down, you have to accept that you are not any good; not a slogan, but a fact. "I don't treat my wife right. I want her at my beckon call. I don't help her with those kids." That may be why you're not getting any, honey! Psalm 69:20, 22 says **Reproach hath broken my heart; and I am full of heaviness: and I looked for some to take pity, but there was none; and for comforters, but I found none. Let their table become a snare before them: and that which should have been for their welfare, let it become a trap.**

RAPUNZEL RAPUNZEL

People do all this talking before they get married, but some seasoned married couples will tell you that you better do what the wife says, man. You can't come out. I got you with text. Got you. You can't watch any game today, because I got you. You have your little man cave downstairs, but it's really just a little corner with a T.V. on top of the box. Got you! But when you go upstairs, it's still peace, isn't it? I said, "Man, you know what, my mother and father, what is up with this?" My mamma is upstairs in her castle, and my daddy is down there in the den. He has it surrounded; got his bookshelves; got everything going on. But they had peace. My daddy would travel up to the Eiffel tower sometimes, and my mamma would let her hair down and bring him on up. Isn't that Rapunzel? Some days she'd just look down like, "Go back down in that room!" You all know it's right. Don't sit there and act like you don't know what I'm saying. Drink ye all of it. Sometimes momma didn't let her hair down for us, and we were her kids. She was like, "Uh huh. Not today. Go on, shut that door. Leave me alone." She was watching her westerns, her skating; Lord, if baseball was on, you better put a note in there, because that wasn't the right time. You husbands know, when those wives have that certain program on, you better leave them alone. You all know just, "That program is on. Ok. Well, I'm going this way." That's right. And some of us wives had to learn that they have been waiting all week for this game on Sunday. So, don't start acting like you are going to breakdown when the game is on, because they're not going to show you any love. They are like, "I will get with you on half time, if you're still alive." Right? It's just learning one another. So, the Lord is telling us drink ye all of it, and you can't drink of something or partake of something you don't have confidence in, you're not sure about, you don't have any knowledge of. The Lord came here and made it very plain to us everything that we would be subjected to, because we followed him. You're drinking of the Lord, or you're drinking of the devil. Some of you are not. Even though you are walking with the Lord, you don't know his fullness, because you won't drink all of it! You just go a little far, dancing around the edges, but you never really have been totally engulfed in it. You've never been submerged, so you still don't trust Him, and you still don't love Him like you should. How can you love a stranger? How can you love somebody that you don't know? It takes intimacy, spending time knowing them. Then, after awhile you begin to recognize that voice. My mother used to be able to tell it was us from our voice and by the way we walked. She knew us. She was acquainted with us. To be able to drink what the Lord is passing on to you tonight, you have to know Him in His sufferings, you have to know what it's like for family and friends to reject you. These things are coming upon you children for His name's sake. Drink ye all of it.

YOUR CUP

What's in that cup you have tonight? Persecutions? Is it rejection from the people you least expect? You have to drink ye all of it. Is the Lord doing you like the boys He did in John the 6th chapter? He's finished playing games. He's just coming straight out, telling you to get right or you're not going to His Heaven. Have you been having those thoughts? Have you been thinking about your mortality? It's not because you have been going to bed with the T.V. on the monster channel. No! God's trying to let you know maybe you only have a few days left, so you better get it together. You better get it together. You have to drink ye all of it. In order for the Lord to help you, you have to first come into the realization that you need help! Why would you let somebody cause you to go to hell? That's what's going. You might be listening to the wrong people, involved in conversations that don't have anything to do with you, being weak when the blood can make you strong, being pitiful when you can be strong in the Lord, and acting like nobody loves you. The Bible says for God so loved the world that He gave His only begotten son. You get mad or hurt, sensitive in your feelings, when they killed Jesus. The Lord, in His death, gave us everything we need to do everything that is required through His name. Yes! It's not easy. We have to get into great discipline in this final hour. If you're not disciplined on your job, they're going to fire you. You keep on going in there late giving them excuses, they don't care anything about you. There are so many people in the unemployment line! You don't have it like that. Don't be deceived and think you do! Don't think these jobs can't roll on without you! They can get a person in there for a third of the price they were paying you. They might just be trying to do that now, and nobody hipped you up to it. They still say "hipped you up to it"? Nobody brought you up on that line. Right? Drink ye all of it; everything that's there, everything that was a part of the Lord's life.

DRINKING AND GETTING DRUNK

Let's look at some people and examples of drinking, getting drunk and water being provided. Because we're talking about drinking, aren't we? "Yeah, I like that Reverend." I can tell when some of this music comes on, yup, they used to club. Them doom doom dooms come on, I be like yup, they use to party. They can't help it. They still have that little way about themselves they use to have when in the world, even though a gospel song is on. Doom, doom, doom. You're not doing it on purpose, but you know you don't want any lullabies, you want some doom, doom, doom, and it just happened to be in that song. But now you're praising God. Right now, you're praising God. Some examples of drinking, getting drunk and water being provided for are in 1st Samuel the 1st chapter. Hannah was accused of being drunk in the temple, but she was simply, earnestly praying. Eli the priest accused her, "Woman, don't you come up in this church drunk." So, how can we say this is new? He already did, right? What made him think she was up in the temple drunk, except it must have happened at sometime or another? So, why are we surprised? Brother, you've been drinking? Yeah, he's been drinking. Genesis 19:32-36, the daughters of Lot got him drunk and both conceived sons. They were talking about how they thought the world was going to come to an end. They had to have some kids. The older daughter went in and got him drunk on the first day. Then, the other daughter followed and got him drunk. They both had a baby by their daddy. So, incest isn't anything new. This generation thinks they created sex. Why are you so quiet?

THIRSTY . . . AGAIN

Exodus 15:22-26, **the people murmured against Moses and Aaron because they didn't have anything to drink. And the only water they had there was bitter waters. The Lord allowed a tree to be cast into the water and sweetened the waters for them.** Drink ye all of it. And in Exodus the 17th chapter, two chapters later, they were thirsty again and had a complaint on their tongue again. Some of y'all are so hard to please. It's so hard to make you happy. When they started complaining, the Lord allowed water to come from a rock. So, how can you say that the Lord doesn't love you? Judges the 7th chapter, verses 5 and 6, The Lord tested the soldiers for Gideon based on the way they drunk water. Were they drinking for self-preservation? Were they drinking to fill themselves up? Or where they drinking just enough, and yet keeping their eye on the enemy? How were they drinking? Were they drinking and watching? Or drinking and gulping? You know how it is. You get real, real thirsty, and water starts running down your neck. You just drink so fast. My nephew, Caleb, when he was a baby, Brigit was breastfeeding him. I don't know if he was thirsty or greedy. I'm confused. They both kind of mimic the same thing. So, Brigit was over at the house, Caleb was latched on to her, trying to draw all the milk out her that he could. Finally, milk was coming down his mouth. He just had his head on the top of her and was just like huggggh! His jaws were locked up. He was just tired from searching. But it wasn't going anywhere. The Lord was so mindful about the way the body is made, that when that milk goes on, there's some more coming. But here, that baby wasn't taking any chances. He was going to get it all! Drink ye all of it.

THE MURDER OF A RIGHTEOUS MAN

In 2nd Samuel 11:11-13, David has a righteous man killed in an attempt to hide his sin by getting Uriah drunk, with the hopes that he would sleep with his wife. Then, they both could hide the fact that Bathsheba was pregnant with David's baby. They were going to try and say that when Uriah was drunk, he slept with his wife. But Uriah was a righteous man. How could he have the enjoyment of his wife when his men and the Ark of the Covenant lay outside on the ground? Drink ye all of it. In Daniel the 5th chapter, Belshazzar causes his lords to drink out of the holy vessels, and he was killed for it. God hath numbered thy kingdom and finished it thou art weighed in the balances and found wanting. In Matthew 26:26, it says, **and as they were eating Jesus took the bread and blessed it and brake it and gave it to the disciples and said, take eat this is my body.** So, we know that the bread signifies the body of our Lord and Saviour, Jesus Christ. And he took the cup and gave thanks, and gave it to them saying, drink ye all of it. I want you to underline that in your Bible. He told them to drink it all. Jesus was so wise and magnificent, He used something as simple as Holy Communion to show how close and intimate He wanted to be with us. Something as simple as eating a piece of cracker and drinking some juice or wine to signify that the cracker represented his body, and the wine or juice represented his blood. But we can only be that intimate if we partake of all of Him. You know how you pray sometimes and sometimes you don't. You know how sometimes you forgive, but sometimes you want to hold on to it, because you think it makes you strong, but it makes you dumb. You know how sometimes you want to have compassion, and the next time you want to put a knot on someone's head. I'll tell you one thing, I learned about being a Pastor, eve n in my own life. You'll never know the value of mercy until you need it. You won't understand the concept of it. You won't understand what it really is for somebody to stand by your side, until you need them to stand by your side. Some things that we go through in life, as much as we try, they don't make sense to us, until we find ourselves in that situation. But when we are in that situation, if we are right with God, we are real glad that He is on our side. You don't know how powerful forgiveness is, until you find yourself really needing forgiveness, not because I burnt your toast, but because the Psalmist said in the 51st number *you're the one I really only sinned against. Nobody else really counts.*

WAITING TO SEE YOU

You hold my soul in your hand. Yes! Yes! Yes! Think about how you need to practice showing mercy, practice showing grace, practice being patient with people, practice just having compassion. So what? You had a messed up day! That has nothing to do with your children. They've been waiting on you all day to see your face. Some parents, their kids don't even care about them. Some kids haven't seen their parents, because they've been in six or eight foster homes in the last six or eight months. Your kids want to see your face; they want to talk to you about their day. And don't forget your character building. If you don't have time for them now, they're not going to have time for you when they're a teenager, and you want to know where they are. They're going to get somebody to listen to them. They're going to get somebody that's going to speak to them on their level, but it just might not be the person you want them to be with. Drink ye all of it. Matthew 26:26 and 28 say, **For this is my blood of the New Testament which is shed for many for the remission of sins.** What does false doctrine do with these scriptures? A doctrine that teaches nobody can live free from sin? What do they do with these scriptures that say, **This is the blood for the New Testament which is shed for many for the remission?** What do they do with these scriptures? **What I say unto you I will not drink henceforth of this fruit of the vine until that day when I drink it new with you in my father's kingdom. And when they had sung a hymn they went out unto the Mount of Olives.** What do they do? What do they do with the scriptures that say, the soul that sinneth it shall die? What do they do? Jesus took the cup after supper. You noticed they drunk the wine last. And all of the disciples had to drink from the same cup of wine. Jesus wants us to drink form the same cup that he partook of; the same cup of humility. Philippians says that the Lord humbled Himself even until His death on the cross.

BETTER, BETTER, BETTER

Some of you could have better marriages, better relationships with your children, and better relationships with your parents, if you would just shut-up and stop telling people what you think! Because telling people what you think is destroying what you think you have. Don't tell your wife you don't like her hair. You have to do that in a diplomatic kind of way, but "don't" cannot be in a sentence. You don't hear me. Don't tell your husband what you really think when he has shaved it all the way down. It's not like he can go in the bathroom and get it off the floor. My God! Why did you do that? You need to be saying, "My God is a good God! Oh yes He is!" It's a simple little thing. You don't know how sensitive people are. It's sort of like my Jeep; it's a truck. But certain people close to me, we might be out driving, they'll point to a truck and say, "Now, you know what? That's a truck." But on my insurance papers and on the bill of sale it says "truck." Once that comes into your mind, it does not matter! Truck, truck; you carry that flash card in your pocket with a truck on it. Truck, right? Man, what a truck we have! Because what she might do on the next birthday is get a real truck. So, I'm telling you, drink ye all of it when you sit down and marinate with the scriptures. You will see you have a lot of power! You have a lot of power to keep things together that are in your control! People might be going through, but they're holding on, because you speak so much positivity. People might feel like they can't make it, but they see you going through, and yet you are still happy, you are still encouraged! People want to serve that God that you keep on worshiping no matter what! Or maybe they don't want to come here, because you keep talking about me. They might think I have big feet and bad breathe. Somebody told me before they came to the ministry that they thought I was a real tall woman. Now, I'm bigger than what I use to be. Come on now, you can say Amen. And I was smaller, a little tad bit smaller, and this person said, before they came into the ministry in the apartment days, that they thought from the way people were describing me, that I was a tall woman. They found out it was just me, but I had a hammer in my mouth (that's what my sister, Loretta, always said. She said my mouth is a hammer, and she just had to accept it.) Drink ye all of it. Again, Jesus had the disciples, all of them, drink out of the same cup. It's the same cup for all of us. It's the same cup.

THE CARPENTER'S SON

The Bible teaches us so well that, whatever they did to Jesus, why should we expect anything less in His hometown? The Bible says He couldn't do many miracles, because they were stuck on the fact that He was the carpenter's son! But He went around to other places performing vast and great miracles. You have to drink all of that. People, all they have for you is your past and what you use to do. But the Bible says in 2nd Corinthians the 5th chapter, verse 17 *you are new!* You have to know what you are and who you are in God! People are going to keep on talking no matter what. You have to know who you are and where you are in God. Some people you just have to stop associating with, so they can stop making you weak. You're only as strong as the company you keep. Can I say that right? If you're hanging out with whores, you're going to start prostituting yourself. Can I say that? I did anyway. You can't hang out with a drunk, or you're going to start spending your rent money. You don't want to talk back to me. Watching that porn site! She's always talking about that porn. Somebody in here is watching porn. I'm not talking to the fan. It's already bare. It's transparent. We can see it. The Lord never gives us something we don't need. Somebody in my ministry is into that porn, and they're going to hell for it! You know you can watch porn on your phone? You can dial it up. You can watch it on your tablet. In hell, you're going to lift up your eyes and still want to see it, but you're not going to be able to satisfy that craving. Cursing, going to church every week and cursing; you're not going to Heaven. You have to drink ye all of it.

THROW STUFF OUT!

We thought we were having company and wanted to clean up our house, because when our company came I wanted to be able to show them what we had accomplished. I couldn't have done this by myself. A bulk of the work we had to do was just throw stuff out. You need to start doing that in your life; just throw stuff out. Stop trying to hold on to stuff, things, and what people have done to you. Just throw it out! You need to throw some stuff out in the alley! Amen Reverend Thomas. You need to throw out what somebody did to you, because as long as you're holding on to what somebody did to you, you can't see what you're doing to others! But if you throw that out, drink ye all of it, you will notice a difference in your life and the way you are around people. Some of you treat stranger's better than you treat your loved ones, kin folks. Sometimes people in the house just need to vent. You know what it's like on these jobs? People are poking you and pushing you, and you can't respond. Sometimes people get home and they're not angry at you, they're just trying to get it out, so they won't have to keep it in and retaliate against you. But you don't have enough wisdom and knowledge to realize all they're trying to do is talk to you. Don't keep shooting them down with negativity! Get the wisdom of the Lord! Sometimes all they want you to do is just rub their back! They don't want your thoughts; just "Honey, it will be all right!" That's it! Some of you with two left feet and two left hands are so critical of other people! You want them to be perfect, but you're far from perfection. What people go through on these jobs, the things they have to deal with just to stay employed, they have to vent somewhere. You don't have to vent every day, let me add that. Sometimes you have those days you're not talking about anybody, you're not angry at anybody, you're not angry at God, but you just have to get it out! And that's it. Don't make it be about you! I'm talking about how the pipe busted at the job, but you're talking about hitting me with a pipe. No! No! Don't make it about you! It's about the job. Don't make everything about you. That's so selfish. Don't make everything about you. People, jobs are hard to get. People are going through a lot to keep these jobs to provide, to share their part in the rent and the mortgage. We have to be more compassionate to each other. There's nothing wrong with crying, just don't keep on crying. Cry! Cry it all out. But don't come back tomorrow at dinner time talking about, "Wait a minute, I have one more thing." No! Be compassionate towards one another. All of us are going through something. It does not matter how we look, we are all trying to make it. That's it. That's all. We are all just trying to survive. We should have more love for one another. People should find more love in this place than anywhere else. It doesn't matter what somebody did, but aren't you glad they came back to God? They made it back. Can you see the miracle in that; in this wicked hour that we're now living in. The powers of the devil are so strong, yet by His grace, He brought them back. They're going to be a better worker, a better witness, because they know there's nothing out there. Right? And I know you've been smoking. You're not going to get a healing like that. Some of you come in and had a tussle and a bustle out there in the car, then you slide in here angry, man! Mad man! Then, you're going to try and act like you're alright. That's the worst thing in the world. It's like a musty person spraying on perfume. The must rises up above, and that funk is still there. You just sprayed something on it. Which did what? Made it worse, right? This is not the time to find out where you stand. You need to know where you are with God. The day is far spent. I want you to review this chapter and go over it.

THE HUMAN CHRIST

Jesus goes down in those final verses, Matthew 26:36-46. The very humanistic side of Him was looking for somebody just to hang with him for a minute. Yes, He was the son of God! Yes, He was the redeemer of the world! But remember, He was as human as you and I. How else in the world would we be able to identify with him? In one of His most perilous times He just wanted a human face and hand. He knew they couldn't die for the whole world. He knew they couldn't go too much further, but just right now, right then. Can you just wait with me? Can you just wait on me? In your relationships, can you wait on a person? Can you give them the benefit? Can you just not ride them today? Can you just wait? Can you be patient? Can you just not rag on them about this thing today? That's all Jesus was saying. Jesus was just saying, *I'm going to die, but can you just wait on me? Can you support me? Can you just encourage me in this endeavour? I'm not asking you to take my place yet?* He said that if we were going to follow Him, we would have to take up the same cross, because He showed us that it was possible for us to carry it. But He said, *Right now, I just want you to stay awake.* Jesus was trying to teach them that if they could just stay awake, then they could have victory. If you can just stay awake, then you won't yield to temptation. Just ask that old boy, Samson. Yield not to temptation, for yielding is a sin. That old Delilah was pretty fine. She was probably was a 36, 24, 36. She had some of that fine silk from across the sea. Queen of Sheba might have left some behind for her. She did more than wrap her face in it. She probably had some cucumber oil, a little honeysuckle, pineapple something. Come on, you all know you pay for that good lotion, not that Jergens. You get a little tiny bottle, and it's twenty dollars, and you only rub it on yourself during certain times. You all know you have those special rings. You don't wear those rings to your job. You don't wear your good watch to work. All He wanted was a human hand; just wanted somebody to understand. And Jesus was telling them, *If you fall asleep, the enemy is going to get you.* That's what Reverend Thomas is telling you. If you don't stay awake, the enemy is going to get you! He's going to get you! He's going to get you! The only way you can stay alert is by coming to every service that you can. You have to persevere. You have to fight! You have to contend to be all God wants you to be! Reverend Thomas, what are you telling me? Drink ye all of it; God's whole will for your life.

CAN HE PAY?

One person came to Jesus, and that's how He started this conversation about drink ye all of it. In that same chapter, a person came there and was asking if their son could sit on the left side of Jesus. Jesus said, *Well, can he pay for it?* Can he pay to sit there? You want to go to Heaven, but can you pay your way? You get on these CTA buses. They're going to put you off if your ticket is not working. You can ram it down that machine as many times as you want to, it's going to keep saying there's no money on it. That's what's going to happen when you get to Heaven's door; you're going to try and swipe that card, and it's going to say "unknown." These are the days of Elijah. These are the days you need to get close to the Lord. Drink ye all of it. The persecutions, the separation, the things we're going to have to go through, and some of you you need to separate from the world. You are so worldly. The things you watch, the people you hang with it, they have so much influence over you. How can you say you are of God? You need to read 1st John. It's a short book. Drink ye all of it. Jesus could have refused to die for us. It was His choice all the way up to when they nailed

Him on the cross. He still had a choice. But think about how deceived the people were in the Garden of Gethsemane when Peter cut that man's ear off. Jesus simply put it back up like it was no big thing; put on the man's ear, and He was on His way to His trial. And we're fussing about making a sacrifice. You didn't used to have anything. You have money to give, because you made a promise to God; that if He will, then you will. Yes you did. Yes you did. And not paying your tithes, I don't understand how you can do it. Peter never thought he would deny the Lord; never thought it, but he didn't know himself. Some of you don't even think the Rapture's going to happen; you foolish thing. You think you have plenty of time. That's because you don't know yourself. You can't see yourself. It's alarming. You can't see yourself. You can't see yourself, cursing right up in the church. It's in you. You can't say you're not going to curse. Because the bible says from the abundance of the heart. If you step on my feet, it's nothing for me to say ouch! Pain goes to my brain like, "Open your mouth and say something, so I can get off your foot." The bible says corrupt communication brings bad habits. People who curse have poor vocabulary. Right? I want you to work on yourself this weekend.

WHERE DO YOU STAND?

Where are you at in all of this that I am saying? Where are you? Where are you in all of this, making the Rapture, Holy Ghost, salvation? Where are you? You tarried at home this week? How much prayer time did you have this week? How much T.V. did you watch? How much food did you eat this week? How much hell did you raise? The scales haven't balanced out, have they? Only what you do for Christ will last. Come on, let's praise the Lord everybody. Yes! Yes! Yes! Yes! Yes! We told the Lord we would do anything if He would heal us, if He would save our souls. We have to pay up. I appreciate each and every one of you. Let's lift our hands and say the sinner's prayer, and get ready to get that great miracle you need tonight. Oh God, please forgive me for sinning against you. But I have come home, never to leave you again. Lord, I have come home to drink all of it. To drink all of your greatness, to drink all of your discipline, to drink all of the fruits of the spirit, and everything else that I need to make the one flight out. Oh God, have mercy on me tonight. Please don't withdraw your spirit from me. Please continue to deal with me, oh Lord. Strengthen me on every side. And by faith in the blood, save me Lord! Save my soul! I need your help tonight Lord. And if you meant that, you have the Lord in your heart tonight. Drink ye all of it. Get back in there with your prayer, get back in there with your fasting time, and get back in there with your concentration and dedication time.

CHAPTER 16
IS GOD A REALITY IN YOUR LIFE?

When I was growing up, I believed in Santa. I still believe in Santa. I just have the truth about him today. As a child, I wondered how he came down that chimney without dying. And you know, I would be right there in front of the T.V. watching when they would show on the news where he would be around the world. Come on, don't play with me. You watched it too. And you looked around to see where he might be. Was he in Australia? Your mind was like, "What a mighty man he must be, because he has to stop by here tonight!" He was as real as you are real to me in this room. As I got older, I realized that there truly was a Santa and found out the truth about that.

IT'S HARD

You know, it's hard to have a relationship with someone. It's hard to be patient with someone. It's hard to have hope. It's hard to have confidence. It's hard to trust somebody if you don't believe in them. It's hard. But you have to get the reality of the Lord in your life, because every one of you sitting in this room; there's going to be a time that's going to come in your life. You're going to have to know God for real, or else you're going to fall flat on your face. Listen, things are going to happen in your life that are going to knock the wind out of you. If you don't know God, you're going to go back, because it's easy. It's easy when things are happening in your life, when you are being tested and when you are being tried, to go back to what you're familiar with. Because that's all you knew. All you knew was pornography. All you knew was cursing and fighting and putting a knot on people's head. All you knew was complaining, drinking, and partying.

Then, you met the Lord, but now you're pressed up against the wall again. Now, you're being challenged. Every time you come to the services, the Lord is trying to give you a little bit more. He's trying to make you a little bit stronger, because as long as you're on this Earth, you're going to have some problems. But if the Lord is not real in your life, you're going to keep on rising and falling. Is God real in your life? This is an hour you can't fake it. They have a slogan in the world that says, "Fake it til you make it." It does not apply to God. Every one of you reading this today, if you haven't been to Gethsemane, you're going. In Gethsemane you can't pretend like you know God. When your child is killed or murdered, you can't pretend that God is with you. He's either with you, or you're alone in that dark night. They're going to lay you off. That's a reality. A lot of stuff starts going through your mind when you have a mortgage, and a car note, and you are the heavy breadwinner in your home. A lot of things start going through your mind, and you start perusing your memory.

THE GREAT I AM

Do you really believe? It's easy to believe, like today when you got in your car and turned it on. Amen Reverend Thomas! It started up, and you came here. But is God a reality in your life when you don't have any way, can't see any way? Is He still *I am the great I am*? Is God real in your life? That's something you can't fake. You cannot pretend to know God. Is God real in your life? Everyday, those of you who are earnestly seeking the Lord, He is seeking to manifest Himself. One of the people who came here one Friday told me the way the Lord is manifesting Himself to him. It's unbelievable! The Rapture will happen in your lifetime, and if it's not real to you, we're not going to even look for you to make the one flight out; because if the Rapture is real to you, you're getting ready. Some of you have some agendas that don't have anything to do with God and His will for your life. Some of you are runners. You just run from this, you just run from that, and you're constantly on the run from yourself. God has to be real to you.

That's where those voices come from; suicidal ideations. That's why you're always getting high. You think it's an escape route, but it's just a route to hell. In hell, you're still going to battle with "Mama didn't love me," and "Daddy didn't care." You're still going to battle with "What happened to me when I was little?" Because everywhere you go, you take you with you. And the only one who can change your predicament right now is God! But if you don't know him, you're going to continue and continue, and continue to struggle, until those negative things you're doing are going to will take you out.

PRESSED FOR THE WORD

There is such a wonderful example in Luke, the 5th chapter in verse 1. It says the first disciples are called. **And it came to pass that as the people pressed upon him to hear the word of God.** This is so powerful. You could read verses, and verses, and verses, but depending on where you are in your life, stuff starts jumping out at you like, "Man! I have read this since I have been reading the Bible!" So when I read this verse, this stood out to me. The Holy Spirit is illuminating this scripture for me. This was for me, and maybe it's for you today. The people pressed Him for the word. They wanted to hear what Jesus had to say. And what did Jesus have to say? Whatever his father gave Him. He never spoke on His own. So, they pressed Him for the words, because the words of God are the words of life. The words that Jesus speaks can heal you. The words that he speaks can save you! Come on somebody! The words that He speaks can put you back together again when it seems impossible, and the doctors have said, "That's it! Go home and make all your goodbyes." The words can say, "Not so!" It said the people pressed Him. And it says that He stood by the lake of Gennesaret and saw two ships standing by the lake, but the fisherman were gone out of them and were washing their nets. As He entered into one of the ships, which was Simon's, He prayed him that he would thrust out a little bit from the land. And He sat down and taught the people out of the ship. Isn't that amazing? That He was in somebody else's boat, and He asked Simon to take Him out a little bit. And the Bible says that He taught the people from the shore. Now, what does that mean Reverend Thomas? You're too close you can't see what is happening. You're too close to some people, and some things, and some stuff, and some ways, and some perceptions, and some attitudes, and some thoughts, and some movies, and some songs. You can't really see it. Jesus can't be a reality to you as long as you have all this stuff! You need to separate more. You want Jesus to be a reality to you? Go out from the shore. You're too close to your stuff and things, and money, and your 401k, and your new car. You're too close, and so you deceive yourself and don't realize that your reliance is upon all of this stuff and not upon God!

KNOW GOD FOR YOURSELF

But I'm telling you, you better know God for yourself. You better learn Him for yourself! You better learn Him for yourself! Notice, Jesus was speaking to a great crowd of people, but at the same time, unknowingly, He was teaching Peter! Because the boat belonged to Peter, and He told Peter to move out a little bit, because they were too close and might not take in all the words that He was saying. *If we are too close, then they're not going to respect me. And if I begin to linger with them, then I might become as them. But let's separate ourselves a little bit.* You're not going to be a soul winner going to the bar with them. You're not going to win them by going to the store to get their beer and cigarettes. You don't understand me? I'm going to wake you up out of that coma you just went in. You're not going to win them. You're not going to win them by letting them shack up in your house! You're not going to win them! The Bible says to go out a little bit from the shore. Go out a little bit. You're too close to people, and you think they're going to be there for you, but they're not!

HURT FEELINGS

Some of you hold on to hurt feelings, depression and sadness. You carry them around like they are a cloak for you in the winter. You need to go out just a little bit from the shore. Jesus' teaching could not have been effective if He was right up on them. But He took the owner of the boat, got on the boat, and told the owner of the boat, *Take me out just a little bit.* Isn't that what it says? It says in verse 3, *and He sat down and He taught the people from the ship.* He had to separate himself from the people to teach them. Nobody is coming to God if y'all act the same, y'all wear the same clothes, y'all talk the same talk, and y'all listen to the same music. What's the use in people [souls] coming, if you are doing the same thing? We're hanging out at the same place, talking the same talk (dirty talk), still involved in gossip, saying nasty jokes. What are those people going to come to God for? You need to get in the boat and go out a little bit into the sea. You have to know God for yourself.

LAUNCH OUT INTO THE DEEP

It goes on to say in Luke 5:4 that when Jesus was done speaking, He was finished. Simon was right with him. He said to Simon, *Launch out into the deep, let down your nets for a drought.* So Jesus was telling him, *Now, look how tenderly the Lord dealt with Peter.* I challenge you this week, everybody, to study the life of Peter. Certainly, you're going to find yourself. He just talked too much. Talk is cheap. Peter was telling the son of God, *You're not going to die. I'm going to be with you. Though all never leave you, I'm going to die with you. I know Lazarus is dead, but let's go in there. You know what? Forget about waking him up. Let's die with him.* You can't die until you're ready to live for the Lord. No! No! So, He met Peter, got in his boat, they moved out a little bit, He gave Peter a little bit of the Word, He said, *Now, I want you to go a little bit further with me.* You see that in your Bible anybody? Once he was finished talking, He told Peter, *Now, I want you to*

316

go out into the deep. He already told him before he went in the deep that he was going to prosper. He already told him that in the deep He was going to be with him, that he didn't have anything to worry about. In order for Him to manifest himself, Peter had to go out into a place where he wasn't in control and had total dependence is on Him. See, on the shore, he could have called his boys. On the shore, he had his net. On the shore, he had his other fishing buddies. But out in the deep, there wasn't anybody but him and God. That's where you have to go in this final hour. That's where you have to go in this final hour.

So, Simon started answering. He just couldn't understand what the Lord was talking about. Simon answered and said unto him, *Master, we have toiled all night and have taken nothing. But I'm going to trust your word. I have done all I can do.* Some of you can say Amen to that today. You have tried it your own way. You have given people your opinion about what you thought. The Lord is encouraging you today to listen to Him for once. You see your way wasn't good enough. But you have to know who He is, and what He will do, and what He won't do. You have to have the reality that God is with you. And if you know that God is with you, and that He will help you then, you need to understand the parameters by which it's required that He can be with you. He does not deal with any darkness. He does not deal with any sin. No! 1ˢᵗ John says, *If we are in the darkness, and we claim that Jesus is with us, that cannot be.* It cannot be. You're walking in darkness, and you say you're with Jesus, but Jesus is of life; the Bible says that cannot be. It says, **the light shineth it darkness but the darkness comprehended it not.** 1ˢᵗ John 4:1 says, **beloved believe not every spirit but try the spirit to see if it's of God.** Don't try what's going on in your life with your spirit, because you might be deceived about yourself. Whatever you see is going to come out the way you want, because you're trying it by your spirit. You have to try it by the Word of God. The Bible said, *In a man's eyes, he's always right.* He always has the answers. But He also said, **Mark the perfect man and the upright.**

So, Simon says, **I then tried it my way but nevertheless at your word.** How are you going to take the Lord at His word if you never tried it? If you never let the Lord exercise your faith? You have to exercise your faith, and the Bible says, **To every man is given a measure of faith.** He said, **If any man lack wisdom let him ask of the Lord who giveth freely and abraideth not and it shall be given unto him.** You're trying to do something that you don't even know anything about. You're trying to drive a jeep, but you think you're still driving a forklift; different mechanics. It's different mechanics. It might be similar, but it's not the same. A jet and a 747 are different. You can't operate them the same. A truck and a van are different. A fifteen passenger and a jeep are different. You can't treat them the same. Your friends and God, they are different. You can't treat God like you treat your friends. You tell your friends you're on your way over, but in your heart, you really mean you'll be there two hours later. You can't do God like that. You lie to your friends, but God said, *All liars are going to be cast into the lake of fire.* He said, *No liars. No liars.* And your friends put up with it, because the say they're your friend.

A TRUE FRIEND

A true friend is going to tell you the truth. A true friend wants you to be right; wants you to be a good man, a good wife, a good son, a good daughter. Yes, true friends. Yes! True friends are not going to tell you to cheat on your wife. That's a dog. That's a punk. Amen. A true friend's wife isn't going to try and hit on you. It's like the air. It's like nothing is happening in this room. Right? He said to beware of whores (whore mongering). When you think about the word "whore?" but mongering means they're going somewhere. What are they doing? Are they moving? Sounds like a traveling caravan or something. But Simon said, *I tried all I can, but let me do what you say.* Verse 6 says, **and when they had done this they enclosed a great multitude of fishes and their net brake.** What do you think this did? What do you think this did for them? No doubt, all of these people were with people when they tried it his way. Peter was a leader, and he didn't even know it yet. He had influence with people, but he wasn't ready to be that leader. It was in him, but he needed to be cultivated, he needed to be purged, he needed to be trained, he needed to be disciplined. But in him, the ability lay dormant. He needed God's power, God's will to evoke it and start it in existence! It's the same way with you. Some of you have talents, skills, and abilities, but they're no good to God until you're right. You need to take a bath. The Bible says, **though your sins be as scarlet I can wash you white as snow.** When the Psalmist had sinned against God in the 51st number, he said **wash me and I shall be clean.** So, he said, *I'm going to do what you said.* Then, in verse 6, *when they did what Jesus said, they were successful.* Study this carefully. At first, Jesus just dealt with Peter. So, God has to be real to you before you can make him real to somebody else. Isn't that what it said in verse number 7? Then, they called the other people to come after the reality had been shown to them.

LET GOD BE REAL TO YOU . . . FIRST

You can't tell somebody about receiving the Holy Ghost if you're not even tarrying. He first has to be a reality in your life. You can't tell somebody about having a good marriage, while yours is tore up from the floor up. You're not in a position. Your words don't carry any weight. You can't tell somebody up in your classroom that you're going to save your body until you get married, while you're looking around for some guy to tell you how thick you are. You need to shut the rascal up! That's when you need to raise your hand and tell the teacher, what's up with dude? That's all it takes. A "hehehe" turns into a "hahaha." Isn't that what happens when you have a baby? They say, "Don't push. Hold it. Hold it." That's a "H," right? Ha ha ha, right? Don't "holler" start with an "H"? Oh God! Oh, this baby! No! And now your fame is abroad, but not for a good reason. "She's easy. Go tap that." And who has to put you back together? Right here. All your problems, mind is messed up, and here you come. Now, you're faithful. Now, you're faithful. Didn't want to pay your tithes. Now, they're talking about how the Sherriff is at your house. You're calling us, "Is there anything you can do?" Isn't it too late? And depending on what's going on in your life when you call us, the first thing I want to know is have you been faithful? I want to know are you a tithe paying member? Because see if you pay your tithes, that means you love this ministry. Whether you like it or not, it's right. Yes!

Notice what this manifestation did for Peter. It said in verse 7, **and they beckoned their partners which were in the other ship that they should come and help them and they came and filled up both ships so that they began to sink.** The Lord manifested Himself to Peter. Peter yielded himself, and then he was able to be a witness for somebody else. But Jesus didn't first call everybody. He just worked on Peter alone. God has to get you right. He has to work on you. When you first get saved, that's not giving you a license to go out and try and save your family. Those are the ones you have to stay away from! They are going to pull you down! When you're saved, let the Lord build you up. Let him strengthen you. Learn the doctrine that you have accepted. Learn what it means to walk with the Lord. Yes, you have enthusiasm. Yes, you're ready to go out, but you need to go out in the prayer closet! Go out, so you can go in the prayer closet. Come out, so you can go in the prayer closet! Go out, so you can go in the fasting room! Go out, so you can go in the shut your mouth room! There is a room. The Bible says there is room at the cross for you. Though millions have come, there's still room for one. Shut your mouth room at the cross. Shut your mind up at the cross. Stop lying, fornicating, cheating and watching porn at the cross. Isn't that what Paul's writing says? He said there was *no strength in the shedding of the blood of bull and goats.* It could not keep people out of sin. It could not keep people out of sin.

START OVER

The Bible says that when you fail God, when you sin against Him, you have to start your first works over again. You can't just jump back up, like we see all over the place, and just go back in your position like nothing. No! You need to do your first works over again. So, they brought the other people, and it says in verse 8, **when Peter saw it he fell down at Jesus' knees saying; depart from me for I am a sinful man oh Lord. For he was astonished** (underline that). **And all that were with him at the drought of the fishes which they had taken.** Then, He told Peter that his life was going to rally, be all about, fishing for men. But He had to use something so simple, but in Peter's mind, it was so vast. It was so great. It seemed so impossible, but he had a willingness in his heart. Get this today. It seemed impossible. Your situation seems impossible; where you're at, living free from all sin. It seems impossible at nineteen and twenty, at thirteen and fourteen. It seems impossible, but let the Lord deal with you where you are. Just be honest with your maker. Be honest with your God.

PRAYER IS FOR . . . YOU

Reverend Thomas, what is prayer for? Prayer is for you, because if you're praying earnestly, the Lord is going to open up your mind and open up your heart. That which is in your heart, it's going to come to your mind, and then out of your mouth. From the abundance of the heart the mouth speaketh. Prayer is not for the Lord, it's for you! Because when you're really praying, prayer is a form of humility. You are recognizing that you are in a state, and that it's some greater power than you that you are looking to. You are acknowledging that, "I'm willing to do whatever You tell me to do, because I know You're the only one who can help me." That's what prayer is for. Prayer is a form of humility; prayer is a form of discipline. You know, God is not going to hear you when you're hitting and missing and praying every blue moon. You have to establish a relationship with Him.

That's what prayer is for. Fasting is so you can use what God has given you. Fasting is so you can stay in remembrance of who He is and who you are. Fasting is to keep everybody in the right spot. That's right. You're struggling in your spiritual walk? Do some Bible fasting. I challenge you to go back and read the whole 5th chapter of Luke. We touched on such a small scale.

A GOOD WITNESS

The Lord wanted Peter so bad. He just knew if He could get Peter in the right spot, the Lord knew Peter would be an excellent witness. People knew how he was and how he acted and what he did, but that didn't matter to the Lord. The Lord wants the "throwaways" of the world. He wants the people whose lives seem as if, "God there's no way for me." He wants those people. He wants people who have low self-esteem, and people who are unsure of themselves, people who have been cast aside and rejected and trodden under the foot of men. He wants those people! Why, Reverend Thomas? Because when He begins to elevate Himself, when He begins to manifest Himself in their lives, it will not be any wonder who's got the power, who's healing, who's delivering, and who's helping people. You know in your own self that it takes a lot of work. It takes a lot of confrontation of self. Where does arrogance come from? It's a lack of reality of self. Where does ego come from? It's a lack of reality of self. Because if you were honest with yourself, you would know there is no way in the world that the things that you have accomplished were by your own hand. You don't have that much sense. But stupid people always think they're smarter than others. Everybody knows their stupid, but them. Come on. The Bible says *that if you humble yourself, He will exhort you in,* what? *Due time.* You have to let the Lord become real in your life. He's not spooky, spooky way up in the sky. God can come right down to this church in all of His fullness, yet still be in Heaven at the same time. He's seeking to manifest Himself more, and more, and more, and more, and more, and more, and more, and more in this final hour. He has to take you down to the banks to try you to see if you are really of God. You are being tried in this hour.

GOD'S POWER

We need God's power. We need Him to manifest Himself in our lives. Zechariah 4:6 says, **things are not done not by might nor by power but by my spirit saith the Lord.** Some of you don't have the baptism in the Holy Ghost. You need to cry out and make sure that you're really saved. How can you really be sho-nuff saved, while you're not seeking with all of your heart? I'm not talking about the few of you who are really seeking with your whole heart, but some of you have not thought about the Holy Ghost since turkey day. If you just keep on going on, after awhile, you're not going to feel anything. You feel so little of the Holy Spirit now. Remember how close you were to God? You could hear these messages, and your heart would just be pounding in your chest while you were sitting in your seat; you just couldn't wait to get up where you could say the sinners' prayer. Well, now you look like that's a bad place to be.

I look into some of your faces when the messages are going forth. and you're just unconcerned, unaware, could care less. That's dangerous, because whether you know it or not, the Rapture's going to happen in your day. Whether you'll accept it or not, no sin is getting into Heaven. It does not matter what you think, or what you say, or how I feel. If you're not paying tithes, you're not going to Heaven. It doesn't matter, because the tenth is His. If you're fussing and fighting at home, you're not going to heaven. You might as well cut that mess out. You're deceiving yourself. Don't lie to yourself about yourself. Some of you just run, run, run, run, run, run, run. You have so many issues and so many problems, that when the Lord just tries to scratch the surface, you run off. All of a sudden, you don't need counseling. You don't only need counseling, but you need some medicine. You might be a little bi-polar. And I'm not cracking any jokes. Some of you have so much hurt in you, so many things have happened to you. You need to go to a professional, to somebody who has studied the mind, and let them help you. Now, what I have told my ministers here is that I believe that God can help you, but if you don't let us help you, then you need to go someplace else. Do something. Do something. Do something about yourself for yourself. Do something about yourself for your family, for your kids who have to live through all this mess. You come in everyday, and you're never happy. You might be walking around with a nervous condition. You don't even know if you should say this or if you should say that. If you call their name, they're jumping. Don't make everybody else miserable, because you're unhappy. Find out what's wrong with you and do something about it! Yes! Why do you do that? Why do you act like that? Why do you just run, run, run, run, run? Why? It's an unresolved issue. That's what it is.

NOT NORMAL

When I was suffering with depression, I was never happy. I was never happy. And I was depressed, because I had been molested when I was a young girl. Don't let people lie to you and tell you that what happened to you when you were little doesn't affect you. That's the biggest lie the devil could have ever told. I had to go get some help. I had to cry out to God. But you know what the most important thing I had to do was? I had to realize that depression isn't normal. Crazy as I may have been during that time, I wasn't crazy enough to not recognize that it is wrong, it is not natural. I had to have courage to say, "I refuse to continue to live my life like this." When that boy was blind in the 9th chapter (you know the story), the people were afraid, because you couldn't even talk about Jesus! What was the reason? Whose fault was it that this man was born blind? They were in a sin filled world.

Before the New Testament, wasn't it the Old Testament? Before the New Testament, wasn't it Adam in the Garden of Eden who failed God? Ever since Adam failed, we've been living in hell, torment and damnation. God does not bring babies into the world deformed; that's the Adamic nature. God didn't give me asthma; I was born in a sin filled world. The two times that I had cancer, I wasn't a sinner, but I was a saint living in a sin-filled world. I was marked by sin, but the power of God set me free! Free! Bad things happen to good people. Bad things happen to good people. But I have the reality of God. My father's rich in health, he's rich in sober-mindedness. I don't have to be depressed. I don't have to be oppressed. I don't have to be sick. I don't have to be wayward. I don't have to be evil. I don't have to be unthankful. I can be grateful. I can be healthy. I can be strong. Why? Because I have the reality that my father's rich! He's owns the cattle on all the hills! He's the great *I am*! He's the *Oh my God*! He's the great *I am*! His whole ministry was about healing.

BASED ON CONDITION

You're not healed today, you don't want to be. He does not heal you in disobedience. Some of you are still smoking cigarettes. They tell you on the package, dummy, this causes cancer. But you don't have the reality of God. You're taking Holy Communion and having sex while you're not married. It's the reality of God. That's why you can't have any success. If God is in your life, you're going to be successful; not according to the world's standards. You need to get somewhere and pray until something happens in your life. You have the Bible to back you up. Jeremiah 29:11-14 says, **if you call on me Joel yes God! He said I'm going to restore what was taken from you.** He said **I will restore what was taken from you!** In Ezekiel the 16th chapter, the Lord said through Ezekiel, **you were born drowning in your own blood but I came by and threw a skirt of love and said it's a time of love.** What are you talking about Reverend Thomas? All the gifts of God operate with His love. People have been getting healings and miracles in every service lately. Have you noticed it? Have you watched it? Have you seen it? Have you tried it? You have to know the reality of God in this final hour. The thing about it is, if you don't let the Lord help you, you're going to be on the side of our enemies, because they are on the way. We're getting right on T.V. and saying "whoring Pastors." I'm going to say what God gives me to say. The Lord promised me, He told me Himself that, as long as I told the truth, He was going to protect me. I'm depending on it everyday of my life. Yes! God becomes a reality in your mind and then in your heart. Acts 7:58-59, Paul had a strong determination and a steadfastness, which carried over into his life for Christ. Until he was on the road to Damascus, the only revelation of God that Paul had seen was one which he had rejected (the revelation of Jesus Christ when Stephen was stoned). Acts 7:58-59 says **the witness laid down their clothes at a young man's feet whose name was Saul.** What was this all about Reverend Thomas? The Lord was manifesting himself to Saul. Do you think Saul ever got away from the fact that he was there when somebody died for the name of the Lord? Can you imagine what his face must have looked like when they were stoning Stephen? He wasn't cursing him. He said, "I see Jesus." How many nights did Saul wake up in a cold sweat thinking, "Man, he was dying, but he said he was seeing Jesus?" This is the way the Lord has worked. This is the way he has always worked. You didn't just wake up one day and say you wanted to be saved. No, he started dropping little crumb seeds; breadcrumbs your favorite. Maybe you like garlic. I just have to tell it like it is.

THEY NEED HELP

You see, all of these people out here didn't start out bad; starting fires and killing people. They need help. The devil gets in there mind and twists their thinking up. A lot of people with mental illness, you check their lives. Somewhere in their life, they went to church. Somewhere in their life, God tried to introduce Himself and was rejected. Amen. We have had some of them up in here. I've told some of them they better stop doing that. Then, they would get with other people and talk about me. I was like, "I wouldn't do that if I were you." I'm not lifting myself up, but I just have the reality of God. I think about those boys Korah—"You take too much upon you". Who in the world would call themselves to be a Pastor up in their right mind, baring the burdens of everyone in their life? I've given my life for this work. I'm giving my life for this work. Who in the world would say, "Oh, I want to be a Pastor" and know the truth about it? There is a charge to keep, and a God I must glorify. I love God, and one day I'm going to see His face. I want Him to be glad that He saved me and that He kept me. I want Him to pull back the curtains of time and show me all the souls that were won, because I stood. Though I was in danger many times, He's a mighty good protector. He's a mighty good provider. This world is fleeting, and soon our journey will be over, and we'll be home.

What will you say about yourself? Will you be able to say it with all that you've been given? People are sitting in church or houses across America today, and they have yet to be given a blood message, yet to be told that the soul that sinneth, it shall die. So many ministers are prophets of the devil. They are apostles of deceit and evangelists of sin, sin, sin, sin, sin, sin, telling everybody that it's ok to live the way you live. God understands that you're shacking up, just leading people to hell. Many of God's people die deceived about salvation. God does not have any other place to put you if you're in sin. There's no other way. There's nothing. There's nothing. There's no other place for you to go. Only the pure in heart will see God. Those who hunger and thirst after righteousness, they shall be fed. Here he is on the road to Damascus in Acts 7:56. At first, Paul thought that Christ was an imposter, but one day he met Him for himself. Some of you still haven't had that. You still haven't met him. You talk of Him, but you don't know Him. You come in and fellowship with people who know Him. You get excited off our experience. Have your own experience. That's what Hannah said, *I just want my breast to swell up with milk and my stomach to stick out while I'm in the market.* Amen, Reverend Thomas. Study the story. She didn't have the baby and want to keep the baby, but she wanted the pride that went along with being able to bare a child and be fruitful. She said, *Lord, I want the experience so bad that, if you let me have a child, when he's weaned, I'll give him back to you.* But because she kept her word, the Lord gave her more children. She just wanted to flaunt her big belly in the market to those people who had cast her down and pushed her aside; to show her swollen breasts and her big nose. Maybe she had to wobble, but she said *I'm strutting my stuff.* She just wanted the experience. You can't live off of my experience, you have to get your own experience. Some of you are not happy. You're just going through the motions. I talk about my marriage, and you just got to say, "That can't be real." Well, if you don't believe it's real, you have to believe this: I can't lie and still be saved. Can I say that? I can't lie and still be saved. "How do we know you're saved?" Come on up in the prayer line today. These people are getting healings and miracles around here. The Lord is working through a liar? The Word says, **Let God be true and every man a liar.** He said if there's somebody among you that I have called, I will come myself. That's what He said. Behold, I see the heavens open and the Son of man standing on the right hand of God. And he knew the reality of God. The Bible says nobody taught Him. He went out into the desert for three years and was taught by the Holy Spirit. But you don't have to go out into a desert. You can have an Eden right on the inside of your life. Acts 1:8 says that he would make you a witness. John, the 16th chapter says, **It is expedient for you that I go away, for if I don't go away the comforter will not come. But if I go away I will pray the father and he will send him to you not to stay with you momentarily but to rest rule and abide with you for** how long? Forever. *I'm standing at the door and knocking,* he said. *If you open up that door,* Matthew the 7th chapter says, *me and my Father are going to come in and stay with you.* Knock and the door shall be opened. Joel said, **Whoever calls on the name of the Lord shall be saved.** You have to have the reality of God for yourself. The hour is late. Some of you are so far behind. Some people file bankruptcy, because they lost their job. Some people file bankruptcy, because they try to keep their house. Under some kind of protection in the bankruptcy laws, if you file bankruptcy, you can keep your home. It protects you. People miss so many payments and get so far behind. Some of you are spiritually bankrupt. You have gone so long, you're so far behind. You're way, way out to sea. You've been so long from praying, you can't tell your spirit from God's spirit.

GOD WAS FORCED

He said because when they knew God they didn't glorify him as God so He was forced to turn them over to a reprobate mind. *So, those things that they think are right are really wrong, but I'm going to let them go.* In Matthew the 25th chapter, it says, **at midnight a cry came forth, behold go out and meet the bridegroom.** It says those that were ready went in and the door was shut. God bless your hearts today. Yes! Yes! Yes! Yes! Yes! Yes!

I encourage all of you to read chapters 7 and 8 of *Untying God's Hands*[11]. You can also read (I happen to know this author) chapter 6 in *Just A Few of My Favorite Things*[12]. Let that be your Bible study this week. It will really bless you, studying the life of Peter. We all find ourselves there. Let's lift those hands and make sure we're saved today. **And I want everybody saying, Oh God! Oh God! Please forgive me for sinning against you. But I have come home, never to leave you again. Lord, I need you to make yourself real to me, and I know that will only happen through fasting and praying and living in the Word. You have declared through Your word that if I draw night to you, that you'll draw night to me. Help me Lord! Help me, oh God! Help me in my thinking and in my believing Lord. And by faith in the blood, save my soul! Save my soul!** And if you mean that today, you have Him. You have Him. The more of you that get the word in you, that will increase your faith. Set aside some time to really fast this week and be in the Word.

[11] *Untying God's Hands,* Reverend Ernest Angley, 1977, 2001, Winston Press
[12] *Just A Few of My Favorite Things,* Reverend Beverly Thomas, 2011, iUniverse

ABOUT THE AUTHOR

Reverend Beverly Denise Thomas is a pastor, evangelist, television producer, writer and celebrated author. Reverend Thomas is the founder and senior pastor of *A Passion For Christ Ministries* in Chicago, Illinois, which has been established for more than 16 years and has been serving at the same location for more than 14 years. Reverend Thomas has been preaching for more than twenty-four years. The Gospel is spread through tapes, music, television, skits and literature all over the city, state and abroad. Reverend Thomas has taken three missionary journeys throughout South Africa, spreading the redemptive message of Jesus Christ. " *The Light Still Shines [PFC]*," broadcast is produced and directed by Rev. Thomas and was broadcasted on **WJYS-62 television** for more than five years and can now be seen on **TLN-"Total Living Network**," Comcast cable channel 138, Mondays at 9:00 a.m. **You can watch live broadcast of "The Light Still Shines [PFC]" over the internet at the same time the program airs on local television by simply going to TLN.com and clicking "Watch TLN Online".**

Reverend Thomas, prior to pastoring at A Passion For Christ Ministries, was associate minister and evangelist at three other churches. She has received such awards from South Shore United Methodist Church in Chicago, Illinois, for supporting "Handel's Messiah."

Pastor Thomas received a certificate in journalism for Roosevelt University in Chicago and took part in an internship in Clinical Pastoral Education at Northwestern Memorial Hospital, Department of Pastoral Services and Education. She received her Certificate of Ordination after completing theological course at the Ernest Angley Bible College in Akron, Ohio. In addition to this current work, Reverend Thomas has published three other books, which are listed at the beginning of this great work.

Through such ministries as *Cater-the-Word*, Reverend Thomas is reaching those who are unable to come out to the church. One of her greatest emphasis is on the youth, through such programs as the *Teen Forum*, the youth are able to come and receive strength from leaders within the church as well as outside leaders who are invited to come and encourage the youth.

Visit www.apassionforchrist.net where you can listen to sermons, view our recent telecasts, read newsletters, request prayer and information, and much more. Please write me at passions@apassionforchrist.org.

More Books by Reverend Beverly D. Thomas

A Long Way from Home

Love Letters to the Bride

Just a Few of My Favorite Things

NOTES

Daniel James "Danny Boy" Green
1991-2012
"Boone"

NOTES

Daniel James "Danny Boy" Green
1991-2012
"Boone"

NOTES

Daniel James "Danny Boy" Green
1991-2012
"Boone"

Daniel James "Danny Boy" Green
1991-2012
"Boone"